Paradigms and Fairy Tales

'*Their equipment, though marvellously fashioned, was quite unfamiliar*'

Paradigms and Fairy Tales

An Introduction to the Science of Meanings

Volume 1

Julienne Ford
*Department of Sociology,
Middlesex Polytechnic*

Routledge & Kegan Paul
London and Boston

First published in 1975
by Routledge & Kegan Paul Ltd
Broadway House, 68–74 Carter Lane,
London EC4V 5EL and
9 Park Street,
Boston, Mass. 02108, USA
Illustrations by Martin Davis and Sally Cutting
Set in Monotype Imprint
and printed in Great Britain by
Western Printing Services Ltd, Bristol
© Julienne Ford 1975
ISBN 0 7100 8068 9 (c)
ISBN 0 7100 8248 7 (p)
ISBN 0 7100 8216 9 (c) THE SET
ISBN 0 7100 8250 9 (p) THE SET

For Box and Bernard

Contents

Reed M.

Preface

Recently I selected a quantity of school textbooks and assorted paperbacks from a large cardboard box at a local jumble sale. Before handing over the ten new pence I was already congratulating myself on my good sense in stocking my library with authoritative sources on practically everything from sixth-form chemistry to *Keeping Poultry and Rabbits on Scraps*. Just then the British Legion lady interrupted my thoughts. 'There's a lot of knowledge in books,' said she.

Even so, when it comes to the embarrassing business of tarring other scholars with the brush of gratitude, it is not mere print but conversation, laughter and head-scratching which seems to have had the most effect on the development of my own stubbornly disrespectful position. Books can't answer back, but people do. The following have done their damndest to destroy my own faith in the credibility of some of the arguments presented in this volume: Peter Blau, Steven Box, Bernard Burgoyne (who also corrected some of my sums), Aaron Cicourel, David Cowell, Len Doyal, Jeff Evans, Sunshine Ford, George Homans, Michael Lane, John Offord, Ray Pahl, Jonathan Powers, Jock Young, and the window-cleaner whose name is Richard. I am only sorry that they were not more successful.

Acknowledgments are due to the following for permission to reproduce illustrations: Collection Haags Gemeentmuseum, The Hague, for the illustration on pages 30–1 (M. C. Escher's 'Bond of Union 1956'); The British Library Board for the illustration on page 37 (Plate by Fludd from the *Musaeum Hermeticum*, Frankfurt, 1749), and on page 59 (drawing by Tenniel from *Alice in Wonderland*).

J.F.

Ponders End

Chapter 1

I Beg Your Pardon

Plac'd in this isthmus of a middle state,
A being darkly wise and rudely great,
With too much knowledge for the sceptic side,
With too much weakness for the stoic pride,
He hangs between; in doubt to act or rest;
In doubt to deem himself a god or beast;
In doubt his Mind or Body to prefer;
Born to die, and reas'ning but to err;
Chaos of Thought and Passion all confus'd,
Still by himself abus'd or disabus'd;
Created half to rise, and half to fall,
Great Lord of all things, yet a prey to all;
Sole judge of Truth, in endless error hurl'd;
The glory, jest and riddle of the world.

(Pope, *An Essay on Man*)

Even today 'the lord of all things' may find that this sentiment can have a very powerful effect on his bowels. And, two centuries after Pope we find Thomas Kuhn reiterating the riddle, though in a less romantically enematic form. Closing the argument of his famous treatise on knowledge, Kuhn asks: *'What must the world be like in order that man may know it?'* He concludes that the problem, 'as old as science itself . . . remains unanswered'.[1]

In a most profound sense, of course, he is right. In fact, as common sense has it, 'the more you know, the more you realize you don't know'. As science enables us to devise more and more sophisticated apparatus with which to grope for the 'truth', it seems only to drive us further away from the homely comfort of knowing-that-we-know-what-we-know. Current advances in the exploration of both outer and inner space – with the aid of rockets, spaceships, psychiatric techniques, and psychotropic drugs – serve only to emphasize how blurred is the line between 'phantasy' and 'reality'. And this dilemma has itself become a major focus of contemporary popular art, particularly in its acetate forms: via films and records we can join vicariously in the soul-cries of those who think they know only one thing for sure, that they do *not* know!

> I've looked at life from both sides now,
> From win and lose, and still somehow
> It's life's illusions I recall,
> I really don't know life at all.
> (Joni Mitchell, *Clouds*)

The question does remain 'unanswered' in this fundamental sense. There is no single solution to the reality-problem that has been found to be universally acceptable. Yet it is the argument of this book that *the question is being answered all the time*. The myriad solutions which men have devised, and are still devising, are the substance of those stocks of knowledge which are called common sense or folk-lore on the one hand, and philosophy, theology, philology, psychology, alchemy, magic, science, etc. on the other.

Kuhn himself has provided us with a brilliant historical account and analysis of the way in which scientists might be said to go about producing their particular sort of answers to that very Original Question. They do so *by creating and maintaining paradigms of thought*.

Thought paradigms – Kuhn calls them simply '*paradigms*' – are conglomerations of exemplary thoughts. They include various fairy tales about what the 'real world' might be like all bound up in cover stories about how it may be known. They consist of thoughts wrapped up in thoughts about thoughts. And these devices serve as patterns both for knowledge itself, and for the acquisition of knowledge.[2]

I am going to suggest that the paradigms of latter-day Western science can be envisaged as having analogues in contemporary Western common sense on the one hand, and in other systems of academic thought on the other. That is to say that the methods of reality construction, the paradigms of thought, employed by modern scientists are formally synonymous with those used – at least since the turn of the seventeenth century in the West[3] – by most philosophers, theologians, and magicians, and by ordinary people in their everyday lives.

But let us begin at the beginning, with the Original Question in a less cryptic form. Let us consider:

WHAT IS REALLY REAL?

What a conundrum! Better minds than yours and mine have pursued this one to the point of sheer lunacy. Of course, Lewis Carroll issued an eloquent warning of that danger in his allegorical nonsense poem, *The*

Hunting of the Snark. But alas! It came too late for some. Here the Baker relates his uncle's advice on the subject of snark hunting:

> 'You may seek it with thimbles – and seek it with care;
> You may hunt it with forks and hope;
> You may threaten its life with a railway share;
> You may charm it with smiles and soap – '

> ('That's exactly the method', the Bellman bold
> In a hasty parenthesis cried,
> 'That's exactly the way I have always been told
> That the capture of snarks should be tried!')

> 'But oh, beamish nephew, beware of the day,
> If your Snark be a Boojum! For then
> You will softly and suddenly vanish away,
> And never be met with again!'

> 'It is this, it is this that oppresses my soul,
> When I think of my uncle's last words:
> And my heart is like nothing so much as a bowl
> Brimming over with quivering curds!'

The unfortunate Baker eventually ran the Snark to ground, but, as you have no doubt guessed:

> In the midst of the word he was trying to say
> In the midst of his laughter and glee,
> He had softly and suddenly vanished away –
> For the Snark *was* a Boojum, you see.

Many others, having more regard for their sanity, have resisted the temptation to get actively involved in the chase. The sociologist, Alfred Schutz, for example, wisely confessed 'I want to say that I am afraid I do not know what reality is, and my only comfort in this unpleasant situation is that I share my ignorance with the greatest philosophers of all time.'[4] In making this confession Schutz follows in a tradition of thought which is usually known as *Phenomenology*. The phenomenologists warn us against the dangers of assuming anything about the 'reality' of those 'facts' which appear to present themselves to us either through the taken-for-granted framework of common sense or through the more seductive reality-maker which nowadays is called science. Yet, while stressing that we cannot, in one fundamental sense, *know* what is really real, they do *not* urge us relentlessly to pursue the Snark, chasing it in ever-decreasing circuits until we inevitably disappear up our own cloacae.[5]

One phenomenological technique which has been suggested to avoid this undignified end is that we resist the bait, yet at the same time keep the problem in mind, through the trick of *bracketing*.[6] Aware that we do not know what is really real, we can none the less get on with the job (whatever it is) by simply putting brackets around whatever-it-is-that-we-take-to-be-reality. You can do this discreetly in your head if you wish, or you can do it when you write, writing '(the world)' thus, so that your reader is warned that you wish him, like you, to suspend judgment on the nature of the (reality) about which you write.

Unfortunately this technique can be a little confusing to read, so I would like to suggest that, instead, we adopt the practice of bracketing those-words-whose-meaning-has-yet-to-be-determined with *question marks*.[7] For example, we can write ¿reality?, ¿fact?, ¿phenomenon?, ¿thing?, ¿knowledge?, ¿science?, etc., and thus we can remind ourselves, and each other, of the uncertainty with which we write.

Now you could be forgiven for thinking that all this is a load of 'philosophical' mumbo-jumbo. If every time you were about to step on a bus you stood pondering as to whether or not the ¿bus? was ¿really? ¿there?, you would find yourself left standing at a very real bus stop, quite probably getting unmistakably wet from what would seem remarkably like real rain. In fact, of course, in the context of our everyday lives we are pretty certain *for the most part* what is 'really real'. Though we may sometimes enclose people, things, and situations in imaginary interrogative brackets, this is only as a preliminary to *finding out* what they are. Moreover we are aware that we *don't* understand what these particular items mean (what they *are*) precisely because they stand out from a background of taken-for-granted 'reality'.

One everyday way of coping with the invisible interrogative brackets around those phenomena, events, and processes whose meaning is as yet unknown has been described by sociologists as *glossing*.[8] An example may be helpful. In the following imaginary conversation B does not know what A is talking about, and apparently does not want to ask A, for reasons which are none of our business. B is bluffing along while trying to get enough clues from what A says to find out what it is that they are both talking about.

A: 'I've had enough of this business.'
B: 'Yeah.'
A: 'I can't stand any more of it.'
B: 'I know what you mean.'
A: 'What can we do about it?'
B: 'Search me. I dunno, I really dunno.'
A: 'No, seriously, I want your advice. We must do *something*.
B: 'Well I don't know where to begin.'
A: 'It's not exactly a complicated issue is it?'

B: 'I suppose not.'
A: 'What do you mean "suppose"! There's no "suppose" about it. It's obvious.'
B: (*Says nothing but shifts from one foot to the other.*)
A: 'We've got to have it out with him.'
B: (*Still says nothing at all. This is the first real clue he has had.*)
A: '*You*'ll have to go, it's better coming from you than from me.'
B: (*Desperate by now*) 'What shall I say?'

At this point A could have said, 'Oh use your bloody head!', in which case B would be right in thinking that he simply did not know what A was talking about. B's luck was in, though, and what A actually said was:

A: 'Oh I'd play it real strong, something like "Look here *Mister* Robinson, putting in extra hours is one thing, but staying 'til eight on a Friday without any sort of overtime is ridiculous. We may not be unionized but you can't get away with that." '

The meaning of the whole setting has now manifested itself to B. ¿Whatever-we-are-talking-about? has now become 'what to do about unpaid overtime work on a Friday'. What is important for our purposes is that B has found out *all that he needs to know* about the situation in question. Whether that conversation ¿really? took place or not doesn't matter; whether B is ¿dreaming? the ¿whole incident?, or whether the ¿conversation? took place ¿not? between ¿A? and ¿B? but between their ¿doppelgangers? in a ¿parallel universe?, it simply doesn't make any difference. B has enough information to feel that he knows what is going on and to decide what to do next, whether this is to tell A to fight his own battles or to tell Mr Robinson where *he* gets off. For B to say that he doesn't know what A is ¿really? talking about would be absurd. (This would also hold for those situations where B does not have the option of asking A directly what he means, as those where, for example, the two people speak different languages.)

The aim of everyday bracketing, for example glossing, is, then, to locate a particular reality-gap in a background of ordinariness and thereby fill it in. For ordinary people in their everyday lives:

THE ¿ *REALITY* ? OF HERE AND NOW DEPENDS UPON THE ¿ *REALITY* ? OF NORMALITY.

When academics take off their white scientific coats and funny philosophical hats they turn into ordinary people too, and like all ordinary people, they have to start somewhere. They must have a background normality about which they have, for the moment, stopped asking questions. Such a ground is a prerequisite for identifying those ¿realities?

that they are still pondering about, as well as a *desideratum* for avoiding the very ¿real? possibility of being dragged away in a straight-jacket.

So if we are to try to do the ¿science? called ¿sociology?, then like other scientists (and the ordinary people that we ¿really? are!) we need to decide on an answer that – as my granny used to say – 'will do to be going on with'. In a sense it is rather silly to offer this working answer in the form of a verbal definition,[9] but in case your ¿scientific? training has led you to expect such definitions, I suggest that, for the moment, we treat reality as '*Whatever appears to be*'.[10] In other words, whatever our senses seem to inform us is 'out there', whatever we cannot simply wish away,[11] is for all everyday purposes, and for our present purposes, *really real*. That is to say,

WHATEVER APPEARS TO BE, IS!

If your reaction to this suggestion is to feel that you ¿know? no more about reality than you did before, then I am pleased that you take my point. Whatever we do we must not lose sight of common sense. As A. N. Whitehead remarked, 'you may polish up common sense, you may contradict it in detail, you may surprise it. But ultimately your whole task is to satisfy it.'[12]

Let us look more closely at the implications of this common-sense answer to the question of what is really real. Is it not an entirely incredible thing that anything should exist at all? Yet some things most emphatically do exist. The reality of everyday life presents you with billions of phenomena ranging from good hot dinners, through desperation, traffic wardens, and embarrassing situations, to the-happiest-day-of-your-life.

Now the commonest approach to the philosophy of science has been an attempt to stand back from this common-sense world by trying to find a way of presenting it as it would appear to a being standing completely outside the scene and recording what that world was like in itself. Those ¿sociologists? who have taken the same view have therefore tried to imagine what ¿social worlds? would look like through a Martian viewfinder. One has even prophesied the development of a neutral ¿scientific? or specifically ¿sociological? language in which to describe those strange scenes.[13]

While there is an appealing simplicity about this aim, the absurdity of it has been made amenable to common sense by a number of writers, one of whom has remarked that:[14]

All said and done, as my dentist pointed out to me the other day, the average man likes to see both ends of the stick. . . . But . . . [this is like] . . . pursuing a will-of-the-wisp. It is impossible for you, who are part of the universe to achieve the viewpoint of an observer standing outside that universe which includes you. You *can* only see one end of the stick; for the other end is you.

Another, somewhat more cumbersome, way of making the same point is to say that the phenomena which make up the reality which manifests itself to any one observer cannot be reduced to properties intrinsic to those phenomena, any more than they can be dismissed as mere products of physiological and neurological processes occurring in that observer.[15]

'Polishing up' common sense, then, we might be left with the following saw.

SEEING IS BELIEVING BUT BELIEVING IS SEEING.

If you agree with what has been said so far, then you will accept that the words 'phenomenon', 'fact', and 'datum' must now take on ¿another-level-of-meaning?. A phenomenon can be viewed as *that which appears or manifests itself to consciousness, that which emerges into view from a ground to become what it is here and now for a subject.*[16] Facts and data can therefore be seen as those phenomena which appear to ordinary people and to scientists. They are matrices of sensations organized into meaningful patterns from some point of view; they are *sense structured from senses,*[17] visual, auditory, olfactory, and tactual; they are seeings and believings. So if you wish to explore that strange zone, which hangs vibrating like an eardrum between inner and outer space, then you must first turn your attention to –

YOUR ATTENTION!

At the moment you are reading this book. Your eyes are moving from left to right and back, again and again. But you have not been noticing the movement of your eyes. Nor have you been noticing the hardness of the chair on which you are sitting, the feel of the paper on which these words are written, or the phenomena which at this very moment could be observed to the left and right of this book. Yet, without moving one muscle, you could have been aware of all these things. Of course now that I have drawn your attention to them they have become real, probably at the expense of you losing the thread of the imaginary argument you were having with me.

Once your attention has been drawn to it, the crucial importance of your attention is perfectly obvious. Most of us have seen diagrams which viewed one 'way' seem to be Grecian urns, yet in a moment turn into faces and back into vases before you can even say 'Gestalt switch!'. And you will be familiar with the sort of visual stimuli which *could* be all sorts of things, and assume a meaning for you only because of the way you look at them. (See the illustration on page 9.) But this now-you-see-it-now-you-don't quality is not special to that ¿photograph?, perception diagrams, Rorschach inkblots, Thematic Apperception Tests, and so on. It is characteristic of everything to which we turn our fickle attention, and is particularly noticeable (if you look for it!) in the realm of ¿social? phenomena. Imagine yourself in the place of the lady whose thoughts are recorded below – I think you will find that you have been there before.[18]

> Is he smiling or smirking?
> What is that look in his eyes?
> How does he see me seeing him?
> Does he *mean* to confuse me?
> Can he see that I am confused?
> Ah. He's smiling.
> No! He's smirking.
> Can I see that he sees my confusion?
> Can I see that he sees my embarrassment?
> Am I blushing?
> Does he see my blushing?
> Is he smiling or smirking?
> *What is that look in his eyes?*

We experience reality, then, through a complex of psychic and bodily processes which both affect and are affected by the focus of our attention.[19] Yet obviously the particular interplay between each human being and the ¿world? outside his head, while in one sense unique to him, cannot be entirely independent of the relationships which other human beings maintain with that ¿same? world. A world peopled by such seeming solipsists would be a cold and lonely place indeed! I am going to argue that we human beings have always avoided that bleak possibility by negotiating more or less consensual realities – common-sense worlds – which demarcate certain fields within which attention is normally directed. Thus while phenomena in general, and ¿social? phenomena in particular, have an emerging or *becoming* quality, they are none the less selections from a frozen background of possibilities, a world-taken-for-granted. The embarrassed lady may have been confused about the behaviour and intentions of the man to which she refers, but, *whatever* she thought he was up to, she had routinely eliminated the possibility of his dancing a hornpipe.

Of course, a multitude of different taken-for-granted worlds reign on this ¿one earth?, and often a number of them seem to coexist on the same ¿physical? territory.[20] Nowadays, mainly as a result of the spectacular rise of the mass media, most of us are well aware that our worlds

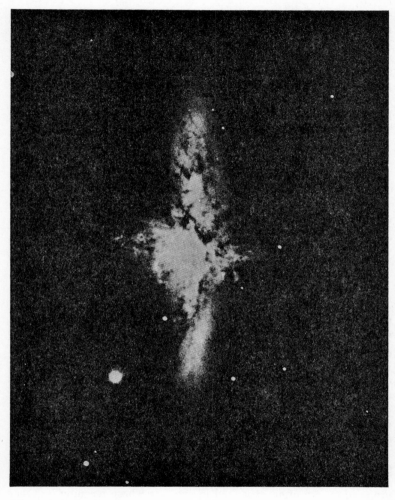

Mysterious Appearances

are vastly different from those assumed by, for example, the Lele, the
Nuer, or the Navajo Indians. Intrepid reporters and some ¿sociologists?
also bring back tales from strange lands which may be no more than a
stone's throw from your own back door: from the lands of hustlers,
professional criminals, Hell's Angels, drug addicts, hippies, and religious maniacs.[21]

So the suggestion that we *define reality as 'whatever appears to be'*
seems to have spiralled up onto ¿another-level-of-meaning?. Normally
people believe what they see, and see what they believe, but the phenomena to which their attention directs them are selected against a
paradigmatic background of expectations, a world-taken-for-granted,
which they share with others of their ilk.[22]

All civilizations set rules concerning what is 'real' and what is not,
what is 'true' and what is 'false'. . . . Our perceptions are narrowly
channeled through concepts and interpretations. What is commonly
thought of as 'reality', that which 'exists', or simply 'is', is a set of
concepts, conceptual frames, assumptions, suppositions, rationaliza-
tions, justifications, defenses, all generally collectively agreed-upon,
which guide and channel each individual's perceptions in a specific
and distinct direction. The specific rules governing the perception of
the universe which man inhabits are more or less arbitrary, a matter
of convention. Every society establishes a kind of epistemological
methodology.

Ever since the so-called Enlightenment the epistemological methodology – the rules of the reality game – to which most[23] people in the
Western world have been prepared to defer has been called *'science'*. Of
course in saying this I do not intend to imply that most ordinary people
in the West are 'scientists', or that the kind of ¿understanding? they have
of their worlds is identical with that for which professional scientists
aim. I will, however, suggest that ¿scientific reasoning? is entirely
commensurable with Western common sense. Indeed, there is a sense
in which 'science' may be regarded as the *reductio ad absurdum* of occi-
dental common sense.

Let me explain. *Science, as it is and has always been practised, is simply
a number of shared beliefs, plus a corpus of well-tried methods for establishing
¿truth?, plus a number of ¿truths? kept-as-knowledge.* While scientific
propositions are often expressed in symbols whose meaning is rather
inaccessible to the layman (esoteric words, formulae, diagrams, mathematical expressions, etc.) there is no doubt that the way in which these
propositions take shape is intrinsically connected with the ordinary
common-sense reasoning of everyday life. In his efforts to ¿discover?,
¿explain?, and ¿control? the parameters of his world, the scientist
generalizes, theorizes, and 'tests his hunches' in much the same way

as the ordinary man.[24] The main difference, apart from the language, is that – from the scientist's point of view – the layman more often makes ¿mistakes?. The layman, realizing this, feels that the scientists are wiser by virtue of their learning, and he is liable to view them as final arbiters in those cases where common-sense theories of the world suddenly seem inadequate or inconsistent.

Yet the development of science has not led to unanimity. While in some spheres there are unquestioned theories which are generally taken to explain the unchallenged facts, there are always some realities which are still in the process of negotiation. Thus most Westerners will accept the same conclusions about the relationship 'dirt–germs–disease', whether or not they follow the reasoning a scientist would employ in explicating that sequence; but, on the other hand, they can select from a variety of scientific assertions regarding such questions as, say, cannabis consumption and heroin addiction, or, say, ethnic status and intelligence.

Nowadays when two laymen enter into a dispute about matters of fact, or about acceptable explanations of mutually agreed facts, they often have no ¿reasonable? means of resolving their argument without recourse to the opinions of some expert. That expert will usually be a scientist or technologist of some kind. And where conflicting expert opinions are available, where ¿truth? is still being negotiated by scientists, ordinary people have no means of checking one expert's story against another's, except by recourse to yet another expert. Thus it comes about that 'Our contemporary pawnbrokers of reality are scientists.'[25]

Now permit me, for the moment, to assume that you accept the equation of appearances and reality which I have proposed, and allow me also to assume that you are prepared – again, just for the moment – to entertain the thought that common sense and science bear some special relationship to one another. It may now occur to you to ask a further question?

You may be wondering how it comes about that, amongst the thoughts we take for granted, is the optimistic presumption that knowledge ¿advances? or ¿progresses? in some way. Of course hardly any of us believe that the route maps we have in our minds for the ¿advance of knowledge? include some end point, some destination, *to* which theorizing is believed to be ¿progressing?. But most of us hold as an article of faith the view that knowledge – both science and common sense – can be regarded as having ¿advanced? *from* various points of definable ignorance in its march 'up' to the present. Contemporary education leads most of us to believe that man (particularly Western man) knows *more* today than he knew yesterday, and that tomorrow he will know *more yet*.

At least since the time of Francis Bacon, this question of ¿theoretical advance? has been one of the major preoccupations of methodologists and philosophers of science. They have seen the development of criteria for assessing ¿theoretical progress? as a necessary corollary of actual substantive intellectual activity. That is to say that they have themselves personally eschewed the acquisition of ¿more knowledge? in favour of clarifying the nature of the rules according to which thoughts may be judged. And I am going to argue that the ¿sociologist? will not find *his* vocation until he also brings himself up against this difficult issue. For only when he has clarified what it is that he means to mean by ¿theoretical progress? will he have the power to peer through the mists of ¿time? and glimpse some little ¿truths?.

Yet if we are to embark upon a quest for some ¿reasonable? way of defining ¿advancing thought?, ¿the growth of knowledge?, etc. we must be prepared to take some fearsome risks. Indeed we shall shortly find that we are on a very strange and dangerous trip!

Now I have claimed that all thought, whether in everyday life, in science, or in any other realm, is paradigmatic. That is to say that all thought is patterned on some mould.

I wonder if you have ever seen those blancmange moulds that are cast in the shapes of rabbits and tortoises? Any blancmange mixture that goes into them is destined to come out shaped like a rabbit or a tortoise, depending on the mould. And so it is with paradigms of thought. Without the paradigm the thoughts cannot take shape, while the shape that they will take is predetermined by the paradigm.

Now (I hope that) you are ¿thinking? that I must have made a ¿mistake? in suggesting that analogy? You are probably bothered by the fact that the ¿progress? of a blancmange tortoise must be slow indeed! We take it for granted that thought ¿advances?, I have said. But we also take it for granted that a blancmange can't go forward of its own accord! Indeed without the help of some external force (such as a breath of wind) it can't muster up so much as a shudder. If you *have* been ¿thinking? like that, then you have been experiencing something akin to the discomfort that has been bothering methodologists and philosophers of science for at least three centuries. Let me restate the dilemma: *if thought is preformed, how can we talk of its ¿advance? ?*

Whatever can I mean when I say that thoughts are preformed? I cannot mean that all thoughts are identical in substance: that would be absurd. It is perfectly obvious that every thought is in one sense unique. That is to say that if you take any two thoughts there will be some respects in which they *differ* from one another. But I want to suggest that – from ¿another point of view? – it is equally obvious that any two thoughts will be *similar* in some respects. Let us consider two thoughts.

THOUGHT A   The probability of selecting four red glass beads from a vessel containing 99 glass beads, two thirds of which are red and one third of which are black, is

$$= P(r_1\ r_2\ r_3\ r_4)$$
$$= P(r_1)P(r_2)P(r_3)P(r_4)$$
$$= \tfrac{66}{99}\ \tfrac{65}{98}\ \tfrac{64}{97}\ \tfrac{63}{96}$$

where r_i is that the ith choice is red, given that choices 1 to (i–1) are all red.

THOUGHT B 'If you don't go to the dentist soon that tooth will fall out.'

At first sight these two thoughts probably look very different to you. In the first place they seem to be about different things. Then, *Thought A* is clearly an 'academic' thought, while *Thought B* is a common-sense sort of a thought. Then, again, *Thought B* hasn't got any sums in it. And you may be able to go on suggesting further differences between them, according to ¿other points of view?.

But, from ¿another point of view?, you could have spotted ¿*similarities*? between the two thoughts. For example, both are probability statements; both are conclusions; both are ¿reasonable?. So, even though the two thoughts are different in some respects, in other respects they are the same. Whether you see them as different or as *similar* depends, simply, on your ¿point of view?.

Now I am going to go so far as to suggest that there are some respects in which *all* thoughts may be viewed as similar. From ¿a certain angle? *Thought A* and *Thought B* may be said to have two further features in common, not only with each other, but with all other thoughts that have ever been thought. In the first place,

ALL THOUGHTS MAY BE EXPRESSED IN SYMBOLS.

This amounts to an assertion that thought cannot be dissociated from language, though some languages, like, say, mathematics, symbolic logic, and music, are expressed not in words, but in non-verbal symbols such as figures, etc.

A second feature which, from ¿this angle?, *Thought A* may be said to have in common with *Thought B* and with all other thoughts, is that none of them makes very much sense on its own. If *Thought A* meant anything to you, it was probably because you have a background grasp of probability theory; if *Thought B* made sense to you it was because you have come to accept certain assumptions about the relationship between rotten teeth and adequate dental care. *Any* thought depends upon a background of other thoughts for its meaning. Without at least some additional thoughts we cannot even *grasp* a particular thought, let alone begin to ponder about whether it might be ¿true?, or even whether it is ¿reasonable?.

A THOUGHT ONLY HAS MEANING IN CONNECTION WITH OTHER THOUGHTS.

I am going to take these two features, dependence on language and dependence on each other, as the *distinguishing characteristics* of thought. That is to say that I shall be limiting my use of the terms 'thoughts' and 'thought' to those intellectual productions which may be regarded as having those two features. From ¿this viewpoint?.

THOUGHT IS A *RESULT* OF ¿THINKING?.

Not all consciousness culminates in thought; thought is simply a clearly identifiable *product* of consciousness. All thoughts may be regarded as similar with regard to two formal characteristics: all thoughts can be expressed in symbols and no thoughts can be regarded as independent of other thoughts.

(BUT THERE IS MORE TO ¿THINKING? THAN THOUGHT as we shall see by and by.)

Now, like any number of differently coloured and flavoured rabbit- or tortoise-shaped blancmanges, once thoughts have been turned out, they *have been* turned out. They are 'mere' objects, they have no life in them.

It is hardly surprising that there is no Society for the Prevention of Cruelty to Thoughts. Thoughts are not like dreams, they can survive anything, you can do what you like with them. You can compare them; dissect them; put selections of them up for show in lifeless menageries; chew them up; digest them; swallow them whole; even put on your wellington boots and jump all over them!

But what is it about the manufacture of thoughts that results in such lifeless travesties? How can thoughts be at once so limp and yet so rigid? How does it come about that we condemn our loftiest aspirations to be confined within paradigms of thought, destined to remain there moribund – mouldering – until at last they are turned out as mere trifles?

'I beg your pardon!' Before I suggest some answers silly enough to do justice to those questions I will regale you with another FAIRY TALE.

Buried deep in a vast wing-chair, his feet resting on the tortoise-shaped supports of the andirons, his wellington boots toasting in front of the crackling logs that shot out bright splashes of mud as if they felt the furious blast of a bellows, Evanid put the insubstantial volume he had been reading down on a table, stretched himself, lit a smoke, and gave himself up to a delicious reverie. His mind was going full tilt in pursuit of certain thoughts which had been buried for months, but which had suddenly been exhumed by some words occurring, for no apparent reason, to his memory.

He found himself staring through the flickering mud onto the mountainous plain beyond. And as he watched he became aware that, though nothing had changed, the peaks on the horizon were sculpted from blancmange. The more he looked the more he saw. All around the blancmange was mocking him.

In a fit of rage he kicked his left foot hard against its iron support. The tortoise-form quivered. And was still again. This was *too much*! His very hands, his ears, his nostrils. . .

'How shall I breathe?' he exclaimed aloud.

'How indeed?' mocked the banished bellows.

In a frenzy the unfortunate began to consume the blancmange that threatened his life. Stuffing blancmange bootful after blancmange bootful he endeavoured to clear a space in which to breathe. But, the greater the effort he put into the task, the less he achieved, and in a little while he realized that he was eating his own body.

'Think, think, THINK!' he screamed. But a faint memory greeted his cry: he had forgotten how to think. Raising blancmange fingers to his head, like met like. And it was all over. Evanid.

At length you will find me asserting that most of the time most of us are Evanid and that it is only through ¿THINKING? that we can ¿transcend? the stifling blancmange of thoughts-already-thought and participate in the recreation of a living world.

But, if you ¿think? that you will have difficulty in swallowing *that* story, I wonder what you will make of what follows?

Chapter 2

Just Another Fairy Tale

Are you sitting comfortably? Then I'll begin.

Still upon a time all paradigms of thought, including whatever we currently take for granted as common sense, may be considered as composed of four elements. The first of these elements I shall call *BASIC BELIEFS*.

BASIC BELIEFS are our most fundamental thoughts about the ultimate nature, or 'essence' of things. They are what philosophers sometimes call *ontological* assumptions. As such they may be regarded as '*essential*' in another sense. For without some *BASIC BELIEFS* no paradigm can maintain its grip on a man's mind. Indeed, it is just because he accepts the beliefs basic to a particular paradigm that a thoughtful person is persuaded to adopt the whole conglomeration of thoughts cast in that same mould.

The *BASIC BELIEFS* which shape our own common-sense world are, of course, rather different from those informing non-Western and pre-modern folk-lore. The latter are of an unashamedly 'religious', 'mystical', or 'metaphysical' character, while we 'wide-awake' modernists tend to blush at the very whisper of such ideas. *We* don't believe in ghosts, gods, fairies, or things that go bump in the night. On the contrary, it is our view that cultures reject animistic notions as they develop and mature, just as children grow out of their belief in Father Christmas. With the exception of some minorities (religious cranks, hippies, and other deviant atavists) we have succeeded in exorcizing the phantoms of idealism from our tidy minds. In their place we find a nice, solid, material cosmos which obliges us by obeying the laws of physics and only rarely behaving in unexpected ways. There is nothing aweful about *our* world, most of it is already familiar, and what we do not know today we shall know tomorrow. No. If there is anything in front of which we stand in awe it is no kind of god. Nor is it a real world of appearances: it is not Maya who has seduced us with her excitement and mystery: after all, we can hardly see her for the plastic amendments with which we have improved her. No. If we experience awe at all it is usually at the achievements of other men, at the thoughts which they have had, and, in particular, *at science*. And, if there is anything we place above *that*, it is the 'spirit' of science, the scientific attitude. This attitude is[1]

> something which only began about four hundred years ago, and which has very special historical associations with England. . . . Men had investigated natural phenomena before, but the scientific *spirit* means very much more than this. It means absolute, unqualified open-mindedness. It means the deletion of the word *belief* from one's vocabulary, and the readiness to unite one's sympathies temporarily with any conceivable hypothesis, for which the barest *prima facie* case can be made out, in order to give that hypothesis a completely unbiased consideration. The rarity of this attitude at present among 'men of science' is of course a sign of the times; but it need not be unduly emphasised at the moment. For if it is true that the pundits of the scientific world are now respected as 'authorities' in much the same way as the Church Fathers once were, it is also true that allegiance is only given to them because they are at any rate in some vague way *believed* to be really open-minded. And that is equally a sign of the times. We are determined to believe something, so we believe this . . . today, while everybody praises the scientific spirit, practically nobody takes the trouble to acquire it.

It has been my argument, then, that *some* belief is basic to any paradigm of thought – even if it is only the belief that beliefs should be banished from thought and statements limited to those which can be established as ¿true? by means of ¿tests?.

Yet while I speak of beliefs as basic to a paradigm, *BASIC BELIEFS* are no *more* fundamental than the second element of thought paradigms which I propose to discuss. I shall refer to this second constituent by a deliberately unusual phrase, *FIGURATION OF FACTS*.[2]

The notion of *FIGURATION OF FACTS* is one which is peculiarly difficult to grasp in an intellectual way, that is to have thoughts *about*. Yet you are *doing* it, simply and unreflexively all the time, including now as you are reading this book. It is through *FIGURATION OF FACTS* that we come to know what is really real; it is through *FIGURATION OF FACTS* that appearances appear; and it is through *FIGURATION OF FACTS* that ordinary, everyday, taken-for-granted thoughts are affirmed as yardsticks against which both the extraordinary-but-indubitable and the utterly-phantastic-and-unreal are compared.

You will remember that I suggested earlier that 'whatever appears to be, really is'? Now, further thought on that thought might lead you to the reflection that some appearances are generally taken to be more real than others. *Are* some realities more real than others?[3]

Look at a rainbow. While it lasts, it is, or appears to be, a great arc of many colours occupying a position out there in space. It touches the horizon between that chimney and that tree; a line drawn from the sun behind you and passing through your head would pierce the centre of the circle of which it is a part. And now, before it fades, recollect all you have ever been told about the rainbow and its causes, and ask yourself the question *Is it really there?*

Of course you know that, if you were to walk to the rainbow's end, it would not be there. You know that the rainbow is the outcome of the raindrops, the sunlight, and your vision. But it does not follow that you could banish the rainbow from the sky by burying your head in the sand. Nor does it follow that there is no difference between that rainbow and a rainbow hallucination or a madman's dream.

The practical difference between the real rainbow and the hallucination or dream of a rainbow is, of course, that the former appearance is 'there for *anyone* to see' while the latter is a somewhat more private illusion. Both are representations, but the former is a *collective representation*. For even if your eyes were firmly shut (to keep out the sand) the rainbow would remain 'in the sky' for any passing wanderer to see (or at least for any passing wanderer who had ever seen a rainbow before).[4]

Now look at a tree. It is very different from a rainbow. If you approach it, it will still be 'there'. Moreover, in this case, you can do more than look at it. You can hear the noise its leaves make in the wind. You can perhaps smell it. You can certainly touch it. Your senses combine to assure you that it is composed of what is called solid matter. . . . Recollect all you have been told about matter and its ultimate structure and ask yourself if the tree is 'really there' . . . the tree *as such*, is a representation. And the difference, for me, between a tree and a complete hallucination of a tree is the same as the difference between a rainbow and an hallucination of a rainbow. In other words a tree which is 'really there' is a collective representation. The fact that a dream tree differs . . . from a real tree, and that it is just silly to try and mix them up, is indeed rather literally a matter of 'common sense'.

And if you are worried that things have suddenly taken a metaphysical turn then you have got hold of the wrong end of an entirely imaginary stick. For metaphysicians don't talk like that, they talk like this:[5]

the objects of knowledge are of two kinds, – only two, – and these totally distinct and different from each other, viz., the percipient nature whose *esse* is *percipere*, and the phenomenal nature whose *esse* is *percipi*, – minds and mental things, – the spirit, on the one hand, which perceives itself as well as its own phenomena, but neither other spirits nor other phenomena, and, on the other hand, these phenomena or sensible objects themselves, often hard, large, and heavy things, which, to the great perplexity of non-metaphysicians, are, by metaphysicians, so commonly called 'ideas', although some of them are mill-stones; and which ideas, we are all conscious, cannot ever perceive either themselves or anything else whatever.

Millstones sink more slowly when it is blancmange that they are being dropped into, but they reach the bottom in the end. And at the rock bottom is the old familiar world-taken-for-granted, the actual system of collective representations that we continually affirm through our *FIGURATION OF FACTS*. For practically any theory of the relationship between mind and matter (whether it is one derived from, say, Aristotle, Aquinas, Kant, Goethe, Marx, Husserl, Bergson, or some, wholly unphilosophical, physiological or psychological construction), practically any theory that you care to adopt would lead you to agree with Owen Barfield that 'the familiar world – that is the world which is apprehended, not through instruments and inference, but simply – is . . . dependent on the percipient'. It is that process of rock-bottom reality construction that is here being termed *FIGURATION OF FACTS*.

Another way of describing the crucial part played by fact figuration in the ongoing creation of shared worlds-taken-for-granted is to point out, as William James did, that percepts without concepts would yield only 'blooming buzzing confusion': it is only when a percept (a sensation or conglomeration of sensations) is combined with a concept (a familiar thought) that *recognition* takes place and we see, hear, touch, smell, or taste a real umbrella, baby crying, marble slab, drift-wood bonfire, or trout in aspic.[6]

When I 'hear a thrush singing', I am hearing, not with my ears alone, but with all sorts of other things like mental habits, memory, imagination, feeling and (to the extent at least that the act of attention involves it) will. Of a man who merely heard in the first sense, it could meaningfully be said that 'having ears' (i.e. not being deaf) 'he heard not'.

I have tried to communicate the notion that it is only through the very *rudimentary* sort of thought which I have called *FIGURATION OF FACTS* that we come to know what appears to be, and that this fundamental ingredient of thought, though elementary, is by no means simple. We do not use our eyes and ears, our fingers, noses, tongues, and brains (and central nervous systems) to make straightforward copies of an independently existing outside world. On the contrary, it is only *because* we use our eyes and ears, our fingers, noses, tongues, and brains (and hearts) in certain habitual ways, that the outside world seems to be as it is.

And, furthermore, it is only because of these habits of perception and conception that the 'outside world' is *'outside'* at all! For there are different ways of figuring facts from those that we 'wide-awake' Westerners routinely effect.

One has only to read the studies of 'totemism' by Durkheim or Lévy-Bruhl to appreciate this. The so-called 'primitives' of which they write turn their eyes in the ¿same direction? as the anthropologists who go to study them and yet see almost nothing of what appears to the latter, while at the same time they see much else of which the anthropologists are quite unaware.

Or, again, you have only to make an attempt to ¿understand? Eastern ways of being in the world to realize that there is another way of having an 'outside' and an 'inside' from the one we take for granted. For the Buddhist, for example, the 'outside' world that appears to the senses is unreality, illusion (Maya). For him reality is 'inside', it is the inner world of consciousness in which the self is immersed when in meditation. The Eastern way of figuring creates a different sort of bond between 'inside' and 'outside', one in which spirit, ideas, the 'unrepresented', are the taken-for-granted reality, while the collective representations, matter, have a status something akin to that which we grant to dreams, phantasies and hallucinations.

But you must have had some difficulty in grasping that attempt to describe the Eastern way of consciousness (unless, of course, you practise some form of oriental meditation in which case you will have had a different sort of difficulty in recognizing the description!). This is because figuring is so fundamental to thought that, where two men cannot take it for granted that they are conceiving and perceiving in the same manner, they cannot share a background of representations; they have no common earth on which to stand; they are 'Worlds Apart'.

I must say a little more about *FIGURATION OF FACTS* before passing on to the third element of thought which I propose to discuss.

You will have concluded from the above that I am maintaining that shared *FIGURATION OF FACTS* is an essential prerequisite for any further ¿reasonable? thought, but that, at the same time, shared *FIGURATION OF FACTS* is at the foundation, the rock bottom, of appearances, that is, of collective representations or commonly taken-for-granted realities. Perhaps it seems to you that I have tried to place *FIGURATION OF FACTS* somewhere *between* 'you' and the 'outside' world that you and I commonly take for granted. So you may now be wondering whether I am supposing *FIGURATION OF FACTS* to be a part of 'you', or a part of the world 'outside'. Then, anticipating my answer that it is 'a part' of *both*, you may be faced with a new conundrum: What has happened to the distinction between thought and appearance, consciousness and actuality, mind and matter, man and nature, etc. After all, if I am right about the normal, everyday, Western way of figuring facts, that sort of distinction is one of the thoughts that you are used to taking for granted?

Well, if that very distinction *is* a thought, then, like other thoughts, its meaningfulness depends upon a background acceptance of other thoughts, indeed upon a whole paradigm of thoughts. Like all the thoughts you have, the very conception of a hiatus between 'I' and 'Not-I' is built upon a dual foundation, a basis of beliefs on the one hand and figured facts on the other. That foundation, that double fulcrum of our universe of thought, might fruitfully be compared with the philosopher's stone of the alchemists. For though we would be doomed to failure if we were to attempt to isolate it – as an identifiable entity – from the whole of which it is a part, none the less we base our feverish hopes upon it. And what a strange *metaphysical* premise it is, this philosopher's stone, tied as it is to a generally essential acceptance of certain *BASIC BELIEFS* from one side, and to a particularly rudimentary *FIGURATION OF FACTS* on the other.

But this is our inheritance and (unless we can ¿transcend? it) we are stuck with it! It is the black hole at the heart of our cosmology. It is the yawning epistemological divide which has divided since the beginning of ¿time? and will go on dividing. It divides men from their nature, author from creation, subject from object and each of *us* from each other.

Yet this malignant and threatening gap, this philosopher's stone, this snark, this BOOJUM, *this* is the legacy of thoughts-already-thought on which we have a mind to stand. For if we accept our inheritance, of common sense, and of science, then this is our estate. And, unless we can ¿think? of some other ways of seeing we shall have to hang on to these thoughts that have been left for us.

And what *can* we see with the eyes and minds and memories which we have inherited from our ancestors? Well, look *out there* at the world which hangs around these thoughts. *Look* at it! It is hard to believe that the source of all *that* can be familiar, or close at hand, isn't it? It is hardly surprising that men feel moved to look *out*, further and further away in the hope that they will ¿understand? more?

But the further you look the more you seem to be surrounded by empty space. You find yourself gazing up at the night sky. And for a little while you are entranced by the mysteries of the stars. They at least are not familiar, they are far, far away. For a long, brief lifetime you are almost dissolved in the idea that those stars are reflections in a sort of ¿transcendental? mirror: a magic clue to the reality beneath your sandalled feet.

But ¿knowledge? has ¿advanced? already! Soon the heavens themselves are swallowed up in a deeper mystery as men first rearrange the
planets, setting the sun (instead of the earth) in the centre. And soon
they become aware again of the limitations of their perspective, they
suspect that what they can actually see 'out there' is less than the whole
of what exists. So they build more and more powerful time-machines
in order to beat the interference of earth's atmosphere and explore
further and further out into space. Some of these time-machines take
intrepid explorers to the nearby orbs to pick up bits of rock and bags
of dust for analysis, but the notion is growing all the ¿time? and it is
surely folly to search so close to earth! Radar telescopes and other
marvellous devices probe deeper and deeper into space. Beyond our
very solar system, beyond the whole galaxy of stars, the mechanical eye
looks out.

And what can be seen *out there*? What news comes back from the
frontiers of science? Where is it all pointing, all this talk of pulsars and
quasars, red shifts and Olber's paradox?

Well, you will probably know that there are two competing cos-
mologies currently held by astronomers, the rather naïve 'big bang'
theory and the more sophisticated, but somewhat clumsy, 'steady
state' theory. Though there are some interesting arguments between
these two schools of thought, both are agreed that there appears to be
some ¿point? from which all the 'elements' of the conceivable universe
are – at this ¿moment? – moving away. And as astronomical research
and calculation seems to zero in on that ¿point? of origin, the evidence
appears to mount up. The appearances in the sky get curiouser and
curiouser and the latest rumour is of 'black holes' which, as they are
approached more and more nearly, seem to be nothing more than the
original sinister grin.[7]

'It's the Cheshire Cat: now I shall have somebody to talk to.'

'How are you getting on?' said the Cat, as soon as there was mouth
enough for it to speak with.

But perhaps you are ¿thinking? that the term 'elements' in the above
paragraph would be better replaced by 'elemental thoughts', since
atoms, protons, neutrons, etc. are at last regarded by physicists as
'mere' analytical notions rather than as minute physical entities? Do
you ¿think? that it could be our *thoughts* with which we have peopled
space; that it could be our *thoughts* which seem to have come from
some ¿point?; that it could be our *thoughts* which have drawn away from
their origin, and are still expanding, receding, expanding? Perhaps, like
Philip Morrison, you consider that[8]

[We can never know that] our preconceptions are allowing us to see
and hear all the evidence given . . . for looking far away, thousands

of millions of light years, we are looking *back* thousands and millions of years. . . . We don't need telescopes to do that. . . . This flower is a product of last summer's growth, faded by now, its atoms took up their partnership only a few months ago . . . my hand is another group of atoms which will last, even the bones, at most tens of years, this rock . . . may have lasted a few hundred billion years. . . . Notice the range: from a tenth of a year . . . less than that, a day, to hundreds of billions of years, the earth itself is only a few times older. The remarkable point is that all of the galaxies we see flying away into the depths of space seem only at most to be a few times older than the oldest rocks on our earth. . . . This is a most remarkable coincidence.

It is indeed!

We shall have occasion to return to the observatory for another look at the stars in chapter 5. But for the moment the point to be grasped is that the figuring we do and hence the cosmos we see (either with our naked eyes or through complicated time-machines such as telescopes) is premissed, like our *BASIC BELIEFS*, on a certain metaphysical drift. Some hole!

Once you begin to trace some of these thoughts to which the notion of *FIGURATION OF FACTS* can be linked, you will notice that like most ¿disturbing? conceptions, this one stirs up more questions than it answers. However I shall be content with drawing your attention to just two more of these issues: the first is still to do with cosmology, the second logic.

If you take your habitual figuration for granted in a normal way then you may find the obliteration of the cleft between appearance and reality poses an even greater puzzle for your ¿reason? than does the metaphysic of the Cheshire Cat. Many people, faced with the phenomenological reduction (the abolition of the 'I'/'Not-I' division), have felt moved to ask what happens to Nature, to appearances, to collective representations, when there is no one around to recognize them. That is certainly a metaphysical cliché – but it is still a good question; and, if you are prepared to look beyond quadrangles, juniper trees, and radar telescopes, you may find some very ¿interesting? answers.[9] But all that will require more than mere thought – it will require ¿THINKING? – so perhaps you had better forget about it for the moment.

The other question to which I shall draw your attention here is this: if *FIGURATION OF FACTS* is a rudimentary form of thought, can figuration be ¿mistaken? ? Evidently so. Addressing this same issue, Barfield reminds us of the following jingle from *Sylvie and Bruno*.

> I thought I saw a banker's clerk
> Descending from a bus,

> I looked again and found it was
> A hippopotamus.

But what can it mean to 'make' a ¿*mistake?*, and how can we know when we have made one? In order to address those questions we must now turn our attention to a third element of thought paradigms.

Now, whether or not what I have been saying about the first two elements of paradigms of thought has meant anything to you, I think you will be inclined to agree that it has not been entirely ¿reasonable?. Indeed if you are now wondering whether or not the thoughts about *BASIC BELIEFS* and *FIGURATION OF FACTS* which I have outlined above are 'acceptable', you are quite probably doing that wondering with your faculty of ¿reason?. It is through ¿reason? that we normally decide which thoughts are sound and which ¿mistaken?.

For according to any paradigm there must be some rules of inference which serve to confine thoughts within certain predefined channels. These are the limits of *reason*: they are the bounds which mark the outskirts of a paradigm. Thoughts posited beyond those bounds forfeit their membership of the paradigm and will be exiled as wanderers: they are crackbrained, shatterpated, weird, illogical, unreasonable, dithyrambic, ¿false?, irrational, paranoid, or just plain *mistaken*.

Since you are adequately versed in common sense, you are already equipped with a very handy set of rules for linking thoughts together and for inferring one set of thoughts from another. I shall refer to these regulations as *RULES OF REASONABLENESS*. And, since anything more that I might say about them here would be, not only unreasonable, but also boring, I shall pass on quickly to the fourth and final element of thought that I propose to discuss.

The final constituent of a paradigm of thought is the one that gives it its content. I am speaking of *KEPT KNOWLEDGE*.

All normal people are engaged in a continuing struggle to link appearances with beliefs and beliefs with appearances, without going outside of the bounds of reason. Whenever we succeed in that aim we are so pleased with the resulting thoughts that we keep them as knowledge. Such judgments kept as knowledge encompass an enormous variety of descriptions, classifications, explanations, proverbs, practical strategies, and so on. In the storehouse of common sense there is, then, a great variety of *KEPT KNOWLEDGE*, including both highly abstract judgments (such as, 'things always get worse before they get better') and thoroughly specific recipes (such as, 'always warm the pot before adding the tea').

Now permit me to recap on 'the story so far'.

REALITIES ARE CONSTRUCTED THROUGH PARADIGMS OF THOUGHT.

Any paradigm which you and I may grasp will be analysable into four constituent elements:

BB BASIC BELIEFS
FF FIGURATION OF FACTS
RR RULES OF REASONABLENESS
KK KEPT KNOWLEDGE

Perhaps it will be helpful to crystallize these thoughts by employing additional mnemonics. Imagine a paradigm – *just for the moment* – to be a sort of triangle, or, if you prefer, a cone. At the 'top' is a conglomeration of *BASIC BELIEFS* (*BB*), ideas like the one Swinburne expressed in these lines:

> Glory to Man in the highest,
> The maker and master of things.

At the 'rock-bottom' is the commonly-taken-for-granted *FIGURA-TION OF FACTS* (*FF*), which literally grounds a paradigm in a world of reality, of appearances. The vertices of the paradigm are the *RULES OF REASONABLENESS* (*RR*) which keep the thoughts 'inside' from wandering off into forbidden regions. These are the 'proper channels', the commonly accepted notions about the correct ways of linking thoughts together. Then 'inside' the cone or pyramid

```
                         B B
                 R R     K K     R R
               R R   K K K K K   R R
              R R   K K K K K K K   R R
             R R   K K K K K K K K K   R R
            R R   K K K K K K K K K K K   R R
           R R   K K K K K K K K K K K K K   R R
          R R   K K K K K K K K K K K K K K K   R R
         R R   K K K K K K K K K K K K K K K K K   R R
        R R   K K K K K K K K K K K K K K K K K K K   R R
       R R   K K K K K K K K K K K K K K K K K K K K K   R R
      R R   K K K K K K K K K K K K K K K K K K K K K K K   R R
     R R   K K K K K K K K K K K K K K K K K K K K K K K K K   R R
    R R   K K K K K K K K K K K K K K K K K K K K K K K K K K K   R R
   R R   K K K K K K K K K K K K K K K K K K K K K K K K K K K K K   R R
 F F   F F   F F   F F   F F   F F   F F   F F   F F   F F   F F   F F   F F
```

FIGURE I

that you are picturing at the moment is a collection of *KEPT KNOW-LEDGE (KK)* of all sorts. In our own common-sense terms these are bits of information about what things happen, how they happen, why they happen, and, of course, how to do all kinds of things from unarmed combat to Fair Isle knitting, and from having-a-baby to behaving-nicely-at-a-funeral.

Topped by *BASIC BELIEFS (BB)*, and confined within the space enclosed by the *RULES OF REASONABLENESS (RR)* and habitual methods of *FIGURING FACTS (FF)*, is the *KEPT KNOWLEDGE (KK)*. This is the substance of common sense, and it, like the form of the paradigm itself, is our collective cultural inheritance.

There they are then. They are 'outside' of each one of us, these the thoughts our fathers left for our delight and entertainment, our ¿tested? and ¿true? FAIRY TALES (Figure 1).

Phew! What a lot of thoughts! I am sorry to say that we are about to find out that those are the sorts of things they keep in libraries.

Chapter 3

A Trip Through the Library

Maybe I am ¿correct? in my appraisal of the way in which you and I habitually use our paradigmatic inheritance to construct and maintain the reality which seems to confront us, even now. If so, then, like the rest of us heirs to this cultural estate, you will find it easier to bring your *BB*, *FF*, *RR* and existing *KK* to bear on anything when both you and it are, so to speak, standing still. That is why I have tried to present you with a static view of a paradigm of thoughts. After all it is hard enough to grasp any set of thoughts which persists in changing all the time, particularly if you can't keep still yourself. But I am asking you to do something even more difficult: I am suggesting that you entertain some thoughts about the very thoughts that you take for granted. To have expected you to begin to do that while both you and the thoughts in question were gadding round a maypole would have been a little impolite.

But, whatever else appears to be, thoughts seem to be ¿advancing? all the ¿time?. We are agreed about that, are we not?

It seems that there is more to be gleaned from the storehouse of common sense today than there was yesterday: we are *gaining* in knowledge all the while. Similarly science has more to offer today than ever before. Indeed, I doubt that you would be surprised to hear that if every scientist who ever died was to return from the other side for a grand ball, they would scarcely fill the Wembley Stadium; and their venerable company would be clearly outnumbered by a gathering of all the scientists alive today. No, we have little doubt that knowledge, whether in science or in everyday life, is moving onward and onward.

Yet, of course, motion, like any other appearance whatever, is a matter of perspective. You have quite probably had the experience of sitting in a railway train which was standing in a station. Looking out of the window to your right you thought the train was moving, but, on glancing out of the other window, you realized that the appearance of motion was a delusion produced by the fact of another train passing on your right. You also know, if you pause to reflect on it, that *you* are moving all the time, even when you seem to be standing still, for the earth is yet circling the sun. And you know that when you are moving upon the earth the appearance of motion is a function of the relative speeds of the *two* bodies, you and the earth and their relation to certain other points of reference. So you will agree that motion, like anything else, is a matter of perspective. And so, of course, is ¿time? itself. For 'An absolute time with an independent flow would seem to require another time in which it flowed and by which its rate of flow was measured, and so on *in infinitum*.'[1]

So, if thoughts are ¿advancing? in ¿time? then we, the beneficiaries of this gratifying appearance, must be continually changing our perspective(s). How do we manage this enchantment?

I suggest that the clue to the mysterious phantom of ¿advancing knowledge? is to be found in that part of a paradigm of thought which I have described as the *RULES OF REASONABLENESS*. It is through *reason* that modern minds maintain their perspective of ¿progress?; thus it is through *reason* that thoughts must seem to ¿advance? and knowledge to ¿grow?, as we 'travel' from yesterday to today and 'on' towards tomorrow.

For reasoning is not – like believing and figuring – an unreflexive kind of thought. To reason is to have thoughts *about* thoughts: it is a *self-conscious* pursuit. And to be conscious of oneself is to be conscious of the independent existence of other selves, of other minds. Through reason we measure our thoughts against the thoughts of others, we compare, contrast, dispute, debate, and argue. We spot mistakes by reference to a background of other thoughts, we suggest corrections, we forge new links between one set of thoughts and another, and, sometimes, we reject old thoughts formerly kept as knowledge, replacing them by newer, better, more ¿advanced? notions.

If it is through reasonable dialogue that thoughts ¿progress?, then our taken-for-granted world – our paradigm – is in constant flux. Change in the *content* of our knowledge (in our *KK*) is happening all the ¿time?, it is an entirely *normal* thing. But this *normal* change or ¿growth? of knowledge takes place within a fixed frame of reference, an unchanging paradigmatic *form* of thought. Indeed it is only because of the constancy of our *BB*, *FF* and *RR* that we perceive a ¿growth? in *KK* at all. So change in the *formal* characteristics of a paradigm is by no means a normal phenomenon; on the contrary it is an entirely *extraordinary* or 'revolutionary' occurrence which, as we shall see, cannot occur unless the taken-for-granted paradigm governing normal thought is ¿transcended? in some way.

While the stock of *KK* enclosed within a paradigm seems, ordinarily, to be *growing* all the ¿time?, then, this is only so because the *BB*, *FF* and *RR* are preserved as fixed points of reference. Within those margins reasonable dialogue can take place, and through such dialogue thoughts may be seen to *advance*, to develop and *progress*. If you and I – or you and anyone else with a 'mind of his own' – are to have a discussion about anything at all, you must do so on the tacit assumption that both share an epistemological methodology. The epistemological methodology from which *we* are jointly bound to begin is the one we have been confronted with since we first opened our eyes upon this world. It is the form of a paradigm of common-sense thought which is founded upon a base union of a certain kind of *BB* with a special sort of *FF*, a union bound by vague but harsh legislation, the *RR*. And, though the *BB*, *FF* and *RR* are *all* taken for granted it is the last, the *RULES OF REASONABLENESS*, which seem to govern the enterprise. It is rather as if the architects of the epistemology of post-Enlightenment thought saw the *RR* as the radii which defined the whole scope of the paradigm. It is almost as though they took their pencils to their drawing boards and began their plans by constructing the vertices of the conical structure first, allowing the angle at the apex of the pyramid (the mitre of *BB*) to be determined by the meeting of those lines of reasoning. Almost. But not *quite*.[2]

Now even the most casual study of the history of thoughts in our own cultural domain leads inevitably to the realization that the paradigms of science and of common sense are somehow implicated with one another. That science grew out of the efforts of ordinary mortals to increase their sense of ¿understanding? and ¿control? over their worlds has never really been denied. That science has an impact on the common-sense reality of everyday life *cannot* be denied. It is obvious to common sense that any science which ignores folk-reasoning is ignorant, yet it is equally obvious from a scientific viewpoint that a culture heedless of the work of its scientists is impotent. Whereas today there are peoples who treat conjunctivitis by a method which results in total blindness in one out of every two cases, premature faith in the omnipotence of science led many Westerners to ignore the already-known curative properties of mouldy bread, that is, until the ¿invention? of penicillin.[3]

Of course, it is a cliché that specialization is rendering even the men of science themselves ignorant of the vaster part of the knowledge to which they could be party,[4] and that scientific advance is proceeding so fast that much of what we laymen learned in school is already ¿false?.[5] Yet there is a sense in which it is still reasonable to hold the view of men like Huxley, Tyndall and Spencer that 'science is but common sense refined and organised.'[6] For we laymen believe that we are separated from the fruits of science only by our ineptitude. On the whole we accept that the reasoning of the scientists would be amenable to us

Bond of Union

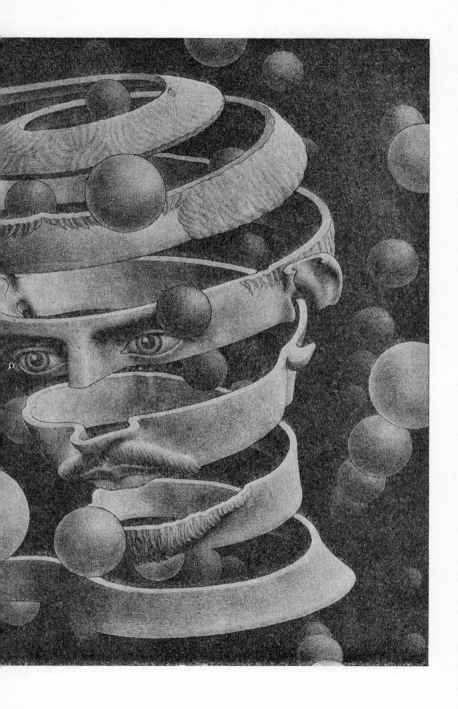

if only our heads were a little fuller and our wits a little sharper. And when 'scientific conclusions' are made available to us in a language we can follow, we accept them, for they have the authority of *reason* about them. In our common-sense culture, as in science itself, there is a respect for the disinterested pursuit of ¿truth?, that is for the *pursuit of knowledge through reason.*

According to the common-sense *RULES OF REASONABLENESS* (which, normally, we all accept) ¿time? 'flows onward', ¿causes? precede ¿effects?, and *more* reason must necessarily yield *more* ¿truths?, *more* knowledge. Thus is our assumption that knowledge advances bound up with our commitment to reason. And thus it comes about that the paradigms of science and common sense seem both to be moving forward in ¿time?. It is as though they describe a complicated involute together, each unravelling the mysteries of the other as they both progress in ¿time?. For their motion with respect to one another is such that *at any particular moment in ¿time?* the view afforded from either perspective gives the distinct impression that:[7]

> '*Yesterday's Common Sense is Less than Today's Common Sense.*'
> '*Today's Common Sense is Less than Tomorrow's Common Sense.*'
> '*Yesterday's Common Sense is Less than Tomorrow's Science.*'
> '*Yesterday's Science is Less than Tomorrow's Common Sense.*'
> '*Yesterday's Science is Less than Today's Science.*'
> '*Today's Science is Less than Tomorrow's Science.*'

Science 'leads' and common sense 'follows'. Yet without common sense science could not have begun. Science must ¿transcend? common sense, yet common sense is the ultimate check on science. Each progresses in ¿time? when viewed from the standpoint of the other. Yet the relationship between the common-sense paradigm of everyday life and that of science is a kind of symbiosis. Like the whorls and tracts of the brains from which they have their common source, they are curiously entangled.

SCIENCE AND COMMON SENSE ARE MUTUALLY INVOLUTED. (See the illustration on pages 30–1.)

Let us just explore a few of the strands of the endless path of thoughts defining the form of those gyrating involutes. Let us look at some of the ways in which common sense and science may be bound together.

The paradigm of common sense contains a background of everyday taken-for-granted *KK*. Though all of this *KK* is available to all of us, each has acquired only some part of it, and what he does know he has not learned in a formal fashion. Rather, each of us has picked up what

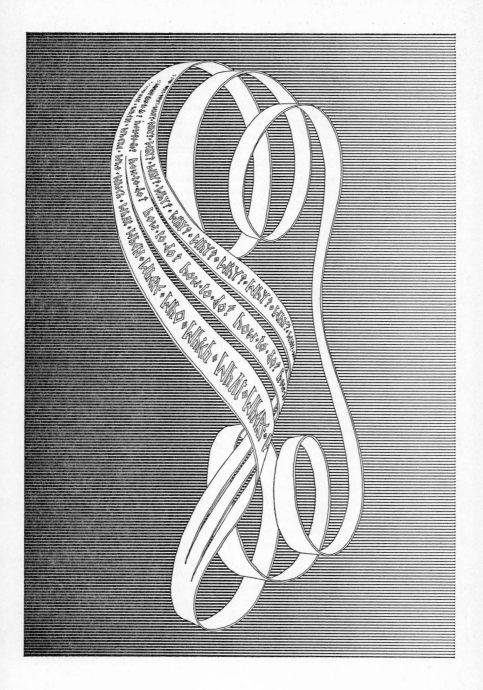

he knows through interaction with other thoughtful people. For example, your knowledge that a poultice of dock leaves and spit will cool the inflammation of a nettle sting was probably not learned from a book. Maybe that information can be found in some book, somewhere, but the odds are that you learned it more directly. My guess is that you first experienced the discomfort of a nettle sting as a fairly small child; then, either at the time or on hearing of your misfortune after the event, some kindly adult or more canny child taught you a useful piece of *KK* (kept knowledge). The stock of information kept as knowledge in the store-house of common sense includes countless similar recipes and remedies for everyday exigencies: it is part of the background reality which we participants in ordinary everyday life in England take for granted; it is part of our *collective* cultural heritage: any one of us may learn any part of it.[8]

But it would be a mistake to think that the questions which present themselves to common sense, in our world or any other, are limited to *practical* issues such as strategies for dealing with annoying or incon-venient occurrences like nettle stings. There are also *factual* questions raised and answered in everyday life, questions like 'Do dock leaves always grow near nettles?', or, 'Do little girls grow up faster than little boys?' These questions of fact, while obviously involving possible implications for practical problems, are not confined to them or necessarily motivated by them. Then there is another type of query which may occur to an ordinary person in the context of his everyday life: the *theoretical* question. Sometimes these questions are also motivated by practical considerations. For example, if young Alice asks 'Why do dock leaves cool the sting?', she may be wondering if the juice of the leaves could be bottled so that she might always have some handy in the pocket of her pinny, and she may be further hypothesizing that the potion might work for insect stings as well as nettle rash. But many theoretical questions of everyday life are motivated simply by the desire for understanding itself, as with 'Why do the stars shine in the night?', 'Why does the rainbow make the colours of my dreams?', and 'Why do butterflies die so soon?'

Common sense, then, throws up three sorts of problems: *practical problems* or How-to-do?-questions, *factual problems* or Who?/Which?/What?/Where?/When?-questions, and *theoretical problems* or Why?-questions. Normally suitably kept answers to all three sorts of questions can be found in the store of common-sense *KK*. Thus children spend more time asking questions than adults do, simply because the latter already know most of the stock answers. Yet, of course, these stock answers are inextricably connected with the scientific storehouse of *KK*. Imagine, for example, the Spock-educated middle-class parent answer-ing a child's dock-leaf queries in terms of alkaline and acid states, or transposing rainbow phantasies and gossamer webs into matters of refraction of light and the biochemistry of the spider.

Now, sometimes, everyday life and thought spit out problems which bother even knowledgeable adults. They want to know How?, Who?, Which?, What?, Where?, When?, or Why?, and going to the common-sense storehouse of kept knowledge they find that comical conical cupboard bare. 'How can this new form of wheat blight be stemmed?'; 'What are the odds on me dying of lung cancer if I carry on smoking forty cigarettes a day?'; 'Are young people who use drugs sick?'; 'Is the disease catching?'; 'How can I prevent my teenage son from going down with it?'; 'Does the new washing powder with Biological Action wash any whiter?'

Of course suitable answers to some of these problems can be *worked out* within the common-sense paradigm even though no relevant stock of knowledge yet exists about them. For example, the housewife who is interested in the last query can simply compare the two kinds of washing powder using the common-sense rules of reasonableness, which would no doubt lead her to attempt to wash similarly soiled sundries in similar suds, varying only the type of detergent. But in other cases the only suitable answer which common sense suggests is '*Ask an expert*'.

Thus some of the problems thrown up by common sense, and the experience of everyday life, become puzzles for scientists. But by no means all of the puzzles of science have such mundane origins; many, indeed most, of the puzzles that scientists face are products of the scientific enterprise itself: there are practical puzzles such as those of measurement and instrument design, factual puzzles of unexplored parameters and unknown variables, and the unending chains of theoretical puzzles that beset the ivory-tower dwellers of our imagination.[9]

Yet the simple queries of everyday life are by no means unimportant to science, and the history of science is full of tales of problems from the parlour, sickroom, or field whose solutions by scientists were keys to further ¿discovery?, ¿invention?, and ¿theoretical advance?. These solutions, translated into the language and physical equipment of everyday life, are then taken into the storehouse of common sense to be kept as knowledge, learnable by any ordinary member of the culture.

To reiterate, one source of the puzzles which provide the rationale for scientific activity is the loose ends which spin off the common-sense way of ¿understanding? the world. Where common sense cannot answer its own queries, either with a stock solution from the storehouse of *KK*, or with a way of working out the answer according to the ordinary *RULES OF REASONABLENESS*, then the ordinary person turns to an expert for ¿explanation?, information, and recipes for action. Today's experts are almost invariably scientists. Their answers are

often a long while coming, but, if and when they do come, they add to
the stock of folk-knowledge and may even modify or extend the ordinary
techniques of folk-reasoning. At the same time it must be recognized
that answers to purely scientific queries may result in innovation for
common sense, even where the latter had recognized no prior problem.
I am told that the gentleman who invented the electric light bulb kept
it dark for nearly twenty years because he could see little use for it![10]
Yet that invention has affected the common-sense world we now take
for granted. For the spread of domestic electricity in these islands has
resulted in the addition of much practical knowledge to our background
of *KK* and, like other technological developments, has even added to
the strategies of reasoning which we have developed within the confines
of *RR*. It is, for example, highly probable that you not only know how
to identify and replace a blown fuse but that you could also *work out*
how to mend an electric fire, smoothing iron, or other domestic device.
Indeed you might well catch yourself modestly disclaiming some in-
credulous lady's admiration of your flair for electrical craft with the
remark, 'It's only common sense'!

But there is an even more *fundamental* way in which the development
of scientific thought continually affects the everyday world of our experience. For judgments kept as knowledge within the paradigm of
science eventually leave their marks upon something more basic than
even our common-sense *KK* – they impress themselves upon our very
FIGURATION OF FACTS. What you see and hear, touch, smell,
taste, and feel in today's ordinary taken-for-granted world is – at least
in part – an assemblage of scientific relics. The solid rock-bottom of
your world is fossiliferous: within it lurk the traces of scientific thoughts-
already-thought. But *you* merely take them for granted, these fossils of
science. *Your* taken-for-granted world is round; everything in it and
beyond it is made up of tiny 'particles of matter' (atoms, neutrons,
protons, etc.); your material universe is expanding; your knowledge is
growing; your culture and civilization are advancing. *All that you take
for granted!* But once upon a time there lived a race of men whose
manifest world was made up out of four elements (earth, air, fire,
water); their universe was God-given; and their wisdom was ever on
the wane since the moment when the first woman treated the first man
to the original naughtiness (see the illustration on page 37).

> her rash hand in evil hour,
> Forth reaching for the fruit, she pluck'd, she eat:
> Earth felt the wound, and Nature from her seat
> Sighing through all her works gave signs of woe
> That all was lost.
>
> (Milton, *Paradise Lost*, ix)

Aftermath

Now, if you have in your mind the image of linked paradigms of thought which I have been trying to convey, you may well be wondering how this has happened. One moment I say that it is impossible for you to see both ends of the stick because the other end is you, then I seem to be trying to show you what scientific and common-sense paradigms of thought might look like if you could somehow ¿transcend? them and look at them with the eyes of a stranger to both. What kind of a trick is *that*?

You are right! It is another illusion, another construction through another paradigm. I have not been offering you a secret view of the ways in which common sense and science *in themselves* relate together. I have been simply suggesting another ¿model?, another perspective on the familiar phenomena of everyday life and on the scientific enterprise which attempts to ¿transcend? them.

What kind of a paradigm could render whole systems of thought and appearances as mere phenomena? From what sort of standpoint could one construct a paradigm of paradigms?[11]

Actually there are a number of answers that could be given to this question. Metaphysicians, Magicians, Theologians, Philosophers of Science, Psychologists, Anthropologists, Anthroposophists, Epistemologists, and many others, all offer methods of building paradigms of paradigms, systems of thoughts about thoughts, theories about how human beings use beliefs, sensations, reason and knowledge, to construct and maintain appearances of reality. Another method – rather a fashionable one in the world which you and I share today – is ¿sociology?.[12]

¿Sociologists?, asked to describe or ¿explain? their activities as ¿sociologists?, are fond of replying that they are out to construct a 'theory of the natives' theories',[13] or a 'typification of their typifications'.[14] Paraphrasing these charters in even more grandiose terms, one might say.

¿SOCIOLOGISTS? SEEK A PARADIGM OF PARADIGMS.[15]

But how *in the world* could such an enterprise begin? Out of what could such a paradigm be constructed? If we wish to do ¿sociology? where do we start?[16]

Well, maybe we would begin with our feet firmly on the ground, clinging unequivocally to that aspect of our common-sense paradigm that we, like any other academics, philosophers, scientists, etc., are least eager to relinquish. We could concentrate on the *FIGURED FACTS* of everyday life which ordinarily anchor our thoughts in a background world-taken-for-granted. Thus we might choose to take the common-sense data of experience as the unproblematic 'givens' from which to launch a paradigm. We cannot know whether you and I see the ¿same? colour when we pronounce, 'That is red', or whether we share an evaluation of it when we exclaim, 'How *red* that is!'; but we do take it for granted that we can communicate our sensations through the shared notion of redness and the shared word 'red'. We are used to taking certain sensations as clues for identifying and communicating supposed qualities of reality. Maybe then we could begin by recording our communicable sensations?

Ponder upon this suggestion for a moment and you will probably agree that it would not get us very far. For, if we were to do this, what would we achieve? On the one hand we might simply give a very boring minute-to-minute commentary on one type of life in one particular world seen from the point of view of a small part of that world. For example, the student wakes up and begins immediately to verbalize his sensations for the benefit of a strategically placed tape-recorder:

'light . . . eyes rub itch rub eyes . . . mouth like bottom of parrots' cage . . . tingle tongue toothpaste . . . bubbly boil . . . coffee tastes . . . etc.' On the other hand we might try to escape the artificiality of language, only to produce gobbledygoop of a different kind: 'Ooooooooooooo! . . . ugh! . . . Brrrrrrrr! . . . Ouch!' Yet we would still be trapped within the mundane world of everyday life: after all 'brrrrr!' means something to you, 'gggggggggggm!', for example, does not.

No. I am going to pretend that you agree with William James that percepts without concepts can yield only 'blooming buzzing confusion'. So I shall proceed as though you accept the assumption that the sensations which we actually experience are heavily dependent upon our attention. Thus our life in the everyday world we have learned to take for granted has taught us to structure our attention in order to select stimuli from within a limited range.

Obviously then we must be more adventurous. We have set ourselves the grandiloquent task of 'building a paradigm of paradigms'; if we rely upon our senses alone we shall not get beyond the appearances.

Perhaps we could try gathering knowledge instead? Maybe if we could gather enough pieces of *KK* we could simply pile them all up into a paradigm? The implication is this. If you want to be a ¿sociologist? forget your own sensations: you are *not* hungry, your feet are *not* cold, your fingers are *not* numb from pressing doorbells and filling in questionnaires: go out into the field and collect some more knowledge. Surely, if you ask enough people you will find out plenty of things that they know about their world?

But unfortunately the Ordinary People know *too much*! They know all sorts of things from the certain fact that the blacks should be sent back where they came from (a piece of knowledge that *you* don't even believe to be ¿true?) to the highly agreeable judgment that you look as though you need a nice hot cup of tea. And if you were blessed with abnormal longevity (and an unnatural thirst for ¿sociology?) you might actually collect all the knowledge to which one Ordinary Person laid claim. You would then, of course, proceed to the second respondent in your sample only to discover that he too had a hoard of knowledge about his world, some of it very much like his neighbour's, but some – like the judgments that, say, he is proud to be black and that he can't stand tea – startlingly different.

And how would you record all this mass of information? How would you process it? What could you make of it?

It is said that Francis Bacon had a similar problem when he wished to gather together the significant parts of the kept knowledge that filled the scientific paradigm of the seventeenth century. As Kuhn has noted, this approach inevitably produces a 'morass. . . . The Baconian histories of heat, colour, wind, mining and so on, are filled with information, some of it recondite. But they juxtapose facts that will later prove revealing (e.g. heating by mixture) with others . . . ', for example the weird judgment that 'water slightly warm is more easily frozen than quite cold'. Kuhn continues:[17]

> In addition, since any description must be partial, the typical natural history often omits from its immensely circumstantial accounts just those details that later scientists will find sources of important illumination. Almost none of the early 'histories' of electricity, for example, mention that chaff, attracted to a rubbed glass rod, bounces off again. That fact seemed mechanical, not electrical. Moreover, since the casual fact-gatherer seldom possesses the time or the tools to be critical, the natural histories often . . . [include] descriptions . . . that we are now quite unable to confirm. Only very occasionally . . . do facts collected with so little guidance from pre-established theory speak with sufficient clarity to permit the emergence of a first paradigm.

Karl Popper has also damned this approach to paradigm building with the memorable pejorative 'bucket theories of the mind'.[18] The implications for the ¿sociologist? inhere in the image of the eager data-collector, 'armed only with common sense and a tape recorder',[19] dashing out into 'the field' to find some pieces of KK, some little bits of culture. The intrepid researcher and his costly assistants return occasionally to the research unit to unload some data. Meanwhile, back at the unit the processing has begun: several professional bucket-men feed the computer with data. The answer is impatiently awaited. (From another dimension Gertrude Stein interjects a dying gasp, 'What was the *question?*'[20]) The wait is punctuated by breakdowns, interpersonal rivalry and Alka Seltzer. Finally the programming is complete. The computer prints out:

+ I + AM + THE + PENULTIMATE + BUCKET +.

Oh no! It is clear that a pile of KKs no more makes a paradigm than two swallows make a summer. What next then? We could try beginning with *BASIC BELIEFS*. Perhaps these would show us a way of making a whole paradigm take form? Perhaps they would, but the pragmatist would point out that such a stratagem would not get us very far in this Age of Reason: we would be labelled as 'ideological', 'political', or perhaps even 'idealistic' and thus stigmatized; no one would take any notice of what we had to say. Moreover if we did adopt that tactic we would never be quite sure that if we had chosen a different set of beliefs (¿chosen? from ¿what? ?) we would have come to the same conclusions.

Apparently there is only one way left. Do you agree that we might

just as well try the last possibility? What would be the consequences of
starting off with the *RULES OF REASONABLENESS*?

The ¿time? is now

YOU: (*Beginning to get interested*) Yes?

ME: Stretching the point, it seems a reasonable place
to commence (*continues changing out of clown
costume*).

YOU: One might, as it were, erect the girders of the
conical structure first, placing the vertical scaffolds
firmly on the rocky ground that is 'given'.
(*At this point Vierkandt, Frege, and Sorokin all
turn in their graves.*)

KARL POPPER: (*Wondering why he has been listening*) The resulting mesh would be like a sort of giant butterfly net
without a stick and could, perhaps be used to catch
the world, or little *KK*s of it?

PYTHAGORAS: (*Dimly from very far away*) And what about the
beliefs? Eh? How do they get in?

A. J. AYER: (*Very slightly intoxicated*) I suppose they sort of
float in at the top, hmmmm. Like Walt Disney
clouds, all pink and blue with angels playing harps.

Enough of this nonsense! It is very dangerous to stretch analogies for
reasons that I hope will become depressingly clear in the following
pages. Disciplined thought is what is required in a situation like this.
We need *reason* (which, of course, is precisely what I was saying when
you all interrupted!). Now,

TURN YOUR ATTENTION TO THE WAY IN WHICH YOU REASON.

Imagine, for example, that you wake up one morning with a belly ache.
There is a piece of reality which you simply cannot wish away, though
you might try! It is a problem and you have decided to make it a puzzle.
You want to solve it, to ¿explain? the event, you ask yourself '*Why* have
I got a belly ache?' Of course, you might ask yourself this question for a
number of motives, the hope of some strategy for relieving the discomfort or at least avoiding the situation in future, might be more
compelling at the ¿time? than your thirst for ¿understanding?: your
'*Why . . . ?*' might really disguise a How?-Question. But what is
¿interesting? now is how you would go about *answering it*.

My guess is that you will seek your answer beyond the event itself in
a more general class of phenomena which you feel you ¿understand?.
You will clutch at a piece of common-sense *KK*. It is well known, for

example, that gut troubles frequently follow unusual gastronomic events. (You hastily dismiss the possibility that this instance is one of those commonly known as 'making a pig of yourself', a category which you know to be very commonly relevant at such times.) You immediately grasp the possibility of a connection between the oyster-eating of last night and the agony of this morning. You are being entirely reasonable. Despite the misery you are bearing so bravely, you are working things out by the common-sense rules of reasonableness. A sensible hypothesis has formed in your mind. Now you devise a simple ¿test?: 'Have my co-oyster-eaters also been afflicted?' A couple of telephone conversations later you would probably have ¿explained? the whole thing:

> 'Marigold, Jeffrey, and Bartholomew are all suffering . . . but Jane is disgustingly healthy . . . she doesn't eat oysters . . . by all accounts she doesn't *need* to . . . [*that is a totally irrelevant piece of* KK *relating to an entirely different puzzle. Common sense is often untidy.*] couldn't have been alcohol . . . then, definitely the oysters . . . you DO have to be very careful with oysters.'

Now let us run through that again in slow motion. You wish to *¿explain?* the occurrence of an event (you have gut trouble). You search the knowledge available to you for a generalization that may be relevant. You find one ('Gut troubles often occur after uncommon dietary experiences'). *Reasonableness links this proposition with that-which-was-to-have-been-explained* (you have gut trouble) *via a number of other judgments* (for example, 'I ate oysters last night', 'Oyster-eating is uncommon for me'). But some of these linking judgments are so obvious that you are never actually conscious of considering them, it is almost as though such judgments as, for example, 'Oyster eating is eating' (i.e. a 'dietary experience') spring from the events themselves. *Now by the same rules, you reason that, if you are correct in your ¿explanation?, then certain other phenomena will also be observable* (e.g. 'People whose present relationship to oyster-eating is equivalent to mine will also have gut ache'). *You therefore have some hypotheses to ¿test?* ('Marigold, Jeffrey, and Bartholomew will also have gut troubles this morning'). You do this by means of the telephone. In the process of testing these hypotheses you also uncover an ¿interesting? additional phenomenon ('Jane does not have gut trouble'). This both reminds you that you forgot to examine the possibility of an alternative explanation (for example that the gut trouble is linked with the heavy drinking that accompanied the oyster orgy) and serves as an unsought ¿test? of a hypothesis that you could have derived from that alternative ('Jane has gut trouble'). *You have generalized in order to ¿explain? a puzzling particular and particularized in order to ¿test? your ¿explanation?.*

Perhaps you would like to stop and consider this. Do *you normally* work things out like that? Is that how you usually reason?

Focusing on the process of ¿explanation? I have suggested that you and I share with other members of our culture a tendency to ¿explain? by subsumption under generalizations. *We feel that we have ¿explained? a previously puzzling phenomenon when we have related it to a background of taken-for-granted generalizations* (KK) *without violating the ordinary* RULES OF REASONABLENESS *in so far as we follow them.* You and I also share a tendency to call such ¿explanations? *theories.* Our world is full of theories: there's Mrs Arkwright's theory about her husband's lack of interest in her, there's the psychiatrist's theory about Mr Arkwright's impotency, there's Mr Arkwright's theory about Mrs Arkwright and the psychiatrist, and there's Ronnie Laing's theory about the lot. And – skipping a few steps – there is *your* theory about my theory about Ronnie Laing's theory. For you, as for me, Ronnie Laing, the psychiatrist, Mrs Arkwright, Old Arkwright, Uncle Tom Cobley and all,

EXPLAINING IS GENERALIZING.
GENERALIZING IS THEORIZING.

To ask for an explanation is to ask for a theory. Theorizing is the linking of observations to generalizations. A successful explanation is one which succeeds in *subsuming* the puzzling particular under a general proposition, or, to put it another way round, in *deducing* the particular from the general.[21] But to be successful an explanation must also be reasonable, it must not violate the *RULES OF REASONABLENESS.* How can we be sure that we are obeying those rules, that we are being reasonable?

One obvious answer to this question lies in the method of formalizing and elaborating upon common-sense reasoning which characterizes the way of science. For the common-sense *RULES OF REASONABLE-NESS* have a formal analogue and extension in that part of the methodology of science which I shall distinguish from the former by the name *RADII OF REASONING.* The scientific *RADII OF REASONING* are analogous to, and commensurable with,[22] the common-sense *RULES OF REASONABLENESS,* but the two are not identical. The proponent of the scientific approach would explain to you that, while the ordinary *RULES OF REASONABLENESS* provide a sufficient guide for determining the reasonableness of simple explanations, they become rather difficult to apply when the issue is more complicated.

For example, if a mistake had occurred in the *oyster-gut-saga* outlined above – if unreasonable reasoning had taken place – it would have been simple enough for us to spot it. But imagine that you wish to devise a more ambitious theory. Suppose, for example, that you were puzzled by the very judgment that 'oysters are dodgy eating' and wished to explain that phenomenon itself.

The advocate of the scientific approach to reality would tell you that, faced with this rather more ¿interesting? puzzle, common-sense thought stands little chance of ending up with an entirely reasonable chain of judgments. Indeed, he would urge that the man-in-the-street should step off the pavement to make way for the professional, the expert, the scientist.

Now reasonable scientists admit that, like any other reasonable people, they are sometimes right and sometimes wrong. But in their own estimation their superiority over the ordinary folk-in-the-road, like you and me, lies in one particular talent: the sure-fire ability to detect their own ¿mistakes?. Unlike you and me, they *know* when they (or more usually their rivals!) are wrong.

If taken into the realm of, say, medical science, then, the query about the relationship between oyster consumption and gastronomic disorders would be treated to a form of analysis similar to – but much more complicated than – our original oyster-gut-saga. For the rules of reasoning which are supposed to arbitrate the rationality of scientific thought are no less than the ordinary common-sense rules of reasonableness in a new guise. It is almost as though the wise old owls of our childhood had swallowed their sadness at finding the nurseries empty and, covering their untidy feathers with neatly-combed legal wigs, had slipped in amongst the grown-ups. Thus attired they now adhere strictly to the formal principles laid down in the judicial rule-books – and their strict wiggings persuade the grown-up professional scientists to avoid harsh sentences by keeping their reasoning legal.

You *may* find such guidance welcome. Perhaps it is better to clutch at a straw than to close your fingers against your empty palm? Anyway there isn't very much else to hang on to within and without the FAIRY-TALE MOUNTAIN of science. That straw rule-book might come in handy sometime – even if it is only to clobber some of the monstrous ¿SPIDERS? that are lurking in wait for you between the pages of the following chapters.

Come on then, let's have a look at the *RADII OF REASONING*. Let us see how the scientists propose to enable us to improve upon the common-sense *RULES OF REASONABLENESS*.

According to the interpreters of the rule-book principles who are currently most influential,[23] the original oyster-gut-saga can be viewed as a rough draft of a perfectly ¿valid?, if rather crude, theory of a sort which they call a *deductive nomological explanation*.

When constructing a *deductive nomological explanation*, the ¿GOLD-STAR? science student begins at the bottom. He starts with the-thing-that-is-to-be-explained, with the puzzle. This he calls the '*explanandum*' or '*E*' for short. He writes it at the bottom of a blank piece of paper and draws a line above it. Above that line he writes a number of sentences which go together to make up what he calls the '*explanans*'. These sentences are of two sorts, some of them are generalizations (statements like 'All mothers-in-law are a pain in the neck'); these he often calls '*laws*' and he labels them 'L_1, L_n etc.'. The other sorts of sentences are simply descriptions of particular phenomena and events (for example, 'Mrs Blenkinsop is my mother-in-law'); these our GOLD-STAR pupil labels 'C_1, C_n etc.'. His task is now simply to check that the *explanandum* (in this case, 'Mrs Blenkinsop is a pain in the neck') is a ¿reasonable? conclusion to draw from the *explanans*. The formula for his theory therefore looks like this:

A DEDUCTIVE NOMOLOGICAL EXPLANATION

L_1, L_2 (*some generalizations*) L_n
   (*e.g.*: All mothers-in-law are a pain in the neck)
C_1, C_2 (*some particulars*) C_n
   (*e.g.*: Mrs Blenkinsop is my mother-in-law)   EXPLANANS
   (premises)

EXPLANANDUM
E (*whatever-was-to-have-been-explained*)   (conclusion
   (*e.g.*: Mrs Blenkinsop is a pain in the neck)   & original
   puzzle)

If you put any theory into this form you should be able to check its ¿reasonableness? quite quickly by using Common Sense as a guide and arbiter of whether E follows 'logically' from L_1 to L_n and C_1 to C_n.

Take, for example, the following unreasonable piece of reasoning:[24]

  (C_1)   The sunlight falls upon the grass;
  (C_2)   It falls upon the tower;
  (C_3)   Upon my spectacles of brass
        It falls with all its power.

  (L_1)   It falls on everything it can,
  (L_2)   For that is how it's made;
  (C_4)   And it would fall on me, except,   EXPLANANS

  (E)   That I am in the shade   EXPLANANDUM

(from Mervyn Peake, *Rhymes without Reason*)

Any reasonable person reading that little rhyme can see at a glance, that as a theory, it is nonsense – glorious nonsense, but nonsense none the less. As an *explanation* of why the writer is in the shade it is a dismal failure whatever its other obvious merits. Perhaps you will protest that you don't need the format of a deductive nomological explanation to spot a load of nonsense when you see it? But perhaps I can persuade you to try an exercise.

EXERCISE

Rewrite the oyster-gut-saga as a deductive nomological explanation.

Did you find that annoying? The GOLD-STAR science pupil could explain to you that, unless you are prepared to use the annoying formulae which characterize the *RADII OF REASONING*, you may be laying yourself open to error. For, whereas assumptions may go unspoken (and perhaps unthought-about) in common-sense explanations, the efficiency of the scientific approach depends upon 'the principle that while hypotheses and theories may be freely invented and proposed in science, they can be accepted into the body of scientific knowledge only if they pass critical scrutiny'.[25] The first step in such critical scrutiny is the check that the information given in the *explanans* is sufficient for any reasonable person to infer from it the *explanandum*. The proposition *Oyster-eating is a dietary experience*, for example, may seem too obvious to bother about on a common-sense level of explanation, but if you undertook the exercise above you will have discovered that the oyster-gut-saga will not 'work' as a theory without it. The *logico-deductive method*, which insists that to be 'scientific' a theory must be stated in a special way, may be rather bothersome to operate in practice, but it certainly does help one to decide whether or not a theory is 'logical', that is whether it is *valid*.

A 'LOGICAL' THEORY IS A VALID THEORY.

Once a theory has been expressed as a deductive nomological explanation it is much easier for the reasonable person, who is not a professional logician, to spot errors of reasoning and detect invalid arguments. Hempel, for example, has exposed the unreasonableness of a certain once-common type of ¿sociological? explanation by simply rewriting it according to the formula.[26] By so doing he has enabled any student to spot the goof for himself.

Let us suppose that a certain silly ¿sociologist?, whom we shall call

Mr Vulgar Functionalist, is interested in explaining the occurrence of a certain feature (say, for example, high religious involvement: Call it *Trait I*), in a certain social location (say the ¿social world? of the Welsh: Call it *System S*), at a certain time (say the nineteenth century: Call it *Time T*), under certain specifiable conditions (which amount to a description of the ordinary context of everyday life in nineteenth-century Wales: Call it a *Setting of C*). Our ignominious functionalist would no doubt express his theory in annoying terminology (he may use words like 'functional prerequisites', 'tension management' and 'equilibrium') but, notwithstanding translation difficulties, we could probably render his explanation in the following form.

(C_1)   At Time T, System S functions adequately in a Setting of C.

(L_1)   System S functions adequately in a Setting of C only when a certain necessary condition, Condition N, is satisfied.

(L_2)   Whenever Trait I is present in System S then, as an effect, Condition N is satisfied.

(E)   (Hence) At Time T, Trait I is present in S.

You may have a number of quibbles about that theory. For example, you may be wondering what 'functions adequately' means, and you may be bothered about what kind of a phenomenon Condition N might be, and how anyone could know if it was there. But without even raising these queries you should be satisfied that you are faced with a thoroughly lousy theory, for it must be perfectly obvious that the *explanandum* cannot be validly deduced from the *explanans*. There is something wrong with the sheer 'logic' of that theory: it is as nonsensical as the poem about the sunshine and the shade.

EXERCISE
Ask yourself the following questions:
1. What is wrong with that theory?
2. How could it be rewritten as a logically valid explanation?
3. What difference would that modification make to the theory?

If you get stuck you can look up the answer.[27] But I think that you will find that it pays to work these things out for yourself.

Well, shall we proceed along these lines? You are in no position to answer – so, by default, the decision is mine. I reckon that we should go on. There is no point in each of us trying to develop a whole set of rules about reasoning, or 'logic', for ourselves. If we were to communicate our thoughts at all we would still have to accept common sense as an arbiter of the reasonableness of our theories. So perhaps for the moment it is best to accept the judgment that cleverer people than you and me have already systematized methods of reasoning which work very successfully, and which are still readily answerable to common sense. The GOLD-STAR science pupil will be our WHITE RABBIT. Let's follow him for a bit and see where we go. Ready? (See the illustration on page 49.)

Once inside the rabbit hole we find that the burrow seems to twist and turn around so that we frequently get the feeling that we are being led back to the part we reached a moment or so ago. Yet, at the same ¿time? it appears that we are ¿progressing? in some sense. We seem to be delving deeper and deeper into the strange world which lurks inside the mysterious conical mountain. Every now and then we come to a fork in the ways. Then, again, there is a choice of ¿directions?. We have just reached another fork.

The first tunnel on the right is marked 'Esoteric Formalism'. Our GOLD-STAR RABBIT stands aside so that we can peep in and see the great warren of funny signs and symbols and odd-looking diagrams and sums that lie through there. Some Very Clever People are working their ways along the walls being very careful not to make any mistakes. 'It took the pioneers a lifetime to get through that lot,' our RABBIT says, 'on the other hand nowadays a good guide can get you through in a fraction of the time.' We are very tempted to have a go, particularly when we spy the luscious conundrum who squats by the entrance to the tunnel; she is wearing a great big button badge which says 'WORK ME OUT!' But the RABBIT is talking again.

> RABBIT: Many who have taken that route have enjoyed the diversion tremendously, but others find it terrifying. They fear that one day they will come to a part where they can't work out the answer, that fear haunts them and taunts them until it drives them right into Confusion's trap.
>
> ME: What is Confusion?
>
> RABBIT: She is a SPIDER. She spins her webs all through the labyrinths of thought. Here in the catacombs of science the warren of esoteric formalism is one of her favourite haunts. For here her battles are in deadly earnest. Those who follow her glistening threads to this nest of logicians and mathematicians meet her at her most desperate. They attack her with all sorts of weapons, like Ockham's famous razor and Ithuriel's rusting spear, but some of them are choked by the tangled ends. And some are so filled with the lust of the game that they choose to stay.

'Let's follow him for a bit'

      ME: Shall we go in, I don't think I am afraid of the spider.
RABBIT: You do as you wish. I shall take the short cut all the
            rabbits use, we made it ourselves by DIGGING. Now
            hurry!

    I think we should follow the RABBITS. So far they have taught us that,
in a deductive nomological explanation, validity can be ascertained by
any reasonable person who considers whether or not the *explanandum*

follows from the *explanans*. In making the decision as to what *follows*, the reasonable person is guided fundamentally by the ordinary common-sense *RULES OF REASONABLENESS* to which even the *RADII OF REASONING* must defer. Now some people think that these rules can themselves be formalized, as they are in the warren of esoteric formalism, but common sense can provide the sense of direction which will give us the confidence to take a short cut.

I am suggesting, then, that we be content to use the formula of a *deductive nomological explanation* to settle the question of the scientific validity of a theory. Indeed we have already employed the logico-deductive method of removing the interrogative brackets around the word ¿explanation?. For logico-deductivists, to explain a phenomenon or event is to render it an *explanandum* and successfully deduce it from an *explanans*. A successfully deduced theory is a valid one, one which involves no 'logical mistakes'. A Proper Explanation and a Real Theory are for the logico-deductivists the same thing.

The Logico-Deductive Creed
To EXPLAIN is
To generalize is
To theorize.
A theory is
A construction in which
Concepts are
Combined into judgments,
And judgments are
Combined into chains
Of judgments,
Which form a
deductive nomological
EXPLANATION
Such that
The EXPLANANDUM
Can be validly deduced
From the
EXPLANANS.

In the catacombs catechisms like this,[28] necessary as they are, echo around rather empty chambers. For of course few of the theories that scientists entertain are Real Theories, few explanations are Proper Explanations. Most of the warrens are jerry built. If we were to exclude from science all theories that do not take a deductive nomological form we would find ourselves with precious little science left. Take away the dodgy bits and the whole warren might cave in. Thus most normal scientists reason that it is better to strengthen the enterprise with weak props than with none at all.

When so few natural scientists are as rigorous as their faith might suggest, those sociologists who have followed our RABBIT right into the mountain tend to look doubly silly, frequently discovering when they come out with their deductive nomological explanations that they have turned into bores in the dark.[29] No one is listening any more; the lime-light is on those theorists whose explanations are deductively doubtful and only casually contingent, those who have forgotten all about the creed and simply 'got on with the job'. So let's not follow our GOLD-STAR scientist any further at the moment, for, as he would have said when he was a RABBIT ,'We are in a hurry!'

I suggest that we accept that many of the explanations that scientists entertain are not GOLD-STAR explanations at all. Many scientific theories are not Proper Theories, though – as we shall see – their efficacy always lies in their potential for being superseded by genuinely deductive explanations. So, in order to outwit confusion for a ¿time?, I shall adopt William James's useful strategy: 'When you meet a contradiction you must make a distinction.'[30] I shall distinguish between those explana-tions which do take a strictly deductive form and those which do not. The former I shall call *EXPLANATORY THEORIES*, and these will be seen in contrast to two other sorts of theories, *IMPLICIT THEORIES* and *ANALYTICAL THEORIES*.[31]

IMPLICIT THEORIES are in abundance, both in the realm of everyday reasoning, and in that of science. They are like the oyster-gut-saga in its original crude form, with all its incompleteness and irrele-vance. Such theories do relate something-to-be-explained to a set of generalizations, whether these latter are scientific or common-sense fragments of *KK*, but they do so in a vague and ambiguous manner. It cannot be said of them that any reasonable person could always act as a judge of their reasoning fouls. In other words it is difficult to tell whether implicit theories are logically valid, and they may therefore be misleading. The everpresent danger with such theories is that hidden assumptions may lurk within them, tricking people to jump to ¿false?[32] conclusions, and fall prey to confusion. One of the most influential interpreters of the deductive rule-book, Carl Hempel, refers to these theories as 'explanatory sketches'. He accepts their usefulness, provided that scientists treat them with caution, recognizing that they are only in-complete or partial explanations.[33]

ANALYTICAL THEORIES are another kind of theory which, while extremely useful to the scientist, must be treated with great wariness. These are not really explanations at all, but representations of whatever-was-to-have-been-explained in terms of some *model*. The strategy for model-building, or analytical theorizing, is this. Suppose that you wish to cope with the puzzle 'Some people behave in a really nutty fashion.' Suppose also that, off-hand, you cannot find a generalization under which you can satisfactorily subsume this judgment. Now it *may* occur to you to pretend that the puzzling phenomenon which you have observed can be treated *as though* it were some *other* phenomenon which you *can* readily explain. This is the advice of the analytical theorist; he says, 'Look at the situation *as if* it were a different one.' In this case, for example, you might look at the phenomenon of nuttiness as though it were like the phenomenon of physical sickness, or – if that ¿model? does not turn you on – you can try treating nuttiness as if it were possession by evil spirits or punishment for the sins of the victim's great-grandparents.[34] In this way you can tentatively ¿understand? the phenomenon that was puzzling you, not by actually explaining it, but by treating it as though it were for all intents and purposes like something else that you *do* ¿understand?.

What you are doing when you reason in this way is *isomorphizing*, thinking in similes or metaphors.[35] You are relating the phenomenon-that-you-would-like-to-be-able-to-explain to entirely explicable things in an ISOMORPHIC fashion. *Models* are ISOMORPHS of reality. This means that they have two features.[36]

ISOMORPHISM   (a) There is a one-to-one relationship between the ¿interesting? *features* of the phenomenon-to-be-explained and those of the model.

(b) The ¿interesting? *relationships* in the original are mirrored in those of the model.

I can best convey the idea of modelling by using a model. Think of the way in which a builder of super-models might construct a model of the British Museum. First, his model is isomorphic in sense (a), everything that he considers ¿interesting? in the museum has a facsimile in the model.

Now, though the level of enthusiasm and skill and the adequacy of the materials of the ordinary model-builder might put limits upon what he could achieve, let us imagine that our super-model-builder has produced a marvellously life-like reading room with readers and books and a man at the door to check people's tickets. He might yet have forgotten entirely about the Elgin Marbles because, for him the ¿interesting? things about the British Museum inhere in its librariness, not its museumness, but no matter. For his purposes his model would be perfectly adequate provided, of course, that it also had feature (b). The relationships between pens, acquisition tickets, catalogues and so on would have to be preserved in the model. Perhaps another model will help you to grasp this model model? Think about *scale* then. If the model museum was 'out of scale', say with tiny little readers and great big books, then, for most conceivable purposes it would not be isomorphic with the real British Museum. For one of the characteristics of the real one, which would be ¿interesting? to almost anyone who wanted to build a physical model of it, is its shape in three-dimensional space.[37]

If, on the other hand, it was a good model then we would probably find that we could work out certain features from the model British Museum which the model-builder had not consciously incorporated into his model but which were observably isomorphic with the real institution. Imagine, for example, that he has included all the books and all the catalogues in the main reading room; they are all there in some amazing miniature form. Then, if we add a remote-controlled miniature reader we could observe his movements in the model library and compare them with those of a real reader in the real British Museum ordering a real copy of the same book. The sheer choreography of the situation would probably be noticeably isomorphic in the real and model settings: the movements of the real and model readers from seat to catalogue to central desk and back to seat would trace a similar pattern in three-dimensional space.[38] (Of course the isomorphism could not be perfect: for example, real readers occasionally blow their noses, argue with librarians and go outside for a cup of tea – but these are features in which the model-builder was not ¿interested?.)

Now that was only a model model: a model bounded by ¿time? and three-dimensional space. The models scientists make and use are *only sometimes* constructed out of tangible materials like ping-pong balls, matchsticks, plastic, and clockwork. Many of their models are simply adopted as full-blown ready-made ways of having thoughts about things. Once you decide to 'look at light as though it were composed of particles', or to 'look at a ¿social world? as though it were a functioning system', you decide to adopt a whole package of ideas which has been developed in some other context, and to apply them to the new one. Such models are isomorphs of realities in a sense which is isomorphic with the sense in which our tangible model British Museum was isomorphic with the real one. But these latter are verbal rather than physical arrangements.

Scientists create other sorts of models in addition to these two. For example, there are the models they construct in two dimensions on paper, using mathematical expressions or diagrams of one sort or other. Then there are also models created through a dialogue with a computer: the simulation games now popular in many fields are an identifiable type of analytical theorizing.

Models of all sorts, second-hand or home-made, are clearly invaluable to scientists. But they are the source of at least two serious forms of confusion.

The first danger with ¿understanding? by model-building or analogizing is that *the model may be wrongly taken for an explanation.* The very complexity of a well-worked model may lead people to forget its humble function, and slip into assuming that it is a valid and ¿true? theory, a satisfactory explanation. Thus, for example, some sociologists have adopted from the natural sciences the evolutionary model, and this has frequently been misconstrued as an *explanation* of social change. But it is no such thing; it is simply a metaphor which may or may not be useful in the *search* for an explanation. Just imagine that because our super-model builder had produced an amazing replica of the British Museum reading room he thought he had explained it! You could no doubt discover how his model readers 'worked' by taking them to pieces, but you would be engulfed in a strange phantasy if you thought that *that* would throw any light upon the way in which the real readers 'worked'. It would not assist you in grasping the motives of the latter in ordering specific books, the consequences of their reading those books, or anything else in which you might be ¿interested?.

A second, and related danger with models lies in something about which we have already had some forewarning. Of course, equipped as you are with the common-sense *RULES OF REASONABLENESS* you do not really need me to remind you of this trap: but I will do so all the same. A small child of my acquaintance can furnish us with an example. It had occurred to her one day as she sat contemplating in her bath that, 'The hot water is like all the good in the world and the cold like the evil. The bath is a mixture of hot and cold, and there is both good and evil in the world.' That is quite sensible analytical theorizing for a seven-year-old. But she had gone on to speculate that, 'Since the water in the bath is getting colder all the time, then the world must be growing more evil.' In deference to her I shall call *the error of over-stretching an isomorphic relationship* the BATHWATER FALLACY.

Models are inherently dangerous but no discipline can do without them, and many scientists are prepared to rely on them. The library of ¿sociological? *KEPT KNOWLEDGE* is crammed full of analytical theories; in fact some ¿sociologists? have complained that the vogue for models is operating to inhibit the development of explanatory theories.[39]

> YOU: Just a minute! Where does that door lead to?
> RABBIT: Only the library. *All* the doors lead to the library around here. In fact, if you go through the library you can get from almost anywhere to almost anywhere else.
> YOU: Shall we go in?
> RABBIT: NOT I! Once I get in there I can scarcely hear myself *thinking* because of the din. But if *you* want to go and catch a headache that's your business. Don't get lost now . . . and hurry!

In the main hall of the library there are leather-bound volumes of *grand models*. If you go over to the ¿sociological? section you can see some examples. This one is called *The Social System* and, like the others, it is supposed to offer an enlightening isomorph of entire ¿social worlds?. The author, Professor Parsons, takes great delight in assimilating into his model any ¿social phenomena? to which his attention is drawn. He follows in a grand tradition of ¿sociological? model-builders who have chosen to view ¿social worlds? as though they were *organic systems*. Some of these writers, like Spencer and Comte, splashed BATHWATER all over the place, sometimes causing the ink on their manuscripts to run so badly that it is difficult to make head or tail of them.[40] But this Professor Parsons has been a little more cautious.

On a near-by shelf stand some volumes of grand models based on a different analogy altogether, that of the *machine*. Still other grand model-fanciers have gone further and used the analogue of the *computer*: they have had great fun creating 'process flow models', and thinking of ¿social worlds? as though they were vast systems of information input and output with plenty of feedback loops. There is also a nice collection of very pleasantly illustrated books in a section sub-titled *dramaturgical models*. These are based on the attractive and well-loved notion of the world-as-a-play.[41]

Now none of these grand models represents a uniquely ¿sociological? way of looking at things. Nor is this sort of grand-model construction an exclusively Western activity. For example, in the Rubaiyat of Omar Khayyam you could have read:

For in and out, above, below
'Tis nothing but a Magic Shadow-show,
Play'd in a Box whose
Candle is the Sun,
Round which we Phantom
Figures come and go.

But you won't find a copy of *that* book in the section of the LIBRARY where they keep the ¿sociological? grand models; though there are plenty of other books around which we are in no position to find at the moment.[42]

If we turn away from the hall of grand models we find that passages full of volumes of *ad hoc* or '*middle range*' analytical theories lead out-wards in all directions. Unlike the grand models these do not involve schemes for relating all things ¿social? to each other. They are less ambitious but more practical strategies for coming to grips with specific ¿social? phenomena. There are the models of 'demographic transition', 'cooling the mark out', 'sponsored and contest mobility norms', 'erotic stratification', 'status crystallization', and numerous other tales, fascinat-ing exercises in isomorphism without which the LIBRARY of ¿sociology? kept-as-knowledge would be the poorer.[43]

But I guess that you are feeling rather uncomfortable now? The
LIBRARY is very ¿interesting? but at the moment it is probably making
you feel like a certain little girl must have felt when she said, 'Somehow
it seems to fill my head with ideas – only I don't exactly know what
they are!' You can't even remember how you got into the LIBRARY in
the first place – and you keep getting the most unpleasant sensation that
there is a SPIDER close behind you and . . .

RABBIT: (*appearing suddenly from behind a huge pair of spectacles,
           the gold star twinkling on his waistcoat*)
           Don't panic! It's only a library, there are always spiders
           in libraries. If you follow the signs saying '*Exit*' you
           will find your way back to the entrance.
YOU: (*walking out of the main reading room at the British
           Museum*)
           I've had quite enough for one day, thank you. I'm going
           to go across the road for a cup of tea. I want to remember
           where I've been today and what has been going on.

Well, once upon a time someone asked a silly question. 'What must
the world be like in order that man may know it?' he said. And, before
you could say 'EPISTEMOLOGICAL DIVIDE!', you were off on a
mad May dance. You found that you were whorling and gyrating around
the very BOOJUM that you had resolved to ignore. There you were,
dancing like a dotty dervish along a strange Möbius route, without
beginning or end, yet somehow seeming always to progress, to advance,
onward and onward in ¿time?.

Of a sudden you felt more than a little dizzy and grabbed the hand
of the partner to your right. What a relief to hold firmly to Common
Sense who, as she spins about you points out the homely facts of everyday life which surround you both. She shakes and spins and shakes the
doubts away. The brackets of uncertainty fly off: ¿reality?, ¿phenomena?,
¿facts?, and ¿things?, unmasked, turn out to be the ordinary familiar
phenomena, facts, and things of long acquaintance.

But the dance continues still. For Common Sense has let your hand
slip, as she grabs a grander partner. Science and Common Sense spin
on together, whorling round the middlemost grin of the CHESHIRE
CAT which seems to be the only appearance around for a ¿time?. You
grab out for some guy, some partner in the dance, and it is Reason who
takes your hand.

'Doubt the rest,' says he, 'but do not doubt your own Reason. I will
hold your head high above the whirlpool of thoughts-already-thought.
Keep fast to me and you will not go down the drain with the dirty
BATHWATER.'

High and dry, you are resting from the dance, congratulating yourself

on your temporary refuge from the greedy vorte
the vague possibility of cleaning some of the bl
wellingtons. Suddenly the WHITE RABBIT appears, th
shining brightly on his waistcoat pocket.

'If the MOUNTAIN will not come to you,' he says, 'th
follow me.' So you followed the WHITE RABBIT into th
MOUNTAIN of Science. And there, in that strange realm of
tunnels and spiralling ways, you saw how the ordinary common-s
RULES OF REASONABLENESS had been captured and, with a f
deft strokes of a magic wand, turned into the RADII OF REASONING,
the logic and methodology of Science.

You guessed that no ¿sociologist? would get far in the MOUNTAIN
unless he learned something of the RADII OF REASONING. So you
began by memorizing the creed that governs scientific theorizing: you
learned how a Proper EXPLANATORY THEORY should be expressed in the format of a deductive nomological explanation, and you
practised the art of checking the validity of such a theory.

But, just as you were feeling that you would be able to hold your own
against the RABBITS in any disputes about the validity of an EXPLANA-
TORY THEORY you found that you had wandered into the LIBRARY.
There you were in that part of the LIBRARY reserved for knowledge-
kept-as-¿sociology? when you discovered, to your great consternation
that there were very few volumes of EXPLANATORY THEORIES
there. Two other kinds of books were crowding out the shelves,
IMPLICIT THEORIES and ANALYTICAL THEORIES. And, all
amongst them, were the most fearful SPIDERS!

You emerged from the horrors of the LIBRARY to find yourself at the
main entrance of an amazingly life-like model British Museum, determined to get across the road and have a real taken-for-granted cup of
tea.

EXERCISE
While you are having that cup of tea, try sketching a map of
the journey that brought you to the LIBRARY of ¿sociology?
kept-as-knowledge. Then summarize what you have discovered
about the theories on the shelves.

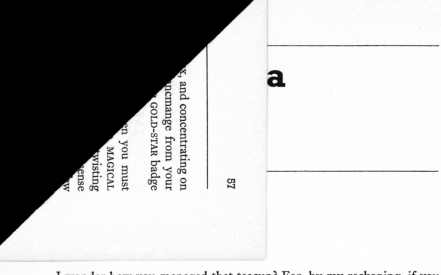

I wonder how you managed that teacup? For, by my reckoning, if you were small enough to get out through the door of the miniature British Museum in the last chapter, then you must have been slightly too short to peer over the brim of an ordinary taken-for-granted teacup – even if you were standing on the tips of your toes.[1] But there is no need to worry about it. Let us take some advice from a certain Caterpillar: he may be able to tell us how a very *extraordinary* kind of 'growth' can transform even the most diminutive thoughts into a taller part of an even loftier whole.

> In a minute or two the Caterpillar took the hookah out of its mouth, and yawned once or twice, and shook itself. Then it got down off the mushroom, and crawled away into the grass, merely remarking as it went, 'One side will make you grow taller and the other side will make you grow shorter.'
> 'One side of *what*? The other side of *what*?' thought Alice to herself.
> 'Of the mushroom,' said the Caterpillar just as if she had asked it out aloud; and in another moment it was out of sight.
> Alice remained looking thoughtfully at the mushroom for a minute, trying to make out which were the two sides of it; and, as it was perfectly round, she found this a very difficult question.
> [See the illustration on page 59.]

Come now! You'll be here all day if you carry on looking *thoughtfully* at the mushroom.

If you are still with me then I must assume that you are prepared – at least for the moment – to entertain the arguments of the preceding chapters. So I will pretend that, for the ¿time? being, you and I can take it for granted that we agree that,

'One side will make you grow . . .'

THOUGHTS ARE STRICTLY LIMITED.

Common-sense thoughts are confined within the boundaries set down by the ordinary *RULES OF REASONABLENESS* of everyday life, and the *RADII OF REASONING* that set the peripheries of science are no less restricting. While you remain *thoughtful*, reason will restrain you from straying into Wonderland. And though the knowledge to which you are party will still seem to carry on growing in the *ordinary* way,[2] nothing *extraordinary* can happen.

Now, if you have ever read any of the tales of great ¿discoveries? or ¿inventions?, the stories of momentous developments in science, you will know that, far from being mere developments from *ordinary thoughts*, these have always been the results of *extraordinary, or 'revolutionary' ¿thinking?*. Scientists – normally the most rational of folk – have not been entirely immune to occasional bouts of feverish imagination, reckless flashes of inspiration, sudden serendipities which have, apparently, burst upon them, shaking them from the ruts of thoughts-already-thought, and lifting them out of the realm of the taken-for-granted into a Eureka-land of awe.[3]

Science, like any other paradigm of thought, has always had its deviants. There have always been ¿thinkers? who have been willing to question what everyone else is happy to continue taking for granted. And some of these heretics seem to have been vindicated by ¿time?. Their audacious and challenging viewpoints have subsequently been hailed as ¿truths?, and their devious wanderings rationally reconstructed as 'revolutionary' or 'progressive' ¿thinking?.

But however do they do it? How do these *extraordinary ¿thinkers?* come to question the thoughts that they have been in the habit of taking for granted? How do they ¿transcend? the dead paradigms of thoughts-already-thought and start the vital process of ¿thinking? ?

Well, there are some mystics who claim that, in order to start ¿thinking? it is necessary to get rid of the thoughts that threaten to enslave us. They claim that we must *make an effort* to empty our minds of all thoughts-already-thought in order to make room for ¿thinking?. Various different ways of achieving this intellectual purification have been suggested. Some say that it is to be accomplished by disciplined meditation, by a deliberate *effort* to wipe the mind-slate clean, to start again with a *tabula rasa*.[4] Others, with a deep commitment to the metaphysic of scientism,[5] urge us to 'let the facts speak for themselves' in the half-articulated belief that by immersing ourselves in appearances we will ¿transcend? the thoughts through which we encounter them.[6] Some of these have invented esoteric rituals which are every bit as weird as the mental gymnastics to which the former exhort us. They propose that we pretend to be engaged in a game of skill in which all conceivable contestants are represented by a mythical beast whose only known tactic is unpredictability. In order to confuse that beast the skilful player is supposed to employ various instruments of randomization, from yarrow sticks, coins and die, to glass beads and probability theory.

Of course these statistical magicians have no more surefire way of knowing when they have achieved their aim than the slate-wipers have of knowing when they have achieved theirs. For just as the thoughtless mind must have ceased to exist for itself at the moment when it banished the thought of itself, so the randomizers' curious beast will have turned into an already-thought SPIDER by the time it has become sufficiently confused to satisfy the statisticians.[7]

No. You cannot abolish thoughts by methodical effort – however hard you try. To do so is to attempt to press reason into the service of its own destruction, and everyone who has ever seriously tried to ¿think? in that way has succeeded only in eliminating *his own credibility*, while the straight-jacket of other people's taken-for-granted methods of reasoning has remained tight about him. In short, he has gone stark staring BONKERS!

Oh dear! Oh dear! Oh dear! We don't want to go bonkers do we? So here we are still staring thoughtfully at that mushroom. We are entirely unable to let go of our thoughts, bound up as they are in the reason that seems to keep us sane.

Now you will remember that the Caterpillar said that the mushroom has two sides. So, though we may have no notion which is which, or why, reason informs us that we can be sure at least that the right side is not the wrong side and the wrong side is not the right side.

> *LOGICIAN:*   Right is not wrong and wrong is not right.
> *YOU:*   But is not-wrong right and not-right wrong?
> *CATERPILLAR:*   Oh for goodness' sake! Try it and see.

There are a growing band of philosophers and methodologists of science who are doing just that at this very moment! They realize the limitations of thoughts-already-thought, and accept that science must aim at more than the mere accumulation of *KK* within the limits of the present *BB*, *FF* and *RR*.[8] They recognize, in short, that,

PARADIGMS OF THOUGHT MAY BE ¿TRANSCENDED?.

They consider that, since today's ¿truth? has ¿transcended? yesterday's ¿truth?, then tomorrow's ¿truth? may ¿transcend? today's. But, lacking the recklessness of insanity, they have chosen to hold fast to the guidelines of reason. Knowing that every past advance of theory can be reconstructed with hindsight as a rational outcome of the inadequacies, inconsistencies and anomalies of the preceding theories, they consider that the sort of reasoning which seems to have made sense of the past should be extended or projected into the future. So, faced with our allegorical mushroom, these rational men have tried to consider coolly the consequences of making a *rational* choice between one side and the other.

In a moment or two I am going to suggest a much more exciting way of viewing the development of paradigms of thought, including science, an all-together more ¿interesting? way of looking at the mushroom. But the puritan – the hard-working and reasonable scholar within me – directs me first to bore you with a review of the arguments of these highly reasonable men who, faced with that same teaser, have chosen to pretend that reason has always been, and must remain, their guide.

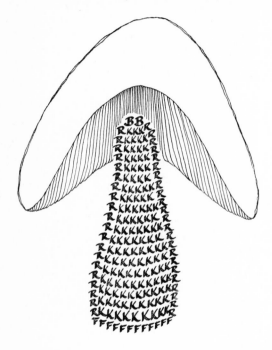

Right now they have all gathered together for a jolly party. Let's slip in and mingle amongst them.

Ah! We have met some of these fellows before (and I should warn you that we will find occasion to bump into some of them again before our travels are done). The atmosphere is pretty tense. Everyone at the party wants to take part in the bun fight which is going on about the nature of the development of knowledge in general, and science in particular. With a single exception,[9] no one wants to be considered unreasonable, but everyone is speaking out of turn.[10]

We have already been introduced to one of the guests of honour, it is Professor Kuhn himself. He has just shocked quite a few people by expounding his views on the nature of *normal* scientific work. He has claimed that scientists normally take a given paradigm of thought and then go about their research work in such a way as to give a ring of ¿truth? to the belief that reality is in accord with that paradigm. As he pounds a mushroom *vol-au-vent* with the palm of his hand and talks of 'bashing reality into line', not a few of the guests are reminded of Kant's view that 'our intellect does not draw its knowledge from nature but imposes its knowledge upon nature.' No one present at the party really wants to disagree with him about *that*. All are happy to accept this 'activist' view of epistemology as it seems altogether more ¿interesting? than the alternative construction in which Nature would be seen as implanting her marks upon perfectly inert minds. But a veritable Babel of voices rises to protest that, on this view of *normal science*, nothing extraordinary could *ever* occur.

'A new paradigm could never emerge from Normal Science as characterized by Kuhn', says Professor Watkins, his words rising momentarily above the background noise.[11] There are some murmurs of agreement. And you and I hear our own voices among them. It certainly seems reasonable to suppose that, while the scientists are busy rushing about tidying up the facts so that they can be stored neatly as *KK* within a precious paradigm, they must inevitably be so blinded by thoughts-already-thought that they will be unable to ¿think? in a novel way. The possibility that what they have been taking for granted might, from some ¿other point of view? turn out to be less than the-¿truth?-they-could-know simply would not occur to them under normal circumstances and when they uncovered mistakes they would be bound to attribute these to the shortcomings of their research instruments, procedures and techniques, or even to personal inadequacies; but they would not be driven to question the paradigm itself. Thus it would seem that scientists are *normally* prisoners of their taken-for-granted conceptual frameworks. Though they may elaborate and develop these frameworks; though they may greatly expand the sheer 'volume' of *KK* that they can fit (skilfully) inside them; they cannot break out.

What a rumpus! Some of the guests are brandishing sausages on sticks, some are handing around great plates of red herrings. No one is quite sure whether Kuhn actually has egg on his face or whether they have been confused by the egg stains on their own spectacles.

Now, several of the brawlers suddenly hit upon the same face-saving gesture: perhaps what Kuhn has described as 'Normal Science' is not normal at all? Perhaps it is a ghastly caricature of scientific work, a sort of sham science, fit only for 'plodding, uncritical minds'?[12] Perhaps there are some hack scientists who *do* behave like that, but the remainder (be they the majority or the minority) keep high the standards of critical precision, and retain the ability to ¿think? for themselves?

Professor Karl Popper feels moved to speak by that point. Grasping one of the delicately plastic-wrapped blancmange trifles provided for the delight and amusement of the guests, he wrenches the absurd plastic container apart, declaring:[13]

> I do admit that at any moment we are prisoners caught in the framework of our theories; our expectations; our past experiences; our language. But we are prisoners in a Pickwickian sense: if we try, we can break out of our framework at any time. Admittedly we shall find ourselves again in a framework, but it will be a better and roomier one; and we can at any moment break out of it again.

Splat! The disgusting confection, free of its original polluting container, has found the limits of another one. The thing has stuck on the ceiling. It wobbles up there for a ghastly moment and then – plop!– part of it breaks free again and, with what seems like a mind and will of its own, it selects the head of the most sophisticated of the guests and nestles affectionately in his hair.

And *what* a sophisticated fellow he is, this Dr Lakatos. Instead of taking the coward's way out (to the cloakroom to clean the blancmange from his coiffure) he turns his plight to his own advantage.[14] Walking gracefully to the centre of the room he proceeds to deliver a short lecture in a quiet and controlled tone of voice. The gist of his argument is that, with a little further thought, the guests could elegantly redeem themselves, and the science for which they speak, from *naïveté* and the vulgar excesses of dogma.

As his arguments are a little involved – at least for those of us who prefer the bawdier pastime of blancmange slapstick – I shall take the liberty of condensing them.

Lakatos begins by reminding his audience that they are all in agreement in their rejection of the sort of passivist epistemology of science which characterizes the scientist as a mere editor and annotator of the facts which, having a voice of their own, should be given the chance to speak. Such a view, and the *inductive* or fact-gathering approach to knowledge which it entails, is naïve, says Lakatos. But by (almost) the same token, those who interpret the *deductive* rules of research too literally are just as deluded, he says. For the view of the scientist as the author of theories which, though quite freely proposed, will be deemed acceptable only if they are in accord with the currently knowable facts, is, at least arguably, as naïve as the inductivist, or 'empiricist' view. Lakatos argues that this sort of dogmatic deductivism involves two highly questionable assumptions.[15]

> The *first assumption* is that there is a natural, psychological borderline between theoretical or speculative propositions on the one hand and factual . . . propositions on the other.

The *second assumption* is that if a proposition satisfies the psychological criterion of being factual . . . then one may say that it was *proved* from the facts.

In making these two assumptions the dogmatic adherent to the rule-book principles, the unquestioning follower of the scientific *RADII OF REASONING*, is *taking it for granted that 'facts are facts and ought not to be ignored'*. To that extent, as Lakatos says, he might just as well be an inductivist because, like the self-admitted inductivist, he will be prepared to question almost anything *but* the facts. And, as we shall see later,[16] this effort to stand up straight by the rules of deductive logic while simultaneously bowing down in the presence of the Imperial Facts leads these narrow-minded scientists to two other absurdities. Lakatos has noticed one of these, the view that 'a theory is scientific if it has an empirical basis'.[17] The other, which Lakatos cannot see from where he is standing at the moment, is the tendency to speak as though the facts and the ¿truth? were one and the same.

But despite his strange failure to analyse what *he* means by the term 'truth' (an omission which, incidentally, none of the other guests at the party seems to have noticed)[18] Lakatos is spinning a very ¿interesting? yarn. Hesitating only to help himself to another sandwich, the sophisticated party-goer now proceeds to make a very elegant point. He says that those two assumptions ('*the naturalistic doctrine of observation*' and '*the doctrine of observational proof*') ought not to be simply taken for granted as they are by the dogmatic rule-followers. Rather, he says, they should be recognized as *arbitrary decisions* which the reasonable scientist makes *for the purposes of a particular programme of research*.

Let me just repeat that important point, in case it has been lost in the general brouhaha. While a scientist is working on a particular research project he must do so within a paradigm of thought, that is within a framework of assumptions which he has, for the ¿time? being, relegated to an unproblematic background of thoughts. The two assumptions that 'facts are facts' and that 'facts ought not to be ignored' are simply two of the thoughts which go to make up the currently favoured *RADII OF REASONING* of science. That is to say that these assumptions are not *normally* questioned by scientists. *Normally* – that is while they are content to work within the given paradigm – scientists simply take these two thoughts for granted in much the same way as they take it for granted that, for example, 'infinity is greater than one', '¿time? moves forward', '¿causes? precede ¿effects?', and that 'a proposition can be either ¿true? or ¿false? but cannot be both ¿true? and ¿false?'. But no open-minded scientist should ever entirely forget that *these are assumptions*, and that *he is not condemned to take them for granted*. The possibility of breaking through a paradigm of thought into a 'roomier' one inheres in the recognition that there may always be some ¿transcendent? theoretical position from which these very assumptions may – like any other taken-for-granted thoughts – become problematics rather than givens.

Now the question of how ¿transcendence? can be attained has still to be answered.

But hush! The man with the sticky hair is still talking. He is telling some hair-raising nineteenth-century ghost stories. Apparently some brave philosophers, notably Poincaré, Milhaud and Le Roy, had called up the spectre of the-man-imprisoned-in-thought which long since appeared to Kant and which Professor Kuhn has dared to invoke again today. But Lakatos considers that, unlike most of the best ghost stories, this one nearly has a happy ending.[19]

> Poincaré's critics refused to accept this idea that, although the scientists build their conceptual frameworks, there comes a time when these frameworks turn into prisons which cannot be demolished. This criticism gave rise to two rival schools of *revolutionary conventionalism*: Duhem's simplicism and Popper's methodological falsificationism.

Lakatos dismisses the first of these schools of *revolutionary conventionalism* as placing too much emphasis on 'subjective taste' in the development of science. Fingering his extremely tasteful tie, he declares that the development of science should be something more than a fashion show. Then, turning to the gentleman in the well-worn umpire's coat who is standing beside him, he waves his half-eaten sandwich in a gesture of approval. 'Popper', he says, 'set out to find a criterion which is both more objective and more hard-hitting.' The Popperian sort of revolutionary conventionalist, as characterized by Lakatos,[20]

> realizes that in the 'experimental techniques' of the scientist fallible theories are involved, 'in the light of which' he interprets the facts. In spite of this he 'applies' these theories, he regards them in the given context not as theories under test but as *unproblematic background knowledge* 'which we accept [tentatively] as unproblematic while we are testing the theory'. He may call these theories – and the statements whose truth-value he decides in their light – 'observational': but this is only a manner of speech which he inherited from naturalistic falsificationism. . . . [He] *uses our most successful theories as extentions of our senses.*

Thus the Popperian saves the 'attractive code of honour' of the GOLD-STAR rule-book: '*that scientific honesty consists in specifying in advance an experiment such that, if the result contradicts the theory, the theory has to be given up.*'[21] This, says Lakatos, is a heroic stance to adopt: it involves the scientist in considerable risks for, unless his theory is at least in principle ¿testable? against a clearly specified range of knowable facts, it will not, by this criterion, be regarded as scientific.

But Popper's dare-devil revolutionary conventionalism is altogether too quixotic for a sophisticate like Lakatos.[22] The latter points out that such harsh methodological standards may result in the premature rejection of ¿interesting? theories. For the proponents of new approaches may at first be unable to work their theories through to the point at which they involve precisely specifiable consequences for the knowable facts, or, on the other hand, they may make mistaken deductions from them, and erroneously reject the theories in the face of evidence which they ¿falsely? consider to contradict them.

So Lakatos exhorts his colleagues at the philosophers' tea-party to abandon their blustering ways and adopt a more urbane attitude towards the scientific code of honour; he extolls the niceties of a position which he chooses to call '*Sophisticated Falsificationism*'. Unlike his naïve colleagues the Sophisticated Falsificationist does not consider that experimental evidence should provide the sole reliable criterion for the (tentative) acceptance of theories. Rather he encourages the 'proliferation of theories'.

Any theory, says Lakatos, which promises excess information in comparison with its predecessors (or its rivals), should be given (temporary) accommodation. A theory which promises to tell us more about appearances, to predict *new facts*, should be entertained and developed even if no one has yet found a way of making that theory consistent with all the *old facts*. Perhaps as the new theory is developed some of the excess information about the world which it seems to provide will be 'corroborated', perhaps, on the other hand, the new theory will eventually be shown to be at variance with the sort of old facts which no one is prepared to give up, but the important thing is that *where they promise excess content – 'progressive problem shifts' – new theories should be given a better chance of survival than that afforded by Popper's tactics.*

So saying Dr Lakatos retires to the cloakroom to ponder on the question of the blancmange which is still clinging obstinately to his hair.

Well I don't know how *you* reacted to those thoughts, but from where I was standing they looked far *too* sophisticated.[23] It seems to be that a science staffed by such sophisticates would be a thoroughly decadent one.[24] For if Lakatos were to have his way then scientists *would* go on a veritable fashion binge. Since they could be confident that any new theory which seemed to be roomier than its competitors would be welcomed and applauded, they would be free to propose all kinds of fantastic ideas.[25] Indeed the greater the fantasy – the higher the level of abstraction – the greater would be the applause! Of course, that is not to say that the applauding colleagues would accord these new theories the status of ¿truth?, or that they would automatically assume that the new theories could *readily* be reconciled with the old facts. But it *is* to say that the new theories would be considered as thoughts, that they would gain some (albeit tentative and temporary) place amongst the other thoughts to which the community of scientists collectively laid claim. Anyone who had a nice roomy theory could bore anyone else with it.

Of course, we are *all* guilty of boring a few close friends with our occasional wild brainchilds! But Lakatos is suggesting that it is perfectly good manners for each of us, *qua* scientists, to do our best to bore the scientific community at large.

In my view Lakatos, or any of the scientists for whom he speaks, has a perfect right to spend his own ¿time? working on his own theories, particularly if they seem to be roomier than any of the acceptable alternatives. (I might almost say that he has a duty to do so.[26]) But I consider that, sophisticated or not, it is very *bad* manners to expect other people to do the hard work on one's own theory. If one cannot get the theory into a researchable state then, in my view, one has no right to foist it upon other people.

To get a theory into a researchable state is – by GOLD-STAR standards – to render it as a proper deductive sequence involving at least some statements which are ¿testable?-in-principle. If one cannot do that with one's theory then, in my view, one ought to pause for a long time before considering boring other people with it by publication. For, by publishing an ¿interesting? theory prematurely, one is only contributing to the obscene mole-hills of half-set blancmange which are threatening to swamp our LIBRARY.

Surely it is just that sort of indiscriminate publishing which has produced the sloppy state of science that we find today. Many ¿sociologists? of science have drawn attention to the vicious circle of publication and specialization which results in a situation in which most of what is written can be understood by only a few narrow specialists.[27] The concomitant lack of dialogue *between* specialist areas can only culminate in a defeat for reason, as more and more people are forced to take more and more specialist knowledge on trust, to accept it on the thoroughly inadequate authority of expertise, because they have no means of judging it for themselves. So the publication of new theories *just* because they seem to be roomier than the current alternatives is, in my view, a waste of ¿time? – and, since it is also a waste of paper, it is also an unwarranted assault on the liberty of trees.

> A wise old owl
> Sat in an oak.
> The more he heard

The less he spoke.
The less he spoke
The more he heard.
Why can't we be more
Like that wise old bird?

Probably because, if we carry on the way we are going, there won't be any oaks left to sit in![28]

Well I did *warn* you that that would be a boring party! Anyway we don't seem to have got hold of any very useful clues from the guests. While everyone else was berating Kuhn for advocating a kind of science which seems actually to inhibit 'revolutionary' developments, none of them has any better plans for inviting such breakthroughs. All are agreed that scientists must aim at ¿transcending? thoughts-already-thought, at producing new and roomier theories, but none can give any very useful tips on how to get hold of such novel ways of looking at things. Popper tells us very clearly what to do when we *have* an ¿interesting? theory, and Lakatos tells us that we might just as well not bother to do it because we might make mistakes. So we have come round in another circle. And here we are again! (See the illustration on page 59.)

But wait a minute! Perhaps that circuitous excursion to the philosophers' tea-party was not such a waste of ¿time? after all? If you *look back* on it you may *remember* that you have been listening to a reasonable debate as a result of which you now know *more* than you would have done if you had, say, lain down under the mushroom and gone to sleep.

I will elaborate. Before we put on our party togs and slipped into the tea-party we had seen that there are two sorts of theoretical development in science: the *normal growth* or progress or advance of knowledge which was discussed in the preceding chapter, and the *extraordinary* or 'revolutionary' *leaps and bounds* which occur from ¿time? to ¿time?.[29] We suspected that the two might bear a very peculiar relationship to one another, but at the same ¿time? we were reasonable enough to allow the philosophers to try to persuade us that reason has something to do with the development of *extraordinary* as well as of *ordinary* science. And now, looking back on that debate with the hindsight that it itself affords, perhaps you will agree that they have, in a sense, succeeded. The philosophers have indicated that reason does have *something* to do with the relationship between normal and extraordinary scientific work.

For, reconstructing that debate with hindsight, it seems that all the party-goers would agree with us if we were to claim that,

ONCE AN EXTRAORDINARY THEORY HAS GAINED ACCEPT-
ANCE WITHIN A PARADIGM, IT IS RATIONALLY RECON-
STRUCTED AS AN ASPECT OF NORMAL PROGRESS.

Thus reason provides a way of linking the extraordinary with the
ordinary in the light of *subsequent* judgments. But *reason cannot provide
guidelines for a movement from the ordinary and taken-for-granted to the
extraordinary*. You cannot get into Wonderland without going outside
of the boundaries of the normal taken-for-granted logic and methodology
of today's science.

In retrospect it seems that reason has tempered our thoughts: through
it we have collectively reconstructed the ebbs and flows of epistemological tides, making them seem to have been a steady progress of development, a progressive evolution from humble maritime beginnings to
the dry complexities of modern thought. These were the legends of
reason.

BUT TO ¿TRANSCEND? THE TAKEN-FOR-GRANTED IS TO
STEP BEYOND THE LIMITS OF REASON.

Now stepping beyond the limits of reason is *not* the same thing as
relaxing logical and methodological standards. Lakatos is, in my view,
badly misguided if he genuinely does believe that the collective coddling
of half-thought-out arguments will somehow result in theoretical breakthroughs. After all, any trip to any of the sections of the LIBRARY of
knowledge kept as science will soon show you that standards are relaxed
enough as it is! Rather – as I shall be arguing in some detail below – it
is *more* stringent methodological standards which can best prepare the
ground for extraordinary developments.

The more serious deductive work scientists do on those theories
which have been proposed already, the more they link one set of
thoughts with another, the more they trace out the implications of
theories in one place for theories in another, and, above all, the more
precisely they specify the points at which the more general and abstract
theories touch upon the unproblematic background of currently knowable facts, then the more likely they will be to discover *mistakes*.[30] This,
in my view, is the proper activity of reason, of logic, and it is a negative
one. *Reason is not a source of theories, it is an arbiter of mistakes*. Mistakes
are the fruits of GOLD-STAR reasoning, and honest scientists should
welcome them.

Mistakes in science are, as we have already seen, the inconsistencies
and incompatibilities between currently existing thoughts which can be
revealed by the ordinary taken-for-granted logic and methodology of

science, the *RADII OF REASONING*. And these inconsistencies (or anomalies as some of the philosophers at the tea-party prefer to call them) should not be regarded as worthless garbage to be thrown out of the back door of science. Rather they should be valued as good manure, as fertile soil in which to plant the seeds of new theorizing.

Of course, many of the mistakes which GOLD-STAR methods uncover may turn out after all to be mere puzzles for normal science. That is to say that they will be deemed solvable within the currently operative paradigm of thought, that they will be resolved as trivial errors of logical deduction, of ¿operationalization?, of ¿instrument design? and ¿measurement? or of over-hasty ¿casual inference? from data. But some of these mistakes will turn out to be more fundamental, they will represent *CONUNDRUMS* for the scientist: teasers which cannot be solved within the bounds of the presently existing framework of thought.

Now the most ¿interesting? thing about a *CONUNDRUM* is that it cannot be finally recognized as such until it is viewed from a perspective which ¿transcends? that of the paradigm which spawned it – and, once thus seen, it is no longer a *CONUNDRUM* but a mere *PARADOX*. Like the progress which characterizes *normal science*, the *CONUNDRUMS* which mark *extraordinary science* can be recognized only with hindsight. It is only from the point of view of a roomier, that is ¿transcendent?, theory that the *CONUNDRUMS* of its predecessors can be distinguished from their ordinary puzzles.[31] Yet by the ¿time? such a perspective has been attained the insolvable *CONUNDRUM* will have been reformulated: it will have dissolved into *PARADOX*. (See the illustration on page 72.)

So, while *normal science* may properly be described as a puzzle-solving enterprise, the *extraordinary science* which results in the identification and resolution of those puzzles which it can reconstruct as *CONUNDRUMS/PARADOXES*, cannot be viewed as a direct, logical, outcome of a puzzle-solving activity. *The attempt to solve a puzzle can never logically entail the creation of a bigger, roomier, or ¿transcendent? theoretical position.* To assume that it can is a bit like taking it for granted that, when a mountaineer is stuck on a difficult face without footholds, he should endeavour to build a platform above his head and then climb up to it.

Yet, once in a blue moon, the reasonable efforts of reasonable men to find solutions to those puzzles which reason has formulated for them do – *incidentally, accidentally, unaccountably* – result in ¿transcendence?. For, pitting their wits against intransigent puzzles, men are sometimes driven to such a pitch of lunacy that they burst through the constraints of thoughts-already-thought and, free at last of the straight-jacket of reason, dream wild dreams.

As the Mad Hatter tried to tell the other philosophers at the tea-party,

The Gyre Ascending

the 'function of rational discourse may consist in increasing the mental
tension that precedes . . . the . . . outburst'.[32] But, on the other hand,
such an increase in mental tension – that results from the successive
frustration of efforts to solve what will, in the end, turn out to be a
CONUNDRUM – is by no means a *necessary* prelude to ¿transcendence?. For wild flashes of inspiration may occur to anyone at any
¿time?. Though reasoning and ¿thinking? involve hard work, serendipities are not granted as long-service medals to those who have

persevered against all the odds. It is one of the harsh conditions of science that inspiration is not attained by hard thought: those who have tried and tried, and thought and thought, have been no more, and are no less, likely to ¿transcend? their taken-for-granted paradigms than those who have not.

'Come, my head's free at last!' said Alice in a tone of delight, which changed into alarm in another moment, when she found that her shoulders were nowhere to be found: all she could see, when she looked down, was an immense length of neck, which seemed to rise like a stalk out of a sea of green leaves that lay far below her.

Hullo! I didn't expect to meet you up here! Can you see what I see? Down there is the mushroom and – oh my syllogisms and statistics! – there are two great big bites out of it. But I *recognize* those teeth-marks. Oh dear, oh dear, oh dear! I must have eaten some of the mushroom without realizing what I was doing. I wonder who took the other bite?

From *this viewpoint* you can clearly make out the writing on the top of the mushroom. One side is neatly labelled ¿THINKING? and the other is richly embroidered with the word 'IMAGINATION'. And there is no doubt about which side has been bitten. For it is only through IMAGINATION that thoughts-already-thought can be *transcended*.

TO TRANSCEND A PARADIGM IS TO MOVE BEYOND IT AND ENGAGE IN AN IMAGINATIVE ENCOUNTER WITH THE ¿UNTHINKABLE?.

Such a trip is nothing at all like the method of reasoning which we are in the habit of taking for granted. Transcendence is attained, as Kuhn says:[33]

not by deliberation and interpretation, but by a relatively sudden and unstructured event like the gestalt switch. Scientists then often speak of the 'scales falling from the eyes' or of the 'lightning flash' that 'inundates' a previously obscure puzzle, enabling its components to be seen in a new way that for the first time permits its solution. On other occasions the relevant illumination comes in sleep.

Or, indeed, in other altered states of consciousness, or 'ASCs' as some scientists prefer to call them.[34] In any case, as Kuhn continues, 'No ordinary sense of the term "interpretation" fits these flashes of intuition through which a new paradigm is born.' Those who have achieved transcendence have not merely reinterpreted the elements of the paradigm which they have left behind, rather they have been awakened from thoughts-already-thought to some vision of a world beyond its limits.

No, imagination is not a sort of reasoning at all, but it is not thereby *un*reasonable. Only reason could be so blind as to divide everything it can grasp into the rational and the 'not-rational', or irrational. Imagination is neither rational nor irrational. It is not what we have learned to take for granted but neither is it the negation of that earthy knowledge. For it is through imagination that all meanings are intuited, including both those which we take for granted and those which, as yet, we find ¿unthinkable?. In imagination sense and nonsense are one. For logic, as Blake knew, is not to be ignored but must be *overcome*. Everything that we take for granted – Nature and our knowledge of her, our laws, our morality, our habits, all our ways of being in the world – all these thoughts-already-thought emanate from the Daughters of Memory.

But in Blake's vision the Daughters of Memory were to be redeemed by the Daughters of Imagination and, as in 'Jerusalem', welded into one.

Ever expanding in the Bosom of God, the Human Imagination.

And now, lacking imagination, I must be literal: I will turn from the sublime to the ridiculous. For, though it is entirely out of place, it should be said that there was not one philosopher at that silly tea-party who would have had the arrogance to deny the reality of the sword in the great poet's hand.

Kuhn, as we have just seen, was outright in his conviction that the birth of new theories is inspirational rather than merely rational. And Popper has said on many occasions that theories may be regarded as the 'free creations of our minds, the result of an almost poetic intuition'.[35] As we shall realize again and again in the following pages, one of the most forceful principles of Popper's methodology is the oft-forgotten wisdom that the sources of the inspiration which gives rise to a theory have nothing at all to do with the *scientific* appraisal of the *acceptability* of that theory.[36] Unless he considers that he is blessed with the gift of poesy, no mere scientist should attempt to convey the visions of his imagination: for he is bound to fail. Unlike the ¿true? poet he should keep quiet about what he has imagined and, unless he is to relinquish the vocation of science, he must start the difficult business of reconciling what he can now conceive with at least some of what he and his peers have been keeping as knowledge. That is to say that he must start ¿thinking?.

Now, before we fall to ¿thinking? about ¿thinking?, let us just reminisce a little! Let us withdraw to our private places and remember a trip we might have had. Let us recall – until we lose all likelihood of ever forgetting – that *it is through imagination and only through imagination that we mortals may transcend the worlds of taken-for-granted-thoughts-already-thought*, that we may rise above the trifling horror of

Evanid's fears; escape Poincaré's ghastly prisons; break out of Lukács's dungeons;[37] and soar away into the freedom of make-believe. For it is there that the FAIRIES dwell.

Do *you* believe in FAIRIES? No – not *normally* anyway? Well let's enjoy ourselves! Let's make believe that we *do* believe in FAIRIES!

Don't worry, I am not by any means suggesting that you should pretend that FAIRIES exist – though you may do so if you like – I am merely asking you to try for a while to consider what it could be like to *believe* in FAIRIES.

What *could* it be like to believe in FAIRIES? The FAIRIES could be neither 'objective' nor 'subjective'. Such beings could find no resting place in the 'objective' worlds of appearances, nor in the 'subjective' worlds of thought. For in the FAIRYLAND you might imagine there would be no 'objective' and 'subjective': all would be as one. Though we may properly speak of *your* thoughts and *my* thoughts, we could not speak of *your* fairies and *my* fairies, of *your* ideas and *my* ideas. Thoughts are property, but not FAIRIES. Thoughts will continue to divide us. But FAIRIES could not be respecters of thoughts. If we were to encounter them in our imagination we would be as one with them; as they would dwell in our imagination so, in our imagination, we would dwell with them. Though we can shape our thoughts within the limits of reason we could not confine FAIRIES in our paradigms. We could only try, as best we could, to reminisce *about* them, to tell FAIRY TALES.

While thoughts are thought,

FAIRIES ARE UNTHINKABLE.

But we are not forbidden to *imagine* such ideas!

Of course, the connection between imagination and ideas has long been expressed in Art. Few are blind enough to deny that Art roams beyond the reaches of reason. Thus, when, for example, Coleridge sought to communicate the nature of vision in the language of taken-for-granted thought, he found that there were no words with which to do so. Undaunted, the poet invented a word, the word 'esemplastic', which he constructed from the Greek phrase meaning 'to mould into one'. And Goethe with his method of the 'exact percipient fancy', as it is usually translated, showed how the esemplastic imagination could be brought from the psychedelic garden of Art to the dark mountain of science.

Goethe could not countenance the view that ideas might be reached by inductive modes of thought. To attempt to discover ideas within the substance of thoughts-already-thought, to reason from particulars to generals, was, for Goethe to 'darken the counsel'. When he encountered the FAIRIES – the '*Urphänomene*' as he called them – Goethe ceased thought. He paused and attempted to sink himself *in* those beings, to become one with them in imagination. Yet it was through this method that he ¿discovered? *new thoughts*, and *even new facts*! Through this apparent repudiation of the normal methods of science Goethe actually placed himself in the position from which he was able to formulate certain thoughts which, even today, no reasonable scientist denies as ¿false?: 'it was by this method that he discovered – not only that there was, but that there *must* be a bone in the human skeleton hitherto unknown to science – the *os intermaxillare*.'[38] And it was by the same method that he formulated the morphological principle, still central to botany, that all the parts of the plant can be regarded as metamorphoses of the leaf.

Now, according to the FAIRY TALE which I am telling in this book, it was not only Goethe but *Einstein* who had been in contact with the FAIRIES. I am making believe that every great theoretical innovation in science was a souvenir of FAIRYLAND. For if novel theories cannot be produced by logic (that is by the common-sense *RULES OF REASON-ABLENESS* or by the scientific *RADII OF REASONING*) then – perhaps – you might just as well believe in FAIRIES.

But of course you *don't*! And *why* not? Not merely because you cannot grasp such FAIRIES directly with the figuration that you have learned to take for granted. After all, have you tried ever to catch hold of 'Liberty', or 'Brotherhood', or 'Democracy'? Can you grasp 'Aliena-tion', 'Racism' or 'Elitism' and give them the good spankings they deserve? And what of the DWARVISH folk who dwell closer to the world that you take for granted? What of 'atoms', 'electricity', 'drug addiction' and 'Dutch Elm Disease'. Can you catch *these* by their pointy ears, or will you know them only through their works? No. If you do not believe in FAIRIES it is *either* because you deny the possibility of abstraction (a denial which can itself be reconstructed as a very complicated FAIRY TALE) *or else* it is because you have had a vision which transcends this story. In the latter case you will see the FAIRIES I have painted as mere idols, as childish reminders of a loftier point of view.

But, like the mere FAIRIES[39] that I have sketched, the loftier ideas, with which *you* have been united in imagination, must remain ¿un-thinkable?. And what I have been saying goes to suggest that

THE UNTHINKABLE CANNOT BE THOUGHT.

How then is a man who has encountered the FAIRIES (or any other, um, imagination, or, um . . .) to return to a world of thought to tell his tale?

Well, of course, it must be said at once that many of the wanderers in FAIRYLAND never do return to tell the tale. Some come back to the taken-for-granted leaving their tales behind them. Such folk continue to suppose that appearances are more real than FAIRIES, and thus do their best to forget their adventures in the upper regions of the lands of make-believe. Others, having tasted of the FAIRY fare,[40] can never return to the worlds of the reasonable. What they say is condemned to remain as gibberish to those who hear it through their thoughts.

Then there are others who, having had a vision of Silence, ever after refrain from mere thoughts, and the words that betray them, in the hope that they may thus speak the greater ¿truth? in deeds.

But there will always be lesser mortals who wish to return to reality, if only to have a cup of tea! Once back in a world-taken-for-granted some of these may be tempted to try to see if they can tell their FAIRY TALES in the language of reason.

Can FAIRY TALES be repeated within the bounds of reason? Can the ordinary language of science permit a rational reconstruction of those most extraordinary – *literally fantastic* – leaps of imagination by which the taken-for-granted is transcended from ¿time? to ¿time? ? I believe that *that* is what ¿*thinking*? is all about![41] And, while I am well aware that not everything I have said so far is reasonable, this belief drives me to deny that it is ¿unthinkable? I *believe* that

THROUGH THINKING THE UNTHINKABLE MAY BE THOUGHT.

Once upon a ¿time? everything that we know today was unthinkable: but now it is thought. And, since it is thought, we no longer think about it, we simply take it for granted. Thinking is the reconciliation of the once unthinkable with the taken-for-granted Here and Now. To think is to unite the originally-unthinkable with the already-thought. It is to resolve *CONUNDRUM* into *PARADOX*. And, in paradox, the one *is* the other, for there is no other but the one. Thus are the greater ¿truths? revealed.

And if this FAIRY TALE is still unthinkable then I do not doubt that it can be thought. I doubt only that I am, *myself*, adequate to the thinking.[42]

I believe that it is via the extraordinary medium of thinking that new theories are articulated in reasonable and sensible ways. Once the thinking has been done then the thoughts are thoughts as any other thoughts and, *qua* thoughts, are amenable to scientific appraisal. At first these new thoughts may be regarded as heresies. But if they survive the harsh initiation ceremonies of science – if they stand up to the ¿tests? of ¿time? – they may come to be accepted as ¿true?. Thus new theories, new knowledge, and even new facts, will have been created.[43] Sometimes these new theories (some of which are already facts) will have been accommodated within an existing paradigm of thought without any radical changes in the *form* (the *BB*, *RR* and *FF*) of that paradigm. But, very occasionally, the thinking of new thoughts cannot take place without radical transformation of the old forms of thought: the ceiling of *BB* may be raised, the lines of *RR* modified and extended, and even the *FIGURATION OF FACTS* itself may undergo metamorphosis in ¿time?. In these ways *extraordinary thinking* is reconciled with *ordinary thought* in the ongoing process of creation which has resulted in the world which we have been prepared to take for granted.

occult - involving the supernatural: mythical, magical, mysterious, beyond the range of ordinary knowledge

THINKING IS MAGIC.

The methods of the occultists and those of the scientists are saturated with the same meanings. Both are ritual techniques for turning fantasies into realities through the disciplined manipulations of human consciousness. For, whether this praxis is scientist or occult, each magician, each *thinker*, effects a miraculous link between the unthinkable and the already-thought. Having first glimpsed a path between them in the visions of imagination, he now proceeds to represent that link in thought by *thinking* it,[44] and so 'turning all the series of external things into copy for his mental manipulation. He thus achieves the wonderful step whereby all objects alike become *his* objects, *his* content of meaning, *his* experience.'[45]

And what are the riches which this magic has brought? I will borrow another example.[46]

one could take Economics. The economic life is today the real bond of the civilised world. The world is held together not by political or religious harmony, but by economic interdependence; . . . Economic theory is bound hand and foot by the static, abstract character of modern thought. On the one hand, everything to do with *industry* and the possibility of substituting human labour by machinery has reached an unexampled pitch of perfection. But when it is a question of *distributing* this potential wealth, when it is demanded of us, therefore, that we think in terms of flow and rate of flow, we cannot even begin to rise to it. The result is that our 'labour-saving' machinery produces, not leisure, but its ghastly caricature, unemployment, while nearly every civilized and half-civilized nation of the world sits helplessly watching the steady growth within itself of a malignant tumour of social discontent. And this increasingly rancorous discontent is fed above all things by a cramping penury, a shortage of the means of livelihood, which arises, not out of the realities of nature, but out of abstract inelastic thoughts about money!

Later I shall examine some of the rewards of ¿sociological? thinking and, in doing so, I hope to underline what I have said about magic. For honest philosophers-of-magic, from Francis Bacon to Stephen Toulmin, have recognized that the goal and motive of science is not wisdom; nor is it knowledge for its own sake: the driving force of science is *power*.[47] Through their rituals and ceremonies, scientists are creating wider and wider circles of influence, they are producing more and more effective modes of controlling appearances, of manipulating data. And with ¿sociology? the gyre has taken another turn, for, as Alvin Gouldner has said, 'The criticism and transformation of society can be divorced only at our peril from the criticism and transformation of theories about society.'[48] The ¿sociologists? are no longer confined to an obscure corner in the MAGICAL MOUNTAIN of science. Over the last couple of decades they have been taking an increasingly important place in the magical establishment. Like other scientists they are eager to export their thoughts, the products of their special ways of thinking; and thus the effects of the new wizardry can be seen abroad.[49] But is this to be welcomed as a blessed enchantment[50] or condemned as witchcraft and caprice? Lacking the perspective of hindsight, how can we judge the ¿sociology? of today? After all, 'No one is a black magician in his own eyes, and modern occultists, whatever their beliefs and practices, think of themselves as high-minded white magicians, not as sinister Brothers of the Left-hand Path.'[51]

Of course, that is not an ordinary puzzle: it is a *CONUNDRUM*.[52] In order to transcend it, it would be necessary to transcend the ordinary, taken-for-granted, ¿sociology? of everyday life and commune with the '*Good*' FAIRIES. Only then, mindful of our *BASIC BELIEFS*, of the timeless ethics of Humanity, could we begin to think again. And *we must think again*! For it is only through thinking that we can 'see clearly how the institutions which make civilisation possible are but the bodies or husks of concrete creative thinking in the past'.[53] It is through that very magical connection that we might yet recall the highest forms of our imagination and so, joining all hands together, 'breathe life into' our world.

Chapter 5

Cross My Heart and Hope to Die

A man is to be cheated into passion, but to be reasoned into truth.
(John Dryden, Preface to *Religio Laici*)

Before *I* started cheating, I hope I had made a fairly reasonable attempt to persuade you that sociology is no snark hunt.

If we persist in seeking the ultimate reality we will only be rewarded with the ultimate sticky end. Common sense provides us with a way of spinning fairy tales about what might be going on 'out there', and while we continue to believe in them we have a firm foothold in reality. At the same time, academics insist that the methods of reasoning on which we rely as real people in the real world can be extended and organized into paradigms which, while still answerable to common sense, yet transcend it. Thus grander FAIRY TALES are spun by strange beings who dwell in tall towers of ivory and saltpetre, tales which are intended as explanations not only of the commonplace things and events of everyday life, but also of the everyday FAIRY TALES themselves. And all the while even stranger sages tell tales which are weirder still, including in their fantasies stories about how the ivory-tower-dwellers come to tell the tales they do. And so they go on, the FAIRY TALES within the legends within the stories we tell all the time.

But, quite close by, I hear a loud and familiar note. The Red King is crumpled up in his tasselled night-cap, snoring and snoring, 'fit to snore his head off!' as Tweedledum has been known to remark.

'He's dreaming now', said Tweedledee: 'and what do you think he is dreaming about?'

Alice said 'Nobody can guess that.'

'Why, about *you*!' Tweedledee exclaimed, clapping his hands triumphantly. 'And if he left off dreaming about you, where do you suppose you'd be?'

'Where I am now, of course,' said Alice.

'Not you!' Tweedledee retorted contemptuously. 'You'd be nowhere. Why, you are only a sort of thing in his dream!'

'If that there King was to wake,' added Tweedledum, 'you'd go
out – bang! – just like a candle!'
'I shouldn't!' Alice exclaimed indignantly.

Now Alice is a sensible child, so whether or not she has guessed it
already, she certainly realizes before breakfast that she can as easily wake
and dismiss the Red King as he can her. She is part of the Red King's
dream only as he is a part of hers.

But there *must* be more to it than *that*? Some dreams and some fairy
tales come *¿TRUE?*.

Human beings, as we have already discovered, have routine methods
of distinguishing fact from fantasy. Both Alice and the Red King may
have been figments of the White Knight's imagination, the White
Knight may have been nothing but a favoured character in a wayward
deacon's FAIRY TALE, but that that reverend gentleman *actually* lived is
what is commonly known as a 'true fact'.

It seems that, whatever else we do both as ordinary people in the
commonplace of everyday life and as academics of divers disciplines,
we *must* find a routine for distinguishing *¿true?* judgments from all other
types of propositions. For while all paradigms, and all the more specific
theories of which they are composed, do have a FAIRY-TALE quality, like
all FAIRY TALES, there are points at which they coincide – either potentially or actually – with observable phenomena.[1]

Let us take another example from the fantasy worlds of English
children. That Father Christmas comes down the chimney to fill each
child's Christmas stocking, is acceptable as a *¿true?* account of events to
most children for as long as the stocking is mysteriously filled. Indeed,
in West Country households, additional *¿evidence?* can usually be gleaned
from the facts that the mincepie and cocoa thoughtfully left by the
fireplace have evidently been consumed. The really sceptical child
would not, however, be content with this *¿proof?* of the legend, he would
choose a more rigorous *¿test?* of the Father Christmas theory. If he
could not stay awake all night in order actually to observe events, he
might devise all manner of ingenious booby traps to catch or otherwise
reveal the hypothesized night caller.[2] And there can be no doubt that
certain *¿evidence?* – to wit a glimpse of his father tip-toeing toward the
end of the bed – would lead him to decide to reject the legend as *¿false?*
once and for all.

What then are we to understand by the terms *¿truth?* and *¿true?*,
¿falsity? and *¿false?*, *¿evidence?*, *¿proof?* and *¿test??*

Let us begin with *¿truth?* and hope that we shall end with nothing
less! The core of most dictionary definitions of this term consists in the
notion of 'agreement with reality', so it should be clear immediately that
we are up against a problem no less daunting than that with which we

began in chapter 1. Yet we must put all snarks out of mind, we dare not toy with the idea of searching for *the essential quality of ¿truth?*, lest we find ourselves in agreement with Keats who, like many scholars as far apart in time and thought as Aquinas and Russell, held that,

> 'Beauty is truth, truth beauty' – that is all
> Ye know on earth, and all ye need to know.

Our present interest is not in some universal quality pertaining to all *¿true?* acts, notions, thoughts or works of Art, it is rather in the criteria by which we come to decide whether or not to accept a single judgment, whole theory or entire paradigm, as *¿true?*.

It seems to me that, in order to uncover these criteria, it is first necessary to make a distinction between two kinds of judgments which occur, both in the paradigms of academia and in those of everyday life. On the one hand are those judgments which are *contingent-upon-something-or-other*, and on the other hand are those judgments which are *contingent-upon-nothing-at-all*.

Judgments which are contingent-upon-something-or-other are propositions which have implications for observable phenomena and events. For example, 'milkmen have two legs each', 'if I drink too much alcohol I get drunk', 'Father Christmas will come down your chimney on Christmas Eve'; each one of these three statements implies something about things you could actually observe: you could find a number of milkmen and count their legs, you could watch me boozing and observe the effects, or you could sit by your chimney all night on Christmas Eve. On the other hand, consider these three statements: 'milkmen have five legs each, two of these are visible as attachments to the lower part of the body, the other three are invisible and their location is as yet unknown'; 'if I drink too much alcohol I get drunk, but I behave in such a drunken manner all the time that it is impossible for anyone else to tell the difference'; 'Father Christmas will only come down your chimney on Christmas Eve if everyone in the house is fast asleep in bed'. These last three judgments may seem, at least at first, to be contingent-upon-nothing-at-all.[3]

Many – indeed in modern times *most* – philosophers of science have maintained that the notion of *¿truth?* can only have any meaning when it is used in reference either to judgments which are contingent-upon-something-or-other or to theories which contain *at least one* such judgment.[4] *¿Truth?*, for these writers, is a term which can only be applied to bodies of concepts which have at least some implications for observable phenomena or events. For them *¿truth?* and *¿testability?* are very closely connected.[5] A *¿true?* statement, on this view, is one which has been *¿tested?* and which has survived the *¿test?*, a *¿true?* theory is one from which has been derived hypotheses which, after *¿testing?* have been pronounced *¿true?*.[6] This view is expressed very clearly in the following passage from Hempel's introductory text.[7]

> no statement or set of statements T can be significantly proposed as a scientific hypothesis or theory unless it is amenable to objective empirical test, at least 'in principle'. This is to say that it must be possible to derive from T, in the broad sense we have considered, certain test implications of the form 'if test conditions C are realized, then outcome E will occur'; but the test conditions need not be realized or technologically realizable at the time when T is propounded or contemplated. Take the hypothesis, for example, that the distance covered in t seconds by a body falling freely from rest near the surface of the moon is $s = 2 \cdot 7\, t^2$ feet. It yields deductively a set of test implications to the effect that the distances covered by such a body in 1, 2, 3 . . . seconds will be $2 \cdot 7$, $10 \cdot 8$, $24 \cdot 3$, . . . feet. Hence, the hypothesis is testable in principle though it is as yet impossible to perform the test here specified.
>
> But if a statement or set of statements is not testable at least in principle, in other words, if it has no test implications at all, then it cannot be significantly proposed or entertained as a scientific hypothesis or theory, for no conceivable empirical finding can then accord or conflict with it. In this case, it has no bearing whatever on empirical phenomena, or as we will say, it lacks *empirical import*.

Hempel goes on to consider what would happen if two alternative theories of the same phenomena were offered yet where both theories lacked 'empirical import':

> Would there be any conceivable way of adjudicating these conflicting views? Clearly not. Neither of them yields any testable implications; no empirical discrimination between them is possible. Not that the issue is 'too deep' for scientific decision: the two verbally conflicting interpretations make no assertions at all. Hence, the question whether they are true or false makes no sense, and that is why scientific inquiry cannot possibly decide between them.

But we are not obliged to accept this limited 'scientistic' approach in which *¿truth?* is equated with 'correctness' in the sense of correspondence with the observable facts,[8] and in which all statements which are not grounded or groundable in *¿evidence?* are regarded as trivial, empty, or meaningless. For we should not be so impressed by what scientists and philosophers of science say that we forget what common sense and experience have already taught us: Neither in common sense nor in the *actual everyday practice* of science[9] are the terms *¿true?* and *¿truth?* strictly reserved for those judgments and theories which rest upon satisfactory ¿evidence? in fact. ¿Truth?, like reality, is as wide as belief, and as elusive.

We do not in our everyday life and thought apply the concepts ¿true? and ¿truth? – and their antonyms ¿false? and ¿falsity? – in a homogeneous manner, and we certainly do not limit these terms to judgments which are contingent-upon-something-or-other. In fact, I would like to suggest that, in addition to the 'strictly scientific' sense described above, we use the word 'true' to describe three sorts of judgments which *may* have no claim to ¿testability? whatever.[10]

In the first instance we may refer to a judgment as 'true' if it is honestly and sincerely held. In this context a 'false' judgment is simply one which has been uttered with the deliberate intent to deceive or mislead. This notion of truth-as-genuineness-of-intention is, however, presumably irrelevant as a criterion for scientific judgments, for, while we may privately suspect the motives of some scientists and academics we usually consider it bad manners actually to challenge their integrity.[11] We are therefore bound, in spite of any misgivings that we may have, to assume that all judgments made in the name of science are 'true' in this sense of the word.

A second additional sense in which we habitually use the adjective 'true' is to refer to judgments which follow from other judgments 'without error'. Our basic reasoning in these instances is that *if* certain judgments hold, *then* certain other judgments are ¿true? even if the latter have never been ¿tested?, or are, indeed ¿untestable?. Most of mathematics, for example, is subject to this kind of 'truth' considerations, whether it is academic (e.g. $e(x; y_1y_2) = e(xz) + e(zy_1) + e(zy_2)$; *but* $e(zy_1) = e(zz') + e(z'y_1)$ *and* $e(zy_2) = e(zz') + e(z'y_2)$; *hence* $e(x; y_1y_2) = e(xz) + 2e(zz') + e(z'y_1) + e(z'y_2)$), or whether it is mundane (e.g. three toffee-apples at twopence each will cost sixpence). Both everyday and academic minds engaging in this kind of truth judgment are wont to forget the implied '*if* . . . *then* . . . ' form of their thought and to slip into supposing that they are deducing one 'truth' from another. Yet it should still be clear that 'truth' is here being used in a purely logical sense, a sense precisely equivalent to that which we encountered in chapter 3 and labelled logical *validity*.[12]

So far, then, no special problems have arisen. '*Truth*' *in the sense of honesty* should give us no trouble because, like other academics we must at least begin with the (perhaps silly) assumption that everything in science is done with the utmost sincerity. Scientists, we are pretending, for the ¿moment?, do not tell lies. '*Truth*' *in the sense of logical adequacy* should not present us with any complications either, for we have already discovered a special word for this and, provided that we are careful about our use of words, we should not run into any difficulties.

There is, however, another sense in which the word 'true' may be attached to judgments which are contingent-upon-nothing-at-all. Frequently we refer to our *BASIC BELIEFS*, or metatheoretical judgments, as 'Truths' (usually in a way which implies a capital 'T'). Many twentieth-century Westerners would, for example, accept the 'Truth' of the view of Captain James Kirk of the Starship *Enterprise*; he holds that 'Nothing is incomprehensible, there are only some things which are temporarily beyond our understanding.'[13] Similarly, for the Christian, the judgment 'God is Love' is one of the great 'Truths' from which other 'truths' may be derived, while for the modern gnostic the pop lyric 'I am you and you are me and we are one together' may have the same status. In the same way 'Truth' is attributed to wise saws which are not only non-contingent but paradoxical or downright 'contradictory' in form. A good example is the Talmudic proverb,

> He who the invisible would find
> Must look before him and behind.

And the folk-thought of every continent and island is rife with 'Truths' like this which involve their own antipodes.[14]

Modern academics – and pragmatically inclined 'plain men' – tend to dismiss such 'Truths' in a most disrespectful fashion; usually only to clear the ground before asserting other 'Truths' for which they seem to claim a similar status![15] Yet it is hard to see how the 'Truth' of a judgment like 'God is Love' can be attacked from a scientific point of view.

Perhaps we should examine this idea further. How might a 'scientific' critic go about the business of dismissing a *metatheoretical judgment* which someone else claimed to be 'True'? The most obvious line he could take would be to make the counter-assertion that, far from being 'True', the judgment is ¿false?. Yet how could he justify this claim? If he tried, first, to show the judgment in question to be *empirically untrue* – that is, in conflict with the available ¿evidence? – he would succeed only in making a fool of himself, for the statement in question is, by definition, contingent-upon-nothing-at-all. If his second tactic was simply to attempt to discredit his opponent personally – to show that he was making a dishonest and *insincere judgment* – then he might or might not succeed, but he would certainly have stepped outside the scientific ring and violated the academic equivalent of the Queensberry rules. If he had not already behaved so ineptly as to disgrace himself entirely in his opponent's eyes, our valiant critic might attempt the third tactic of demonstrating the *logical invalidity* of the 'Truth' in question. But it is unlikely that such a 'Truth' could be successfully exploded in this manner either. For, on the one hand many metatheoretical judgments are asserted *a priori*, they follow from nothing else at all, and therefore the question of logical adequacy does not arise. On the other hand, however, some metatheoretical judgments are treated as derivative from other more fundamental 'Truths' so that in this case the question of logical adequacy can legitimately be raised. Our critic might just be lucky and discover that he was dealing with a metatheoretical judgment which had been deduced invalidly from a more fundamental *a priori*; but this would presumably only be the case if the judgment in question was a relatively 'original' or newly derived one: an invalidly deduced proposition would hardly have stood the '¿test? of ¿time?'.

Once he had exhausted these three tactics the critic might be reduced to attempting to support his counter-assertion that the judgment in question is ¿false? by the not-so-simple-minded method of *denying his personal belief* in it. The stockbroker might, for example, say to the hippie, 'You are entitled to your belief that the purpose of life on earth is love, but you are none the less mistaken. The most fundamental Truth on this earth is that men cannot live without food, shelter and clothing, it is through work that we earn these rewards, *that* is the purpose of life – work!'[16] But, of course, this tactic (though it might work in some cases) rests upon the fundamental admission that metatheoretical 'Truths' *can*, in principle, be stated meaningfully. The critic is not quibbling about the status of the judgment in question, but merely denying that it falls within that group of 'Truths' which he feels *personally* inclined to accept.

The only other line of attack which seems to be open to the critic of a given metatheoretical judgment is the more thoroughly 'scientific' claim, not that the judgment is ¿false?, but that questions of 'truth' and 'falsity' are irrelevant to it, that it is *inconsequential*, meaningless or, as Hempel says, lacking in 'empirical import'. Of course, this is a most influential view and it is one that, in Western societies, seems to be threatening to overflow the scientific edifices and flood the commonsense houses of reason.

But is a judgment which is contingent-upon-nothing-at-all necessarily *consequential-for-nothing-at-all*? I do not believe so. For metatheoretical 'Truths' are a part of 'the world of daily life which the wide-awake, grown-up man who acts in it and upon it amidst his fellow man, experiences within the natural attitude as reality'.[17] As we have already seen, our *BASIC BELIEFS* help to shape what we see, hear, feel, smell, or taste. The relationship between our senses and our understanding might be less usefully termed 'cognition' than *REcognition*. It is, at least partly, in terms of the assumed consequences of our metatheoretical judgments (*BB*) that we *recognize* phenomena as real. Thus, where one mortal gazes upon the unfathomable miracle of life, another sees a pitiful contribution to world overpopulation; where one hearkens to the revelations of a saint, another pales at the gall of a heretic; for one the proverbial glass is half full, for another it is half empty. Are these judgments meaningless or inconsequential? Not in my view. I believe that we *act upon* our own ¿true? beliefs, not other people's ¿false? ones.

After all we know well that in our interpersonal behaviour, for example, many *a priori* judgments, while ¿untestable? and in that sense *contingent*-upon-nothing-at-all, are ¿true? and in that sense *consequential*-for-all-sorts-of-things. Think of the effect of your own unspoken assumptions on your behaviour towards other people; or consider one of Laing's ballads of Jack and Jill.[18]

> *JACK:* You are a pain in the neck.
> To stop *you* giving me a pain in the neck
> I protect my neck by tightening my neck muscles,
> which gives me the pain in the neck
> you are.
>
> *JILL:* My head aches through trying to stop you
> giving me a headache.

Such interpersonal beliefs are ¿true? because they are self-fulfilling; or are they self-fulfilling because they are ¿true? ? In the same way the most basic metatheoretical judgments, the Great Truths, which men have created throughout history are anything but inconsequential, anything but meaningless! Such 'Truths' as Blake knew, 'can never be told so as to be understood and not be believed':[19] they contain their own fulfilment, they both describe and create.

Who would deny the opposing consequentiality of these two totally untestable 'Truths'?

> Better to reign in Hell than serve in Heaven
>
> (Milton, *Paradise Lost*)

> The soul goes round upon a wheel of stars and all things return. . . . Good and evil go round in a wheel that is one thing and not many. Do you not realise in your heart, do you not believe behind all your beliefs, that there is but one reality and we are its shadows; and all things are but aspects of one thing.
>
> (G. K. Chesterton, *The Dagger with Wings*)

One may deny his *belief* in these judgments – as C. S. Lewis did for the first, or Chesterton's Father Brown did for the second – but it is hard to gainsay their *consequentiality* for believers. And 'Truth' in this so-called metaphysical sense is not monopolized by theologians and mystics. For men like Marx and Sartre believed in the 'Truth' of the judgment that 'Man is, *essentially*, creative' because they considered that the ¿evidence? for such a belief was to be found in *the consequences of the belief itself*.[20]

I am claiming, then, that we human beings are prepared to evaluate the 'Truth' of certain non-contingent judgments in terms of our beliefs regarding their consequentiality. If we believe that the consequences of acting upon certain assumptions are desirable then we are prepared to accept those assumptions as 'True'. But, of course, our criteria for judging the relative desirability of certain outcomes of beliefs are themselves deduced from those most fundamental metatheoretical judgments which we hold to be 'True'. Therefore, in a most profound sense, there are certain judgments in which *we believe because we believe*.[21]

What, then, is a ¿true? judgment? I have suggested that there are four different senses in which a judgment may be said to be 'true'. First, those judgments which are contingent-upon-something-or-other are described as 'true' when they do not conflict with observations of reality which have been made by way of ¿testing?. Perhaps it will be helpful to distinguish this particular 'scientific' conception of ¿truth? by labelling it truth$_4$, and opposing it to falsity$_4$. In his *Astrological Almanac* for 1971 Raphael predicted 'a severe cut in government grants for education creating a severe shortage of teachers for elementary and secondary schools coupled with a deliberate lowering of teaching standards in all state aided schools': at the ¿time? of reading this paragraph you will know whether this judgment is true$_4$ or false$_4$.

Second, a judgment may be described as true$_2$, whether or not it is contingent-upon-something-or-other, if we consider it to have been uttered sincerely. Conversely such a judgment is regarded as false$_2$ if it is stated with deliberate intent to deceive. The notion of truth$_2$ is a difficult one to apply and, although we do it all the time, it is not easy to specify the criteria we use. The claim is often made that falsity$_2$ does not normally occur within the 'scientific community', but nowadays this view is meeting a new challenge, particularly from ¿sociologists?. It will be necessary to return to this important issue later.

The third sense of the word 'true' is true$_3$ meaning logically valid. Whether or not a judgment is contingent-upon-something-or-other, if it is erroneously deduced from a more general proposition it is false$_3$. Consider the following:

> All flowers are coloured
> Some colours are blue
> Dandelions are flowers
> ―――――――――――――
> Hence, dandelions are blue.

The judgment 'Dandelions are blue' is obviously false$_3$ (as well as being false$_4$). The judgment 'Dandelions might be blue' would, however, be true$_3$ if used to replace the original version.

Finally, I have suggested that there is a fourth sense in which we use the word 'truth'. A judgment which is contingent-upon-nothing-at-all may none the less be $True_1$ simply by virtue of the strength of people's faith in it. No human beings can, in my view, avoid making assessments in terms of $Truth_1$ even if these culminate in the firm belief that all judgments which cannot be shown to be either $true_4$ or $false_4$ are meaningless!

EXERCISE

Next time you read *any* book underline the words 'true', 'truth', 'false', and 'falsity' wherever these occur. Attach one of the numbers '1', '2', '3', or '4' to each underlined term, according to the meaning which you think the author intends. Where the meaning of an underlined word is not clear indicate this by interrogative bracketing.

In distinguishing these four conceptions of 'truth' I have done no more than suggest some ways in which we routinely employ the term. So, although I shall from now on refer to '$Truth_1$', '$truth_2$', '$truth_3$' or '$truth_4$' without brackets, I do not mean to give the impression that I have in any sense disposed of the problem posed by the original bracketing. For ¿truth? like ¿reality? can never be seen naked. If we strip her of her brackets we expose only the folly of her undergarments, and the display is not at all shocking, it is merely profoundly embarrassing. The glamorous wench we had imagined is nothing more than an ungainly assemblage of external appearances held in position with whalebone and stout elastic!

Yet we can transcend this seedy tragicomedy. For this is no more naked ¿truth? than was the glittering sequined thing that first fired our imaginations: this is merely the dreary view through the pragmatist's binoculars. We still retain the power to change the view. In the end we can always put the brackets on again so that, at some other point in ¿time? and ¿space? we can be titillated by a different denouement. And there is no end to transcendence:

THERE IS NO ¿TRUTH? THAT CANNOT BE TRANSCENDED.

Yet, from any particular point of view, we are always entitled to make judgments about $Truth_1$, $truth_2$, $truth_3$ or $truth_4$ and from my vantage point it seems that, however we go about this, the decisive element is always that of belief.

WHATEVER IS BELIEVED IS TAKEN TO BE TRUE$_1$
AND/OR TRUE$_2$
AND/OR TRUE$_3$
AND/OR TRUE$_4$.

That is to say that belief bestows 'truth' in four ways. First, our most *BASIC BELIEFS* ensure that the mysterious realms of metatheory are a source of Truth$_1$. For such Truth$_1$ contains its own fulfilment. In Truth$_1$ revelation is actualization, theory is *praxis*, to know is to make, to be: to *create*.

Second, all the thoughts which compose a paradigm may be considered as arranged according to *levels of analysis*, or planes of generality. Thus a pyramid of knowledge may be pictured as a vertical stack of horizontal *levels of analysis*. According to this model the 'lower', more specific, or more *particular* levels are progressively subsumed under ones of 'higher' orders of *generality*, as in Figure 2.

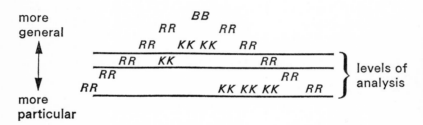

FIGURE 2

Now it is our belief in the reasonableness of this verticality (as form-alized in the *RADII OF REASONING*) which provides the sense of ¿direction? necessary to move from one level of analysis to another. It is logic and methodology which define the ladders of truth$_3$. For GOLD-STAR RABBITS place no intrinsic value upon truth$_3$ for its own sake, but regard truths$_3$ as an assessment of the reasonableness of the assumption that there is a relationship between one level and another. Thus through truths$_3$, the guidelines of logic and methodology which are set parallel to the *RADII OF REASONING*, RABBITS may find their way from one set of *KK* to another. And so great is their faith in the efficacy of true$_3$ ¿directions? that they believe that ladders may be set truly$_3$ between the very highest levels of Truth$_1$ and the lowest of truths$_4$ and vice versa (Figure 3).

Third, *belief* in the sense of *interpersonal trust* is, of course, the source

of truth$_2$. Now judgments about truth$_2$ are generally supposed to be of
real value only in the worlds of everyday life, where they are the substance of both order and change. In the abstract paradigm of science
which transcends the common-sense worlds, truth$_2$ is usually treated
as though it is distinct from, and irrelevant to, Truth$_1$, truth$_3$ and truth$_4$.
Yet citation studies give some ¿evidence? that this view may be false$_2$
and false$_4$, for what academics say they do is not necessarily what they
actually do!²² *Qua* scientists we may mouth our common-sense belief
that 'Honesty is the best policy', but the remainder of that old saw has
not been kept as knowledge: ' . . . but he is not an honest man who is
honest for that reason'!

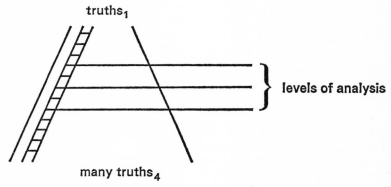

truths$_1$

levels of analysis

many truths$_4$

FIGURE 3

Finally, belief in the methods of science ensures that certain rituals
of research will lead to ¿evidence? believed to be indicative of Truth$_1$. At
the points where various paradigms make statements about the real
world, that is at the points where they generate judgments which are
contingent-upon-something-or-other, we can indulge in a game called
¿testing?. Having first committed ourselves to accept the outcome as
the truth$_4$, we settle our arguments in a sort of sophisticated tick-tack-
toe, where winning paradigms are eternally at risk of being subjected
to challenge from some new contender.

THE METHODS AND TECHNIQUES OF SCIENCE ARE DEVICES FOR MAKING DECISIONS ABOUT TRUTH$_4$.

Thus most scientists and philosophers of science see the aims and
rationale of scientific activity as the establishment of bodies of knowledge (that is of *KK*) which effectively link plausible FAIRY TALES with

truths$_4$. In this way, they claim, human beings can increase both their *understanding* of and their *control* over reality. ¿*Testing?* is continually accomplished by the ritual methods and techniques of science and ¿*evidence?* is obtained from which the truth$_4$ of certain propositions and theories is inferred. Once believed to be true$_4$ these FAIRY TALES and their contingent propositions are then used to make further predictions about reality, or are taken as the basis for action programmes to alter reality in some way.

For example, the judgment 'X increases as Y increases' may be taken to be true$_4$ (or, perhaps, to be probably true$_4$),[23] either because it has been satisfactorily ¿*tested?*, or because it has been validly – that is truly$_3$ – deduced from a theory that is taken to be true$_4$. So this statement, like the theory from which it itself was derived, may be used to *predict* other events: one will tend to expect increases in X to be accompanied or followed by increases in Y. And that judgment might lead one to expect certain other occurrences as well. Also the true$_4$ judgment may be taken as a basis for action: *if* one wishes to increase Y *then* one should increase X.

In Western culture the interrelationship between science and common sense is so salient that the methods and techniques of ¿*testing?* and the criteria by which we assess ¿*evidence?* in the world of everyday life are formally identical with those of science, though they may be less rigorous. For, as I have already implied, there is a growing tendency amongst laymen in our world to accept the 'scientistic' view of ¿*truth?*. Thus, in cases of dispute most of us seek to pin our disagreements down to questions of truth$_4$ for we are prepared to believe that these questions can, at least 'in principle', be settled ¿*objectively?* by the scientific process of ¿*testing?*. Yet, while it is hard for us to imagine worlds where truths$_4$ are not valued as bases for prediction and policy, many writers have described cultures where the ritual methods of establishing truth$_4$ are not those of science.[24]

EXERCISE
Think about the ways in which truth$_4$ is established as a basis for prediction and action in non-scientific cultures (e.g. in so-called primitive societies, or in mystical and millenarian subcultures in Western societies).

In our world we like to believe that we are reasonable. Though we do not deny the force of emotional tactics in arguments, we none the less prefer to be 'reasoned into truth'. But, of course, we are not always able to judge the ¿*truth?* of the scientific theories which we are prepared to take for granted. Thus we are often content to accept the truths$_4$ that these theories profess, not on the grounds of our own judgments, but on the weight of authority. We 'take the experts' word for it'. As we defer to the expertise of others we are acting on the belief that those experts are telling us the truth$_2$. Truths$_2$ become the link between our own thoughts taken for granted and those Truths$_1$, truths$_3$ and truths$_4$ which seem to be beyond our understanding.

Now this must place a very special responsibility on the scientists, the 'experts' to whom the rest of us normally defer. In the first place they have a responsibility to expose their theories to the maximum risk of criticism from their colleagues so that their judgments of truth$_3$ may be open to scrutiny by others. That of course amounts to an assertion that GOLD-STAR methodology should be upheld, that scientists ought as far as possible to formulate their theories as proper *EXPLANATORY THEORIES* whose truth$_3$ values can be readily checked. In the second place experts and putative experts must be careful that the ritual methods of assessing truth$_4$ are properly performed in a true GOLD-STAR spirit. That is to say that they must adopt the GOLD-STAR methods of ¿testing? theories and assessing the ¿evidence? obtained from such ¿tests?.

What are the GOLD-STAR ritual methods of ¿testing? theories. How do GOLD-STAR RABBITS make judgments about the truth$_4$ of FAIRY TALES? In order to find out we must explore a little more of the strange MAGICAL MOUNTAIN whose peaks are turrets of ivory and nitre.

Chapter 6

Testing Rituals

'How is *¿testing?* accomplished and the *¿evidence?* obtained from which inferences can acceptably be drawn about the truth$_4$ of a paradigm, specific theory, or single proposition?' I put this question to a familiar-looking bob-tailed fellow dressed in a white overall, occasionally gaping open to give intermittent flashes of a neat red waistcoat embellished with a gold star.

The eminent scientist's first response was to ask me if I was aware that theories are *contingent-upon-something-or-other*, and therefore *¿testable?* only at certain points, and that the remainder of their fabric is the pure gossamer of the very best fairy tales and is only *¿testable?* by remote inference from the contingent parts. I said that I was. He then asked me if I was familiar with the *radii of reasoning* by which the contingent parts, or *hypotheses* can be related to the theories by which they are explained. I nodded my head, somewhat overconfidently. 'In that case,' he replied, 'you may be in a position to learn the ways of testing and the drawing of inferences from evidence. Now follow me – and *hurry*!'

The RABBIT led the way through brightly lit chambers lined with benches at which rows and rows of scientists were at work amidst the comforting paraphernalia of test-tubes, retorts, and bunsen burners. I felt smug: these chaps were *¿testing?* of course; that was obvious to anyone with an elementary knowledge of science. I began to think that this was all going to be very easy. Then I noticed that the laboratory-corridors were getting narrower and dimmer; the scientists were more strangely clad; and their equipment, though marvellously fashioned, was quite unfamiliar. (See frontispiece.) We came into a very dark passage, no more than five feet wide. There were some candles on the roughly hewn wooden bench, a pile of strange old manuscripts, and some eerie pieces of organic matter in a stone crucible. My guide did not stop, but, twitching a cobweb from his rabbity nose, he picked up a candle and passed into the blackness. As he moved forward with the light I could see an iron staircase spiralling precariously up and out of sight. I went quickly back to the bench to grab a candle and then started up the swaying stairs after the tireless scientist.

The climb seemed endless. But, just as my candle was threatening to burn my fingers, I noticed that the white furry legs were no longer above me. Pulling myself up by my arms, I emerged into a dome-shaped chamber which seemed to be roofed by the deep night sky, and set with twinkling stars. Incredible stars they were, in a class quite different from my guide's waistcoat badge! I heard my own anxious voice: 'Where are we?'

'In the observatory.' Something urged me to ask the ¿time?.

'Approximately 1220 A.D.,' the RABBIT muttered (as he replaced his great gold watch in his waistcoat pocket) 'though I may be a little slow.'

'Be quiet now!' he added. 'They are about to begin.'

What took place then seemed at first to have very little to do with science at all, and even less to do with test tubes, periodic tables, and centrifuges. A number of gentlemen in monkish garb were gathered together in the observatory with the urgent purpose of discussing the relative merits of two different astronomical FAIRY TALES. On the one hand was the ingenious theory of Ptolemy of Alexandria.[1] He held that all the patterns of the heavenly bodies, those which the astronomers could all see from the observatory, could be described and explained by a single pretence: that the sky was ordered by a choreography that included epicyclic and eccentric gyrations, and numerous orbits. On the other hand the assembled company had to consider an alternative theory put forward by a gentleman from the East called al-Bitrogi. This bejewelled and ambitious man had studied together with Averroës in the school of the fat old Islamic philosopher known as ibn-Tofail. According to the Arabic theory the correct picture of the heavens was one of homocentric spheres, and, for al-Bitrogi, *this was no fairy tale*! Unlike Ptolemy he had claimed that his theory could actually be *proved* to be true$_4$.[2]

Unfortunately, neither Ptolemy nor al-Bitrogi could be present at the discussion, as both had made irreversible journeys to the heavens themselves. But the astronomers present were treated instead to the sight of one Bernard of Verdun, frenetically unrolling a manuscript.[3] He began to read. His first claim was that the phenomena, which 'every reasonable man is bound to concede' as observable in the sky, contradict the theory of al-Bitrogi and, far from proving it true$_4$, show it to be false$_4$.

At this all the 'reasonable men' present nodded in agreement (they didn't really think much of the Arab astronomers anyway). But then the gawky Bernard made an unforgivable blunder, he went on to say:[4]

It remains therefore that the second way [Ptolemy's] . . . is *necessary*.

On this theory all the disadvantages we have just been talking about are avoided and the appearances [I have just] listed are saved. By adopting it as our starting point we are able to determine and predict everything that can possibly be known about the celestial motions as well as the distances and magnitudes of the celestial bodies. And up to our time these predictions have proved exact; which could not have happened if this principle had been false; for, in every department, a small error in the beginning becomes a big one in the end.

Everything that appears in the heavens agrees with this theory and contradicts the other. And just as it is necessary to defend the *truths of observation* previously enumerated, so it is necessary to concede the *correctness* of the present theory, and this by the same necessity that forces us to admit the celestial movements in all nature.

At this point a great mumbling could be heard and many wise old heads were shaking under the stars. Then one man came to the fore of the disgruntled gathering. He looked more amused than irritated, and I noticed with astonishment that he was wearing a halo above his cowl. 'Who's that?' I whispered, rather too loudly. 'Sssssssh!' my guide hissed through rabbity teeth. 'It is Thomas Aquinas. Listen very carefully to what he has to say.'

Aquinas began by putting Bernard at his ease and agreeing with him that Ptolemy's theory did indeed make a better job of 'saving the appearances', that is, of accounting for the patterns that astronomers believed they could see in the sky. But he went on to argue most strongly that this did not necessarily make Ptolemy's assumptions $true_4$, in fact no *proof* of $truth_4$ could ever be given for an astronomical theory, for '*one might conceivably be able to explain the apparent motions of the stars in some other way of which men have not as yet thought.*'[5]

The saintly scholar then began to talk about physics[6] but he was suddenly interrupted by the opening of a trap-door in the floor at his feet. A most flamboyant character leapt out, and, with a flourish of his plumed hat, announced himself as Galileo Galilei.

'Oh bother!' the RABBIT hissed in my ear. 'He's over three hundred years too early again. Every time anyone mentions physics he pops up. He simply won't accept that anyone can get along without him – even before tea.'

The ill-mannered Italian ignored Aquinas and began to address the scholars. He claimed that *he* once believed Ptolemy's version of the heavenly ballet, but that there was a superior system developed by Copernicus which could be *proved* correct. He started to talk about demonstrating $truth_4$ through physics,[7] but my head began to swim and I found myself wondering if the RABBIT had been right: *was* the famous physicist too early, or was he too *late*? Since everyone had now begun to

jabber at once and there seemed little point in remaining silent, I turned
to speak to my guide. But I could find neither my furry friend nor the
spiral staircase up which we had come. In desperation I made for
Galileo's trap-door, and, imagining that I felt the top rung of a wooden
ladder beneath me, began my descent.

'Down, down, down. Would the fall *never* come to an end?' I was
just remembering that I had heard that said somewhere before, when I
landed with a splash in a muddy puddle. 'Galileo has calculated that
your fall will have taken three quarters of a century plus the same proportion of an hour',[8] said a voice behind me; but I could see no one at
all.

Of course, you don't believe me; and even if I could show you the
mud on my feet, the stub of a candle I later found in my pocket, or the
feather I pinched from Galileo's hat, you still would not believe me.
For, though I can deduce the presence of mud, candle and feather
from my FAIRY TALE there is nothing whatever to prevent you from inventing a totally different story to explain the same facts. And however
many more hypotheses I deduce from my theory, and however much
more ¿*evidence*? I produce (for example, a frog's leg from the dingy
laboratory, a piece torn from Aquinas's manuscript, etc.), it would be
very arrogant of me to assume that I had *proved* my theory. *You* could
go on inventing alternative FAIRY TALES as fast as I can go on collecting
¿*evidence*?. As Duhem pointed out,[9]

> No matter how numerous and exact the confirmations that are
> brought to a theory by experience, the hypotheses supporting the
> theory never attain to the certainty of commonsense truths. It would
> be a very serious mistake to think that they do, and Bernard of Verdun,
> who did think so, was to that extent quite naïve. To defend such a
> position in our day, after history has witnessed the collapse of so
> many theories long accepted without dispute, one would have to be
> even more naïve. Yet how many of our contemporaries, the very ones
> who think of themselves as tough-minded, accord scientific theories
> the same unquestioning confidence as did the humble Franciscan
> friar of the thirteenth century.

Let us see how many of them do! First, excuse me for a moment
while I clean off some of this mud, then we will pay a visit on a well-
known scientific umpire, Professor Karl Popper. He lives in one of the
towers at the top of the MOUNTAIN but, luckily, there is no need for us
to go through all those dreary laboratories to get there: we can get to
his door by climbing up the outside of the MOUNTAIN and walking across
a sloping CRICKET PITCH.

Popper is ready to admit that among many players in the ¿*test*? game
there exists the uncritical attitude which attributes Truth$_1$ to conven-

tionally accepted theories.[10] He is also well aware of the dangers of thinking that because a particular FAIRY TALE is capable of 'saving the appearances', it is therefore necessarily true$_4$. In fact, according to Popper's version of the rules, attempts to prove a theory by pointing to corroborating instances are foul play. The heroes in this game are the ones who take the biggest risks. Theorists should constantly attempt to derive *hypotheses* from their theories, that is to make their FAIRY TALES yield judgments which are contingent-upon-something-or-other. These hypotheses should, moreover, be genuinely *risky*, that is they should be statements which absolutely *forbid* certain facts to appear. And wherever the gallant scientists make observations which contradict their theories, wherever reality violates their prohibitions, the theories in question should be deemed to have failed the ¿test? and must be discarded.

Thus, for Popper, the proper way to ¿test? a theory is not to attempt to *prove* it but to try to *disprove* it. *In submitting a theory to genuinely risky test the well-behaved scientist attempts to falsify it.* Clearly if he is successful in this attempt he must then admit that the theory is false$_4$ and either discard it completely or modify it in order to test it in a new form.[11]

> (*The scene is set in Popper's parlour*)
>
> ME: Yeah, I think I see what you mean. Once we had a theory that led us to think that if you put jam, washing-up liquid, molasses, bleach, and blancmange powder in a jam jar with some warm tea something interesting ought to happen.
>
> POPPER: Did you have any idea what sort of interesting thing ought to happen?
>
> ME: Well yeah, you know, it might explode, or turn into jelly, or fizz over the top and keep on growing, or turn a pretty colour or something.
>
> POPPER: But was there *anything* that your theory forbade your horrid concoction to do?
>
> ME: Oh yeah! It wasn't allowed to just sit there and do NOTHING.
>
> POPPER: (*Yawning*) What happened?
>
> ME: Nothing.
>
> POPPER: I take it that you discarded your theory?
>
> ME: No. We reckoned we'd made a mistake in the ingredients. Ken went and got some colourless smelly liquid in a bottle, then he poured it into the jar and it all got hot and fizzy and foamy and pale at the top and dark at the bottom and spilling all over the top and the jar broke.

Some theories, like our freak-out jam jar theory, are in Popper's view, most unscientific not because they use jam jars, or say, historical analysis,[12] instead of test tubes but because they fail to forbid very much. Almost anything (and sometimes literally *anything*) that could happen might be taken as support for such theories – and this just isn't cricket because it gives the home team too great an advantage. Popper's ruling is clear:

EVERY SCIENTIFIC TEST OF A THEORY IS AN ATTEMPT TO FALSIFY IT, OR REFUTE IT.

He believes that the more genuine risks a theory takes – the more it forbids – the more *$useful$?* it will be *if* it manages to stand up to those tests. This methodological view may be termed '*Falsificationism*'.

So much for the umpire's tough-minded view, but what do the players actually *do*? Kuhn reckons that Popper has been watching some '*extraordinary*' cricket matches. In his view it is only on rare and memorable occasions that scientists actually keep to Popper's rules of play.[13]

At such times rigorous attempts to falsify theories (and sometimes accidental findings) lead to the recording of observations which run counter to the theories' hypothesized prohibitions. These, at first perhaps unwelcome, findings give rise to some recognition that the favoured paradigm contains anomalies. The paradigm, and its attendant theories, fails to save *all* the appearances, it cannot be reconciled with *all* the known facts. In these circumstances a theory or group of theories may eventually be discarded or modified, but Kuhn considers that these circumstances are rare.

In more '*normal*' times things are different. Just as our common-sense paradigm colours what we believe to be true$_4$ during our mundane experiences of everyday life, so when we play at being scientists our paradigms (and the specific theories which we believe them to engender) act as grids through which we filter what we observe.[14] Thus Kuhn considers that the ordinary run-of-the-mill scientist is not likely to have a truly$_2$ falsificationist attitude towards his work, for, not unnaturally, he hopes to find support for his theory. Such a scientist is likely to be somewhat attached to his paradigm – whether he has invented it himself, or simply picked it up from someone else – so it is a little unrealistic to imagine that he is engaged in a continuing attempt to destroy it.

In fact the bulk of most scientists' work is taken up with efforts to solve puzzles generated by their favoured paradigms rather than with constantly renewed attempts to assess the truth$_4$ of genuinely risky propositions derived from those paradigms. And, while Popper would be utterly disillusioned with scientific practice if he believed that such behaviour was usual, and other umpires like Watkins would rue the

degenerate activity which is fit only for 'plodding, uncritical'[15] RABBITS,
Kuhn considers that, 'Frameworks must be lived with and explored
before they can be broken.'[16] In Kuhn's view, then, the high ideals
entertained by the professional scientific umpires in their ivory towers
become relevant only at times of scientific revolution.

Of course what we require now is a true₂ British compromise. The
RABBITS must be allowed to continue playing the game as they know it,
but – for the sake of UMPIRES, spectators, and RABBITS alike – we need
some clarification of the relationship between the basic rules which are
believed to govern the play and the actual behaviour that we can observe
on the PITCH.[17]

Both Feyerabend and Lakatos reckon that if Popper and Kuhn had
been paying proper attention to the games they would have realized
that such a compromise is practically always evident in science. For, if
one observes a sufficient number of matches,[18] it becomes abundantly
clear that 'proliferation and tenacity do not belong to *successive* periods
in the history of science, but are always *copresent*.'[19] It is because there
will always be some RABBITS who are ready to behave in a most un-
rabbity fashion by introducing rival theories that aspects of what Kuhn
calls 'revolutionary' science are everpresent. Competing theories are
nearly always available to scientists. Thus, whether they like it or not,
they must be continually aware of the possibilities of bringing alternative
theoretical schemes to bear on their particular research problems. This
constant competition between theoretical perspectives can only generate
a series of dialogues which, taken together, give some guarantee that at
least the spirit of 'fair play' is maintained. In this competitive atmosphere
the individual scientist, however much he may desire to protect his
theory, cannot help but develop a *falsificationist attitude of mind*: he must
always be aware of the possibility of other scientists making observations
which produce appearances that cannot be saved by their theory.

It is not that scientists produce *one* theory from *one* universally
acceptable paradigm and then sweat their guts out trying to think up
ways in which their theory could be contradicted by appearances.
Rather, what happens is that scientists develop 'a maze of theories'[20]
from which can be deduced an array of conflicting expectations about
observations that could be made in the real world. It is the continual
attempts to resolve these inconsistencies that guarantees a net falsificationist effect in practice. And, in Lakatos's view, these attempts also
ensure that energy will be directed towards the goal of transcending
specific theories (and even, perhaps, paradigms) by more general or
'roomier' ones which are capable of saving more of the appearances at
once.[21]

THE COEXISTENCE OF CONFLICTING THEORETICAL APPROACHES IN SCIENCE GUARANTEES THAT AT LEAST SOME HYPOTHESES WILL BE AT RISK OF REFUTATION.

Just as the economist is perfectly entitled to describe the collective economic behaviour of housewives in terms of 'laws' of supply and demand, without ever making the assumption that individual house-wives are deliberately following these laws, so it seems reasonable to approach our RABBITS in the same spirit. We do not need to assume that each RABBIT is a diligent Popperian, yet we can still understand the terms *'test'*, *'testing'*, and *'testable'*, and the associated term *'evidence'*, in a sense which follows from a falsificationist approach to the philosophy of science.[22]

So, for our present purposes, a genuinely scientific theory is a deductively valid explanation which generates hypotheses. A hypothesis is a *testable* judgment, that is to say a judgment which is contingent-upon-something-or-other. To *test* such a judgment one searches systematically for appearances that contradict it. The information that one gathers in this *testing* process may be termed *evidence*. But evidence is not proof. Any search for proofs is, from the falsificationist perspective, misguided: no hypothesis, theory, or whole paradigm can be proved $true_4$. The only inference that the scientific community as a whole may legitimately draw from a test is that certain hypotheses, and thence certain theories, have or have not been falsified. That a theory has not been falsified can, of course, never be taken as a certain indication that the theory is $True_1$, for some other explanation may yet be offered which is equally capable of saving the same appearances, and which may even predict other appearances that could not have been deduced from the original theory. In sum,

NO THEORY CAN EVER BE *PROVED* $TRUE_4$.

But this does not mean that there is no point in testing theories. For the more tests a theory has withstood the better basis it affords for making predictions about events in the real world. Just as certain folk-beliefs are 'well tried and tested' so are many scientific theories and the specific predictions which they engender. These scientific FAIRY TALES, like the folk-beliefs, can thus provide quite reasonable bases for guessing what is going to 'happen' in the real world. I am, for example, well prepared to believe that, provided my point of departure is, say, sea level, then 'What goes up must come down.'[23]

Of course the GOLD-STAR RABBIT is entirely *au fait* with this falsificationist methodology, he always acts in such a way as to expose his validly deduced hypotheses, and thence his theories, to maximum risk. But the ordinary run-of-the-mill or '*normal*' RABBIT in his misguided search for proof cannot entirely protect his theories from the risky situations which inevitably arise in the war of all against all that is eternally raging in the spiral warrens of science.

What then of the sociologist with rabbity aspirations? If he wishes to help build a way of looking at the world which gives some reasonable bases for predictions it seems clear what he *should* do. He should avoid consorting with the '*normal*' RABBITS who blunder on amongst the SPIDER's webs, now-and-then succeeding in doing a bit of testing, often by accident. Instead he should search out some GOLD-STAR RABBITS and emulate their methods. But *can* this be done? Is it possible for the sociologist to derive hypotheses from his theories and subject them to genuinely risky test? Let's go back to the sociological LIBRARY and see if we can find any examples.

Well, it is certainly hard to find instances of GOLD-STAR *rabbity behaviour* in these books! So many sociologists, in so far as they have tried to be RABBITS at all,[24] have followed the '*normal*' fellows. Rather than courting falsification in a true$_2$ dialogue about truths$_4$, they have sought verification. They have engaged in a number of rituals which are distinctly '*normal*' rabbity behaviour.[25] For example, they have spent a great deal of time making, sharpening, and polishing their sociological tools and these efforts to invent or improve measuring instruments have not gone unrecorded.[26] They have also spent some time 'gathering' facts, either in the naïve belief that theory will somehow emerge from them, or in the equally vain hope of proving or 'demonstrating' some model or conceptual scheme.[27] There *are* some who have spent their time more fruitfully! These have gone into the LIBRARY itself with large feather-dusters and attempted to tidy up and clear some of the cobwebs away. As a result many sociological theories have been rendered more true$_3$, and their testable implications have been exposed more cleanly to the light of day.[28] But examples of actual testing seem rare indeed. By the look of the records in the LIBRARY not many hypotheses have been exposed to serious risk in the whole history of sociology.[29] More often, 'evidence' has been collected and notions about truth$_4$ have been loosely inferred from this in a manner that would cause any GOLD-STAR RABBIT to wiggle his whiskers in wonder.

However, the situation is not entirely hopeless. Cases of genuine testing can be found in the social science literature if one looks hard enough, and presumably what has been done occasionally in the past could be done more often in the future. Here is an example from the work of a scholar who would probably prefer to be called an anthropologist rather than a sociologist.[30]

Nadel developed a theory to explain an observable relationship between cultural background and cognitive functioning. According to this theory the structure of the world which a child learns to take-for-granted is intimately related to the way in which his mind functions to make sense of stimuli. In cultures where everyday FAIRY TALES structure the world in a highly ordered and systematic way, individual members tend to organize stimuli in their heads in terms of general patterns and relationships. Where, on the other hand, everyday FAIRY TALES offer specific but 'unrelated' explanations of phenomena[31] no such 'analytical' thinking will develop; members of cultures like this will tend to think in terms of 'details' rather than 'patterns'. From this theory two testable hypotheses can be deduced:

HYPOTHESIS 1: *If children from the Yoruba tribe are told a story and then asked to repeat it, they will retell it in a highly structured way, relating the gist of the story rather than the specific details.*

(The Yoruba believe in a series of gods who are clearly related together in a functional and status hierarchy.)

HYPOTHESIS 2: *If the same story is told to children from the Nape tribe they will retell it as a series of 'unrelated' episodes and 'details'.*

(The gods of the Nape have discrete and isolated functions.)

Nadel genuinely put his theory at risk by testing these hypotheses. For if the children had retold their stories in any of the ways forbidden by his hypotheses he would have been forced to reject his theory, either wholly or in part.

Now notice that in that example it was predicted that something would happen *in the future* (*first* you tell the children a story, and *then* they repeat it in a certain way). But it is very important to realize that for a prediction to be genuinely risky it is not necessary for it to refer to something in the future. The process, or phenomenon, or value for a ¿variable? which is predicted by the theory may have already 'occurred', but – so long as the theorist does not *know* this – it is still feasible to talk about prediction. If, for example, I hypothesize that your eating habits will be related to your income in a certain way, I may measure both these variables *simultaneously* and then predict the value of the former on the basis of the latter. I *don't* have to measure your income and *then* hang around waiting for you to eat something.

Thus Piliavin and Briar hypothesized that the disposition of police officers towards young people coming under suspicion varies with the opinion the police have of the demeanour of the youths in question.[32] Evidence about both ¿variables? (police disposition and youths' demeanour-as-seen-by-police) could be collected simultaneously during the course of a study of a number of police encounters with juveniles, and genuine risks could be taken by plotting these two ¿*variables?* against one another in a table. The result of this test is shown in Table I which certainly gives no obvious reason for supposing that the hypothesis in question is false$_4$.[33]

TABLE I   *Severity of police disposition by youths' demeanour*

	Youths' demeanour		
Severity of police disposition	*Co-operative*	*Unco-operative*	*Total*
Arrest (most severe)	2	14	16
Citation or official reprimand	4	5	9
Informal reprimand	15	1	16
Admonish and release (least severe)	24	1	25
Total	45	21	66

Now let us think for a moment about what happens when a theory *fails* a test like this; when it forbids something which, to the researcher's great inconvenience, happens; then appearances conflict with predictions. Does the sociologist in these circumstances immediately throw his theory away?

No. Of course, he doesn't! One typical stratagem employed by the '*normal*' *rabbity* sociologist is to convince himself that the research hasn't 'worked' and try it again. Small boys in school chemistry laboratories can never do anything other than demonstrate yet again that a certain theory can't be falsified – if they succeeded in falsifying it their experiments would have 'failed', and they would be called dull, lazy, or mischievous. This is also so for the ordinary run-of-the-mill sociologist. He considers his research a success only if he fails to falsify his hypotheses (indeed he usually manages to con himself into believing that he has *proved* those hypotheses), and his career success depends on 'positive' rather than 'negative' findings.[34] But if the real world of appearances persistently refuses to be beaten into line, to stop doing the things the theory forbids it to do, then (after tearing his hair and seriously considering inventing all the figures) even the '*normal*' *rabbity* sociologist is forced to think again.

But this rethinking need not necessarily be very radical, even for the GOLD-STAR fellow. All he knows is that he has deduced, from one or more of the theories encompassed by his paradigm, some hypotheses which conflict with the observable facts. Provided that he has not made any logical mistakes (that is, provided that his hypotheses truly$_3$ follow from his premises) and provided also that he is satisfied with his research methods, procedures, and techniques,[35] then he must admit that something is fishy somewhere. Yet in rewriting the theory in order both to save all the known appearances and to generate some new risky hypotheses the theorist does not reject his entire paradigm. He simply attempts to forge new links between what he can observe and what he believes to be $True_1$ within the boundaries of the original paradigm. His metatheoretical judgments, which form the most general propositions at the top of all his theories, are no more likely to be affected by the results of his tests of specific hypotheses than are his basic commitment to the methodology of science, or his acceptance of common-sense ways of grounding his ideas in reality.

Thus, although a metatheory does in some sense determine the form of the theories which it generates, these theories are not strictly *deduceable* from the metatheory – at least not in the same way as the *explanandum* of a theory is deduceable from the *explanans*. Therefore, rejection of a theory or part of a theory, as a result of falsification of a hypothesis or hypotheses, does not logically entail rejection of the metatheory. Just as several different theories may be capable of saving the same appearances, so may several different and conflicting theories be drawn from the same metatheory.

You may find it helpful to consider a sociological example.

Homans and I once set about devising a testable theory of occupational choice. Not surprisingly this specific theory was deduced from Homans's general theory of human behaviour which is itself ultimately attributable to his metatheoretical belief in the rationality of mankind. The theory looked like this.

METATHEORETICAL JUDGMENT	1. The more valuable the reward of an activity is to a person the more likely he is to perform the activity. (Homans)
GENERAL THEORETICAL JUDGMENT	2. In choosing between alternative actions, a person will choose the one for which, as perceived by him, the (mathematical) value of $p \times v$ is the greater, where p is the probability of the action being successful in getting a given reward, and v is the value of the reward. (Homans)
SPECIFIC THEORETICAL JUDGMENTS	3. In choosing between alternative occupations, a person will rank the occupations in terms of the relation between his values and the perceived characteristics of the occupation; the higher the coincidence between the characteristics and his values the higher the rank.
	4. The higher the person perceives the

> probability that he will obtain employ-
> ment in the higher-ranked occupation,
> the more likely he is to choose that
> occupation.   (Homans and Ford)

Luckily for me the research designed to test hypotheses deduced from that theory was a 'success' – the hypotheses were not falsified.[36] But suppose that these tests had 'failed', would this have falsified the metatheory? To put it another way, would Homans have said to me, 'You have shaken my belief in the rationality of man – all my books are wrong!'? *Or* would he have said 'Idiot! You have cocked up the variables again, you've ruined the research!'?

In the end, if we couldn't bash reality back into the paradigm by analysing the *¿data?* in a different way, we would have had to write another theory. But we would not have abandoned the metatheory, merely forged new explanatory links between it and the real world, invented new causal chains, and deduced new hypotheses to be put at risk. It takes more than a bit of research to shake a man's faith in his beliefs about the nature of man! Metatheories are immune from the risks of testing.

NO THEORY CAN EVER BE *PROVED* FALSE$_1$.

So when we talk about testing sociological theories we are not referring to anything as fundamental as 'finding out the *¿truth?*'. We know that the criteria of truth$_2$, truth$_3$ and Truth$_1$ have nothing to do with testing as it has been defined here, and as far as truth$_4$ is concerned the best that we can ever know for certain is that a specific theory has led to deductions which are false$_4$. We have to be content with matching low-level generalizations, or hypotheses, against appearances and, in so far as we fail to falsify these, we presume that our theories 'will do to be going on with'.

A theory which 'will do to be going on with' is one which is both *plausible* and *useful*. It is *plausible* because it has not yet been shown to conflict with any observations which have been made of reality, it saves the appearance. It is *useful* because from it can be derived predictions about patterns and relationships which 'ought' to obtain in the real world.

For example, if a certain theory – let's call it T – generates the hypothesis '*An increase in A causes an increase in B*', and if thorough research has failed to falsify this hypothesis, then we can take it as a pretty reasonable assumption that if we observe an increase in A there is certainly at least a sporting chance that an increase in B will appear, either simultaneously or subsequently. This gives us a basis for action too. For *if* we wished to change the value of B in the real world we would have a fairly good idea that one way to go about it might be to change the value of A in a certain direction.[37] But a theory like T is even more useful than that: it should generate *further* predictions which no one had envisaged before. For example, T may lead to the additional hypothesis that '*Increases in D are a cause of decreases in A*'. Once tested, this and other hypotheses derived from T, could also be taken as reasonable bases for action in the real world.

So a test of a theory is not merely a test of the credibility of a FAIRY TALE about what the real world *might* be like; it can also be a test – in the sense of a trial run – of what the real world *could* be like.

TESTING IS A RITUAL MEANS OF JUDGING PLAUSIBILITY AND UTILITY.

Though they can never know if a theory is true$_4$ RABBITS are prepared to accept the rituals of testing as an adjudication of theories. '*Normal*' RABBITS and run-of-the-mill sociologists allow themselves to slip into assuming that they can equate plausibility and utility with truth$_4$, but GOLD-STAR RABBITS, and some sociologists, prefer the formula,

JUDGMENTS OF PLAUSIBILITY AND UTILITY AFFECT OUR WILLINGNESS TO BELIEVE.

You may or may not consider that what the RABBITS and UMPIRES have revealed about testing is sufficient to lead you to want to know more about it. Just as some people are attracted to the way of understanding the world, and the potential power over that world, that can be gained from a knowledge of witchcraft, so others are attracted to science. If, as Goode says, 'our contemporary pawnbrokers of reality are scientists' rather than witches, then the lure of science must be almost irresistible for the humble sociologist who, like you and me, naïvely hopes 'to do some good in the world'.[38]

You feel something tugging at you, eh? Something is drawing you back towards the MOUNTAIN? O.K. let's go and find out something about the ritual methods of testing.

There are three basic methods for manipulating ¿*variables?* to test theories and all three of these methods are used by sociologists.

First, there is the method which most of us have learned, from our experiences in school, to equate with science itself: the experiment. It is fortunate that you are already familiar with this method. For, as you will see, both the other methods, and all the specific procedures and techniques which are ever employed in testing, are derived from this one basic form of reasoning.

Think for a moment about the *experimental method*. Really it is a method of *do-it-and-see*. If you want to test the hypothesis that '*X causes Y*' then basically what you do is to make X happen and then watch out to see if Y happens. But it is necessary to do this in a fairly systematic way in order to rule out, as far as you can, any irrelevant occurrences that might 'accidentally' cause the happening Y. For example, if you were horrid enough to wish to test the hypothesis that '*Putting nail varnish in a goldfish bowl kills the goldfish*', you would presumably want to do more than simply add some nail varnish to the unlucky fish's water. You would also need to take some rudimentary precautions to ensure that, as far as it is possible for you to tell, no other factor was operating which could cause the fish to die.

You would therefore probably obtain two fish and two bowls, dooming one fish with nail varnish and doing nothing at all to the other. This way you would rule out the possibility that, for example, rather than the nail varnish, the sight of your face through the glass was the fatal factor. Yet even this would not be an adequate test of the disgusting hypothesis, unless you were careful to match other factors between the two bowls. You would need to make certain that there was about the same amount of water in each bowl, that both were at the same temperature, that both bowls contained a similar medley of weeds and bits of old rubbish at the bottom, and that you didn't accidentally spill some detergent in one bowl . . . and so on. In other words you would have to ensure that, as far as you could tell, the only thing that was likely to have produced the difference between the 'experimental' goldfish bowl (plus nail varnish) and the '*control*' bowl (minus nail varnish) was the nail varnish.

The essence of the experimental method, then, consists of the attempt to produce systematic variations in one or more interesting ¿*variables*? (nail-varnish-content-of-water), and the observation of the effect(s) on some other ¿*variable(s)*? (life of fish), while the effect of any extraneous ¿*variables*? (your face, weeds, temperature, etc.) is controlled.

Though psychologists have not, on the whole, had too many qualms about treating their subject-matter (animal brains and human minds) like goldfish,[39] there are a number of good reasons why sociologists have generally considered the method of experimentation impractical, or undesirable, or both. For one thing many of the ¿*variables*? involved in sociological hypotheses cannot possibly be manipulated physically: you can't change the social class composition of a mental hospital, the socialization of a policeman, or the age of a voter. Also many of the causal relationships which sociologists hypothesize are supposed to occur over such a long span of ¿time? that only a Rumpelstiltskin could hang around to observe the results. Then, in addition, when one is testing theories about the ways human beings organize their worlds it is not only impossible to control all the relevant extraneous *¿variables?* experimentally, but also the experiment itself may be a crucial extraneous factor.[40] Suppose, for example, that you hypothesized that the availability of oral contraceptives is an inducement to 'promiscuous' behaviour in females. You could hardly take two groups of women, give one group 'The Pill', lock both groups away to make certain no other *¿variables?* were operating to influence them, and observe their sexual exploits. For, apart from all other absurdities, the fact of locking the ladies away would itself have a very relevant effect.

The final good reason why sociologists have tended to avoid the experimentation ritual is that not a few of them are human beings themselves and have moral objections to messing about with other people – at least in so crude a manner! In the library of sociology, then, experimental tests of hypotheses are few and far between. However, there are two alternatives to the do-it-and-see method of testing which sociologists have not been slow to adopt. Neither of these alternatives involves the actual *physical manipulation of ¿variables?*, though both are *symbolic simulations of experimentation*.

Let us consider the *method of 'mental experimentation'* first. This is the method which sociologists have usually employed when they were interested in testing theories about the causal relationships between major institutions in society. Max Weber, for example, wished to test his theory that the Protestant Ethic was a major cause of the development of capitalist economic structures in the West. First, Weber related some information which he claimed supported his theory, for instance, he claimed that history showed that capitalism in Western countries was always preceded by the development of the specific puritan ideology which he called the Protestant Ethic. But, of course, this adducing of 'evidence' in support of his theory is no kind of test – in order to test the theory Weber had to put forward some genuinely risky hypotheses. One hypothesis that suggested itself to him can be expressed like this: *'In those countries where capitalist economic structures have not developed no preexisting Protestant Ethic will be found.'* He then proposed to test this hypothesis by relating detailed case-studies of the religious systems of some non-Western cultures.

How then did Weber attempt to control the influence of any extraneous *¿variables?* which might have been argued to affect either the Protestant Ethic, or capitalism, or the relationship between them? He did this by choosing for his analysis some countries (only his studies of China and India were actually completed) which he claimed were similar to Western Europe in terms of all other relevant *¿variables?*. He claimed that in these two societies the combination of 'material' factors was at least as favourable to the development of capitalism as in the West, thus he considered that all non-religious *¿variables?* were effectively controlled and that the relationship between religious ideology and economic structure could be examined.[41]

This, then, is the very crudest way of simulating physical manipulation of variables to test a hypothesis. You simply *imagine* that you are doing an experiment and select cases from the real world in such a way as to hold all other factors as 'still' as you can get them, while you compare the values of the ¿*variables?* you are postulating as causes (that is, *independent* ¿*variables?*, for example, Protestant Ethic or nail varnish) and as effects (that is, *dependent* ¿*variables?*, for example, capitalism or dead fish).

This method, sometimes known as the 'case-study' method, has not been reserved solely for the study of grand-scale phenomena in the historical development of societies. It is also used to test hypotheses about variations in the characteristics and behaviour of individual people, groups of people, organizations, or communities, etc. In such studies data are collated from various sources (for example, from prison records, biographies, autobiographies, diaries, letters, interviews, or direct observation, etc.) and cases are grouped together for comparison in terms of the ¿*variables?* that the researcher considers to be relevant.[42] The number of cases compared in studies like this is usually fairly small (rarely exceeding fifty), but it is obviously larger than is usually the case for comparisons of whole societies, like Weber's.

How does simulation of the experiment by selection of cases for comparison compare with actual experimentation? Is this method of *pretend-to-do-it-and-see* much different from the method of do-it-and-see? Well, unfortunately for the rabbity aspirations of sociologists, the ritual of mental experiment is a poor substitute for the ritual of physical experiment. There are several reasons for this, two of which are worth noting here.

First, mental experimentation relies more heavily on the assumption that the researcher *knows* all the relevant ¿*variables?* than does actual experimentation. In the physical method extraneous ¿*variables?* unbeknown to the researcher *may* be operating to confuse the relationship between the experimental ¿*variables?*, but the use of control groups carefully prepared in a manner identical with the experimental groups must eliminate many of the possible confounding ¿*variables?* which the researcher had not even considered. Think back to the sordid goldfish example: you had *unwittingly* removed the risk that the difference between the dead and live fishes might be a result of the size of the surface area of the water, because you had used identical bowls and filled them to roughly the same level. Weber on the other hand, was only able to control for the effects of those ¿*variables?* that he had actually thought about. Thus you or I could, perhaps, have made him blush by suggesting that the Indians and Chinese differ significantly from the

Western Europeans as a result of the amount of rice in their diets. (After all, we might be considering an alternative FAIRY TALE to save the same appearances, namely that, eaten in sufficient quantities, rice turns you on – and turned-on people could never become capitalists![43])

A second problem with mental experimentation is that it is even more difficult to perform this ritual in a genuinely falsificationist frame of mind than is the case with a real experiment. Of course, rivals may oblige by selecting counter-instances, but even so, it is difficult to get the sensation that anything has really been put at risk. This is largely because the researcher almost always has some idea in advance of the value of all the ¿variables? involved.[44] (Weber did not exactly search diligently for societies with relevant values on his independent and control ¿variables? and '*look to see*' if capitalism had emerged in those societies – he already *knew* the answer!) This may be less of a problem where data is drawn from records about individual people or groups, etc., but even here it is likely that familiarity with the cases in advance of performing the pretending-experiment drastically reduces the *risk* that the researcher is taking, and hence the heroism of his test. So, while mental simulation of the experiment by selection of cases may be a valuable ritual from which to draw *inspiration for the creation of theories*, it seems often to fall rather short of the rabbity ideal for *testing theories*.[45]

A much more rigorous method of simulating actual physical manipulation of ¿variables? to test a theory is the *statistical method*.[46] Again the mode of reasoning employed is based on the logic of experimentation.

Suppose that, on the basis of some theory of mine, I hypothesize that eating makes adults fat, in fact I say categorically that '*The more people eat the fatter they get*'. In order to test this hypothesis I might simply ¿measure? both the fatness and the eating habits of a number of different people. I could then, say, punch this information on computer cards. There would be one card for each person. Each card would bear a score for eating habits (perhaps a very simple one like, $1 =$ virtually starving, $2 =$ average eating, $3 =$ absolute gluttony), and a score for fatness (perhaps, $1 =$ thin, $2 =$ medium, $3 =$ fat).

The next stage would be to sort out my pack of cards into groups on the basis of the scores for the two ¿variables?, eating and fatness. First I would sort my cards into three piles according to eating habits, then, taking each of these three piles in turn, I would sort them again according to fatness scores. This would obviously give me nine 'piles' of cards, though some of these 'piles' might be 'empty'. These nine 'piles' could then be easily represented on paper as a *table* with nine *cells*, and the number of cards in each 'pile' could be filled in, in the cells in the table at the top of page 112.

Now, if my hypothesis was false$_4$ the numbers of cards in the various 'piles', and hence the figures in the various cells of the table, would be

	Fatness		
	(thin) 1	(medium) 2	(fat) 3
(starving,and virtually starving) 1			
(average eating) 2			
(absolute gluttony) 3			

(table row label: Eating)

distributed in a haphazard fashion. On the other hand if *most* of the
cards were represented in the diagonal cells of the table like this:

	Fatness		
	1	2	3
Eating 1	(30)	9	7
Eating 2	4	(28)	3
Eating 3	5	8	(45)

I would have no obvious reason to reject my hypothesis. This result
would be precisely similar to that of an experiment in which, say, I had
heated a number of different metal strips and made systematic observations of their temperature and length, finally recording my finding that
increases in length were associated with increases in temperature.

So far so good? One can examine the relationship between an independent ¿*variable?* (say, eating) and a dependent ¿*variable?* (say, fatness)
by taking a number of real people, ¿*measuring?* their relevant characteristics, and then making a pretending-person (a computer card) for each
real person, making certain that the pretending-person resembles the
real person on which it was modelled in respect of all relevant characteristics (the card is punched with values for all relevant ¿*variables?*). Then,
instead of messing about with the people themselves, one can mess
about with their stand-ins, the cards. *But* how does one control for all
the extraneous ¿*variables?* that could be invoked in alternative FAIRY
TALES to explain the relationship in question.

Extraneous *¿variables?* may for the moment be divided into two sorts: on the one hand are *those we know about*, or can guess might be important, and on the other hand, are those *¿variables? which have not even occurred to us so far* but which always figure in alternative explanations of the appearances in which we are interested.

Let us look first at the way in which it is possible to control the influence of any extraneous *¿variables?* which we have actually realized may be important. In testing my eating-and-fatness hypothesis, for example, it might well occur to me that exercise is an important determinant of fatness too, and that this factor might be operating to *confound* the relationship between fatness and eating: people who eat less may be more figure-conscious and therefore take more exercise. Somehow I would need to find out what appears to happen to the relationship between eating and fatness when this *¿variable?* is kept 'still'.

One way of doing this is to *control by selection*. I might, for example, only choose people for my study who did very little exercise and in this way I could reasonably assume that any relationship between eating and fatness was not produced by variations in exercise habits. Obviously I could produce the same effect by choosing people who all did a lot of exercise, or people who were all medium exercisers. But it might be difficult to find a group of people for analysis who were homogeneous with regard to their exercising habits.

The alternative procedure I could try in order to hold this *¿variable?*, exercise, 'still', or *constant*, is *to control by systematic cutting*.

This is a simple operation. Provided I had thought about this problem in advance and recorded some score for exercise on the cards (say, 1 = sedentary, 2 = moderate exercise, 3 = hearty exercise) I could easily produce the effect of holding this *¿variable?* 'still' by cutting my pack of cards according to exercise as well as eating and fatness. Instead of cutting my cards twice I would now do it three times, thus producing 27 'piles', or a table with 27 cells. Such a table might look like the one below.

| | | Exercise | | | | | | | | |
| | | 1 | | | 2 | | | 3 | | |
Fatness		1	2	3	1	2	3	1	2	3
	1									
Eating	2									
	3									

It should be clear that it is possible from such a table to tell what is the relationship between two ¿*variables?* when a third ¿*variable?* is *held constant,* or kept 'still'. Thus, for example, you could look at the relationship between eating and fatness for, say, hearty exercisers only, by considering the last three vertical columns in the table above. In this way it is possible to simulate the experimental method of 'varying' and 'controlling' ¿*variables?*.

But, unfortunately, no sociologist has ever faced a research problem as simple as that example! Normally quite a number of ¿*variables?* are involved, and the researcher often finds it necessary to control several ¿*variables?* simultaneously. In these circumstances, as you can probably guess, he often finds himself with far too few cards to put in his 'piles', and with tables full of empty cells he has to think of tricks to enable him to overcome this difficulty. But let us leave these unpleasant technicalities until later and turn to the problems of simulating control in the case of those ¿*variables?* which, while beyond our present powers of imagination, might still be messing up a test.

The problem is not simply that certain other ¿*variables?* may be varying in ways which have not yet occurred to us. What causes the difficulty for testing is that these undreamt-of ¿*variables?* may be varying in ways which are *systematically related* to the variation of our independent and dependent ¿*variables?*. So the easiest way to mitigate the effect of these nuisance ¿*variables?* is not to try to identify and 'catch' them so that they can be, as it were, tied-down and held 'still', it is simply to take care to ensure that one can reasonably make the assumption that their variance is *irrelevant* to the variations which are being examined. In other words, if the researcher could always assume that all unanticipated extraneous ¿*variables?* were varying *randomly,* rather than in ways which might relate systematically to the patterns in which he was interested, then he could legitimately forget all about them.

Generally the GOLD-STAR researcher attempts to *randomize the influence of unknown and uncontrolled ¿variables?* by taking the greatest possible care how he chooses his cases for study. He tries to choose a *random sample* of cases, that is to select his cases purely ¿*by chance?* as though he were picking pieces of paper from a hat. In this way he hopes to be able to assume that all differences between groups (other than those attributable to the ¿*variables?* that he has actually 'caught' by ¿*measurement?*) are irrelevant to the analysis. Later he will employ special statistical rituals (called 'significance tests') to decide whether or not the patterns which appear in his data can be explained away as mere 'accidents', that is as happenings that could reasonably have been expected to occur purely ¿*by chance?* as a result of the unpredictable and haphazard influences of the unknown ¿*variables?*.

Of course the statistical method of simulating experiments is much more complicated than that, and the tactics I have outlined so far (particularly randomization) often raise more problems for the researcher than they solve. But the purpose of this preliminary exploration of methods of testing has simply been to indicate that,

TESTING MAY BE ATTEMPTED BY MANIPULATING ?*VARIABLES*? THROUGH PHYSICAL, MENTAL, OR STATISTICAL RITUALS.

On the basis of such tests the researcher is prepared to judge the plausibility and utility of his theory. All three methods *can* be used in a genuine attempt to falsify hypotheses derived from a theory though, as we have seen already, and shall see again, they are not always undertaken in this spirit. Unlike the '*normal*' *rabbity* fellow, the sensible scientist does not wrap his theory up in cotton wool to protect it (and himself) from being battered and shaken by awkward appearances, nor does he go on believing in his theory until he accidentally makes observations which conflict with it. Instead he deliberately *tries* to destroy it, rather as you might jump very hard on a home-made bedstead in order to test its strength before trusting your delicate self to it. (Imagine yourself doing that: you would probably subject the bed to much more strain than you expect it ever to have to take, so that, if it gives it gives *now*, not when it matters.) When a theory has withstood pretty hefty assaults – a succession of really risky tests – then it increases in both plausibility and utility.

A theory which has stood up to such tests generally finds its way into the scientific storehouse of kept knowledge (KK), where belief will continue to ensure its truth$_4$ until such time as it may be shown to be false$_4$.

THE THREE RITUAL METHODS OF TESTING ARE SCIENTIFIC CONVENTIONS FOR THE ARBITRATION OF TRUTHS$_4$.

Perhaps you now feel that, given some ¿*variables*?, you would have some idea what to do with them if you wanted to test a FAIRY TALE. But some more problems present themselves: what (on earth?) are ¿*variables*? and how do you 'catch' or ¿*measure*? them?

Chapter 7

The Worlds of
Why-Because

Before a sociologist – or any other RABBIT – can dress up his *¿variables?*
in suitable regalia and press them through his testing rituals, he must,
of course, catch them. But *¿variables?*-catching is not at all like collecting newts in jam jars or enticing slow-worms with vermilion. For
¿variables?, unlike newts and slow-worms do not belong in real worlds
at all. Like 'factors', 'qualities', 'attributes', 'traits', and 'properties',
they refer not to things-in-themselves but to notions we have about
reality, to ideas which we attribute to phenomena from the standpoint
of some paradigm.

¿Variables?, then, are not of the worlds of appearances but of the
worlds of fairy stories and theories. Thus sociological *¿variables?* – ideas
like social class, relative deprivation, status inconsistency, in-group
preference and so on – cannot be directly apprehended in the worlds
that we or any other people take for granted. They live only in the minds
and works of sociologists.[1]

So, if we are to discover anything about the methods which sociological RABBITS have developed for waylaying *¿variables?* we had better
return to the LIBRARY for a moment. You will probably remember that
there are three sorts of sociological theories to be found in the library,
IMPLICIT THEORIES, ANALYTICAL THEORIES, and *EX-
PLANATORY THEORIES*. You may also remember that the GOLD-
STAR RABBITS expressed a distinct preference for the last sort of theories,
though these are in fact the rarest in the LIBRARY. Now before we can
proceed any further with our hunt for ways-of-catching-*¿variables?* we
must find out why this is. We must discover why GOLD-STAR RABBITS
consider that,

ONLY EXPLANATORY THEORIES ACTUALLY EXPLAIN.

Why do they reckon that implicit and analytical theories are only
partial explanations, distinctly inferior kinds of FAIRY TALES? If GOLD-

STAR RABBITS are more interested in deductive validity or truth$_3$ than in the pretty images of the model-builders, why is this?

> RABBIT: (*Suddenly emerging from behind a giant butterfly net*) What did you say?
> ME: I said, 'Why . . .'
> RABBIT: A very good word that: Say it again.
> ME: *Why?*

Indeed it *is* a good word, for, if you think about it, it yields a clue:

'WHY . . . ?'

When we start a query like that we are hoping for an answer beginning with the word,

'BECAUSE . . . '

and ending with a full stop. If we don't get such an answer we will probably go on demanding 'Why, *why*, WHY?' until we either get a satisfactory account of the puzzle or wear ourselves out with wondering. And I am going to suggest that both scientists and laymen tend to regard a 'satisfactory account' as one which suggests plausible reasons or ¿causes? for the occurrence of the events in question.[2]

We have already seen that a deductive nomological explanation consists of a series of judgments which amount to generalizations under which puzzling events can be subsumed. So we are faced with the question of whether an event 'can be completely explained without subsuming it under a universal law licensing its deduction, and consequently showing that *it had to happen*'.[3] And, if we are to adopt GOLD-STAR rabbity criteria for the adequacy of explanations, our answer must be 'NO'. No explanation is complete in a deductive sense until it succeeds in linking the thing-to-be-explained (the *explanandum*) with a series of propositions (the *explanans*) from which it *inevitably* follows.[4] And I am further going to argue that these propositions have the form of a complete account, in the sense mentioned above, only when they are statements about the reasons or ¿causes? for the occurrence of the happening in question. In other words, I am suggesting that,

SATISFACTORY EXPLANATORY THEORIES ALWAYS INCLUDE JUDGMENTS ABOUT ¿CAUSES?.

Three considerations may be regarded as having ¿caused? me to make that bold statement. The first springs from judgments about common sense, the second from notions about science, and the third from some metatheoretical beliefs about the nature of the relationship between the other two.

In the language of common sense the word '*because*' (that is, by-cause)

usually precedes an answer to a Why-question and serves as a signal for the beginning of a story about a particular ¿cause? or set of ¿causes?. A ¿happening? is felt to be explained when its ¿causes? are understood, that is, when some reasonable tale about *what made it happen* has been produced.

In so-called primitive cultures the notions which are invoked as ¿causative? agents are quite commonly of a 'spiritual' or 'occult' nature. Thus gods, winds, fairies, and demons are regarded as ¿causes? of all sorts of everyday phenomena and events from childbirth or crop failure to the appearance of iron birds in the sky. In several centuries of Western thought such explanations have been gradually supplemented by a different collection of fictions whose explanatory power has expanded to such an extent that they have almost entirely replaced the prettier, but not therefore more mysterious, FAIRY TALES of old. These are the fictions of physical, chemical, and biochemical forces which form the bulk of scientific explanations and inform an increasing number of common-sense theories of everyday happenings and puzzles.[5]

In addition to these impersonal and suprapersonal ¿causative? fictions, men, in both 'primitive' and 'scientific' cultures, also tell stories about another agent who is attributed varying degrees of power to make events happen. They claim that man himself may ¿cause? things to be, or change, or go on being. His too are magical powers like those of the gods or mechanical forces. But the extent of his relative strength in the kingdom of ¿causes? varies from culture to culture, paradigm to paradigm and theory to theory.[6]

But wait! This flight into the realms of everyday fancies should not be sufficient to persuade you that ¿causative? fictions are pervasive in science. It might be the case that ¿causes? are 'primitive' notions belonging to 'primitive' thought, notions for which a developed science has no use. This is the view of one writer, Mario Bunge, who claims that:[7]

> It seems, in fact, characteristic of primitive mentality, at least at a certain stage of its evolution, to assign a cause to everything that is, begins to be, or passes away, . . . A second typical characteristic of primitive mentality is the ignorance of chance, the refusal to believe in mere conjunctions and fortuitous coincidences, and the complementary belief that all events are causally connected, whether in an overt or in a hidden (magical) way. This belief in the universal causal interconnection – a belief probably born in prehistoric times – was adopted in antiquity by Stoicism and is nowadays held by the continuers of prehistoric thought.

Why then have I identified GOLD-STAR explanations with ¿causal? explanations? Am I suggesting that RABBITS, particularly GOLD-STAR RABBITS, are 'continuers of prehistoric thought'?

Well, in a sense, yes. For scientists, however long they may be in the tooth, are also humans and I am suggesting that humans naturally desire to invoke causes in their attempts to explain events. But, while it would be foolish to deny the relevance of common-sense modes of reasoning to the way in which real scientists actually go about thinking about things, it would be equally foolish to assume that, by citing this connection, I have given you sufficient ¿cause? for accepting my belief that adequate explanation requires ¿causal? notions.[8] Common sense is not enough. Science, as we have already seen, aspires to *transcend* common sense.

For, from the standpoint of common sense alone we would have to say that an account of an event was satisfactory when it was felt that the puzzle had been explained. The criterion for adequacy of an explanation in common sense is therefore no more than the subjective sense of understanding. There are some very run-of-the-mill RABBITS who are happy to accept this as a criterion in science too. One of these holds that 'the essence of explanation consists in reducing a situation to elements with which we are so familiar that we accept them as a matter of course so that our curiosity rests.'[9] But, of course, a GOLD-STAR scientist would not accept this view of explanation at all. For on this view it is the level of knowledge and understanding of the questioner, rather than the nature of the theory suggested, which sets the standards of adequacy. Thus, for example, the blueness of a glass vase might be taken by some idiot to be an acceptable ¿cause? of its having been stolen, while the same idiot might fail to accept a proper deductive nomological explanation of the same event, simply because he could not understand it.

Turning from common sense to science it seems appropriate to ask whether the history of science has in fact been characterized by a predominance of ¿causal? explanations, and whether ¿causal? judgments are either common or desirable in contemporary scientific theories.

These questions are not easily answered. For, of course, information about the history of scientific thought can no more be directly collected from the real world than can any other sort of facts. And, in so far as any researcher is limited in energy and resources, he must necessarily rely upon the work of others in his search for relevant material. So the facts he obtains will be coloured not only by his own paradigmatic assumptions but also by those of the other scholars upon whose work he draws. It is therefore hardly surprising that the debate about the frequency and utility of ¿causal? assumptions in science has been dogged by confusion and misunderstanding.

From my perspective it appears that one of the major misunderstandings has arisen as a result of neglect of the lessons we learnt in the observatory. For many commentators seem to believe that ¿causal? links are things which exist in the real world. Of course they are not.

Anyone who was paying attention to the debate in the observatory before the intrusion of the gaudy Galileo would realize that ¿causes?, like ¿variables?, exist only in a fairy-tale world. They are notions that people invent in their attempts to grasp, order, and explain reality. Questions about the frequency and utility of ¿causal? ideas are not questions about relationships in the real world but questions about linkages in the world of theory. That is to say they belong to the realm of epistemology rather than that of ontology.[10]

But is it necessary for scientists to invent these notions in order to construct their theories? Such questions cannot be answered while the words ¿cause?, ¿causal?, ¿caused?, ¿causative? and so on, remain occluded by interrogative brackets. And, of course, the answer anyone chooses to give will depend upon the angle from which he removes those brackets, upon the way he defines the term ¿cause?. I suggest the following definition,

A CAUSE IS WHATEVER IS BELIEVED TO MAKE A ¿HAPPENING?.

Obviously the term ¿happening? is not being limited here to the sort of occasion that might be exemplified by a freak-out at Glastonbury or a Situationist assault on the stock exchange, though its sense would include similar occurrences. A ¿happening? is simply any event which becomes an object of thought. When someone notices some occurrence then, in reality, there is a ¿happening?. But as well as happening in the world of reality or appearances, ¿happenings? also happen in fairy tales. These give no direct evidences of themselves to spectators – only to thinkers. Gods may be angered, molecular activity may increase, or the intelligence of a child may be depressed: none of these events can be detected with the senses, yet their happening is postulated in the world of theory, usually to explain something which *can* be identified in the world of appearances, for example a flood, a change in the state of a solid, or a sudden fall in school grades.[11] So,

HAPPENINGS ARE EVENTS WHICH COME TO BE IDENTIFIED BY PEOPLE THROUGH PARADIGMS.

Happenings are linked together in theories by means of ideas about causes. One happening (real or imagined) is said to have *made* another happening; or a whole sequence of happenings (some in the world of appearances and some in fairy tales) are connected together by a series of causal links. But are happenings ever related together in scientific theories by *different* sorts of links? Do scientists even dispense with ideas of happenings *making* each other happen? And can happenings be satisfactorily explained *without* involving notions about some things making other things happen?

I believe that, faced with these questions, we have only two options. On the one hand we may be prepared to commit ourselves to Tychism, that is to the metatheoretical view that all happenings are mere accidents, predictable only in the limited ways dice or poker hands are predictable.[12] On the other hand, if we reject this belief in the omnipotence of an inexplicable and uncontrollable fortune, we must invest causal sequences to satisfy our quest for scientific understandings: we must pose and answer questions about what made things happen.

Very few scientists who have adopted the first course have managed to maintain their accidentalism with any consistency. But those who have opted for causal fictions have certainly not behaved uniformly: in the current stocks of kept knowledge there is a bewildering variety of different sorts of judgments about the makings of happenings. Many of these differ as much from the straightforward suggestion that one-thing-made-another-thing-happen as RABBITS differ from SPIDERS.

In order to grasp this great variety of different forms of causal judgments it may be useful to classify them. For our purposes such judgments may be treated as differing in three ways, according to the type of happenings involved, according to the number of causes suggested, and according to the *¿directions?* in which those causes are said to operate.

First, happenings may be posited as either *beings* or *becomings*; they may refer on the one hand to the mere existence of something, or, on the other, to some change in its characteristics, behaviour, or relationship to other phenomena. For example, the question '*Why does the social institution called the family exist in the majority of known societies?*' is a question about *being*. On the other hand the question '*Why has the role structure of the typical British working-class family altered over the last hundred years?*' is a question about *becoming*.[13] The first question asks for an explanation of why something is there in the first place, the second asks for an explanation of why something has changed.

Second, causal judgments or whole theories may differ according to whether they posit a single causative agent or involve stories about a number of causes which link together to make a happening. The former will be called *monocausal* and the latter *multicausal*.

Finally propositions and theories may be classified according to whether they suggest *uni-¿directional?* or *multi-¿directional?* causal influence. The notion of *¿direction?* of causation is a very difficult one for, since we are talking about 'movement' in the world of FAIRY TALES, this idea of *¿direction?* must be something different from the notion of 'direction' which we apply to our conception of movement in the three-dimensional space of the world of appearances. But let us sidestep this awkward question for a moment and be content with regarding our everyday conception of 'direction' as a simple *model* for the notion involved here. Thus, without delving any deeper into the matter, we can easily recognize that, for example, the statement '*X causes an increase in Z*', when taken in conjunction with the statement '*Y causes a decrease in Z*', implies the idea that X and Y are operating in opposite ¿directions? with respect to Z. For simplicity the question marks will be removed from the terms 'unidirectional' and 'multidirectional', but the interrogative brackets around the word '¿direction?' itself will be retained as a reminder of the curious meaning of the term.

These three distinctions can be combined together to produce the following typology of causal stories.

Types of causal explanations

		Beings	Becomings
Monocausal	Unidirectional	I	2
	Multidirectional	3	4
Multicausal	Unidirectional	5	6
	Multidirectional	7	8

The simplest kind of causal story is the straightforward idea that one phenomenon, say C, makes another phenomenon, say E, come into being. Such an idea says nothing at all about the causal relationships between any other phenomena or events and implies that *whatever else* goes on C is a necessary and sufficient cause of E: C is the only thing that can make E happen, and it can do so unaided. This is a *TYPE 1* causal story and it may be expressed diagrammatically like this, where the arrow indicates the *¿direction?* of causation:

C ————▶ E

A *TYPE 3* story is almost as simple. Here again one cause, C, is posited but this time it is said to have the power to make not just one but several happenings. A *TYPE 3* causal story may be expressed as in the diagram at the top of the page.

Causal stories of *TYPE 2* and *TYPE 4* are less simple. In a *TYPE 2*

story the single cause, C, is seen as perpetuating a change, movement, or progression in E. C makes the change in the sense of 'pushing' E along in a certain ¿direction?:

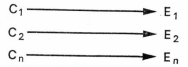

E therefore changes with ¿time? in the ¿direction? of the movement of C. In a *TYPE 4* causal story this picture is either multiplied – one C simultaneously 'pushing' several Es in different ¿directions? – or else C is said to change its ¿direction? producing concomitant changes in the state of E.

Stories of *TYPES 2* and *4* are, however, rather difficult to grasp[14] and it is hardly surprising that, when speaking about becomings rather than beings, scientists have generally tended to invoke whole matrices of causes with mutual influences and interrelations, rather than to develop tortuous explanations based upon a single cause.[15]

The notion of multicausation is not, however, entirely restricted to discussions of happenings of the becoming type, for stories of *TYPE 5* and *TYPE 7* are logically possible and do occasionally occur in science. In a *TYPE 5* story several causes are said to move in the same direction producing several effects, for example:

$$C_1 \longrightarrow E_1$$
$$C_2 \longrightarrow E_2$$
$$C_n \longrightarrow E_n$$

And in a *TYPE 7* story several causes move in different directions, either producing a number of differing effects or, perhaps, converging to produce one effect, as in Figure 4.

But the vast bulk of scientific stories about the causes of happenings are covered by the remaining two types, *TYPE 6* and *TYPE 8*. These are both concerned with explaining why things alter rather than why things came into existence in the first place, and both sorts of stories are set in the context of a vast matrix of other causal influences. In these stories things are not believed to happen in isolation from one another but are considered to occur in contexts. An everyday example may serve as a preliminary illustration. Suppose that Alice has just been sick on the tablecloth! I would not be prepared to accept that the happening *Alice-just-ate-three-teaspoonsful-of-raspberry-jam* is an adequate cause of the phenomenon in question, that simple *TYPE 2* story would not seem plausible to me. However the happening concerning the raspberry jam, when taken in conjunction with some others (*Alice-previously-ate-sixteen-egg-sandwiches-three-jellies-and-two-meringues* and *Alice-took-time-off-from-eating-to-run-around-the-table-seven-times-in-the-same-direction*, plus a number of routine everyday assumptions about the causes of sickness in small girls) could form part of a more complicated causal story which seems to me quite adequate to explain the mess on the tablecloth.

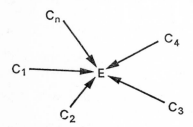

FIGURE 4

Let us briefly review some of these more complicated types of causal FAIRY TALES.

In a *TYPE 6* story the happening, E, which is to be a victim of change is construed as already 'moving' in some ¿direction?. The cause in which the theorist is interested, C, is then conceived as acting upon E in some other ¿direction?. Thus C combines with the antecedent factors to 'push' E in a new ¿direction?. This kind of causal fiction can be crudely represented in terms of a simple addition of vectors (Figure 5).

All other sorts of explanations may be regarded as versions of causal stories of *TYPE 8*. They posit a complex web or network of causal influences moving in several ¿directions? with respect to one another and combining together in various ways to effect changes in existing states of affairs. Since the ¿directions? of these forces cannot be treated like ordinary directions it is usually fruitless to attempt to represent *TYPE 8* stories in precise two-dimensional diagrams. However, crude approximations, or *causal sketches* can be devised in order to aid the memory or speed up the process of communication. One of the most popular ways of

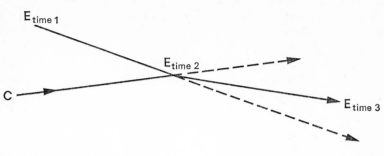

FIGURE 5

drawing a rough causal sketch is to represent features of happenings
as boxes, and draw in the supposed causal links – however vaguely these
are conceived – as lines or arrows. Figure 6 is a very simple example.

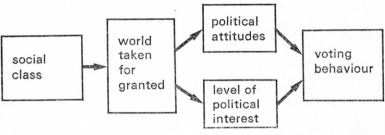

FIGURE 6

This FAIRY TALE is a thoroughly incomplete one, for it does not say
much about the ¿directions? of the causal influences that are implied or
their relative importance. It does, however, provide a useful map of a
simple story which says that a man's social class will have an influence
on the world he takes for granted, and that this world-view will affect
both his political attitudes and his level of political interest, while both
attitudes and interest will influence his voting behaviour.

Unfortunately it is rare that such a simple causal story seems adequate
to explain the complexity of relationships amongst happenings in the
real world. The notion of one thing 'affecting' another, and of this *in
turn* affecting another, vague though it is, is still too restrictive to express
the full richness of scientists' ideas about how things interact with one
another to produce happenings.[16] For example, many *TYPE 8* stories
involve the additional complication of *mutual influences* and *feedback
effects*, so that what is an 'effect' at one stage in a causal FAIRY TALE

becomes a 'cause' at another. Perhaps it is worth our while to make a quick visit to the sociological LIBRARY to find an example of this sort of story. One comes readily to hand.[17]

In outline, the theory is as follows. For diverse causes – biological, psychological, and/or social – most individuals at some time or other engage in *residual rule-breaking* or unusual behavior that is potentially definable by some members of society as abnormal or wrong. (These 'diverse causes', of course, call for the plugging in of sociological and psychological theories of strain generation.) Most such residual rule-breaking is *denied*, not defined or reacted to as of consequence, and is thus not amplified; it is transitory and without issue. On the other hand, depending on the status of the individual, the visibility of his residual rule-breaking, community tolerance level, and so on, his behavior and its effects on family or friends may lead to a 'public crisis' wherein it comes to be defined and 'labeled' as 'mental illness'. These social responses of others significant to him, in conjunction with his own suggestibility at such a time of stress, and along with the stereotyped behaviors of the mentally disturbed he has learned during the normal socialization process, all contribute to his definition of himself as deviant. (This is very much the same process whereby *any* aspect of one's role and self-conception are socially elaborated, though without the stress and crisis.) Inasmuch as this is unsettling to an already disturbed person, his self-control is further impaired, making further episodes of 'unusual' behavior likely. A deviation-amplifying feedback loop is thus set up . . . reverberating from 'ego' and his behavior to significant others, to the public such as psychiatrist, court judge, family physician, or solicitous neighbor, and back to ego's self-conception. Ego's advance into overt deviant role-playing is furthered when the psychiatrist, for example, attempts to fit ego's presumed symptomatic behaviors into traditional clinical categories, and inadvertently rewards ego for the 'correct' behavior symptoms and verbal responses and punishes him for attempting to deny his deviant role. This also constitutes a potential deviation-amplifying source, contributing to the final stabilization of ego into the career deviant role – the neurotic or psychotic. Finally, the aggregation of such deviant roles has its feedback effects on the community, its structure, its tolerance level, and the consequent nature of the 'societal reaction' to further deviance.

The causal sketch in Figure 7 is then offered to clarify the story.

As you will find out for yourself if you begin to play with causal diagrams, even that was a relatively *simple* story! Sometimes you may find yourself having to invent new ways of expressing different sorts of complicated feedback loops – say with double arrows, or with funny wiggly lines. And if you like, then, of course, you can delve into the storehouse of the mathematicians and borrow some of their ways of expressing relationships between causes and effects. You may, for example, identify some happening which has a 'logarithmic' effect on another, or find that what you are trying to say is best expressed by simultaneous equations, or in terms of a graph.[18]

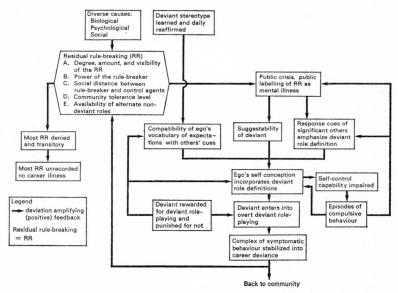

FIGURE 7   *Stabilization of deviance in social system* (Buckley, after Scheff)

But BEWARE! There are dangers involved with this, as with any other, sort of analogical thinking. Certain sorts of relationships which you find to hold in your model may be irrelevant to the characteristics of reality which you were hoping to represent. It may appear from your model that a change in one ¿variable?, say T, will produce a concomitant change in another ¿variable?, say D. But you might have fallen prey to the BATHWATER FALLACY for, according to your original causal story, T may be connected with D in a causal chain but never in a way that implies that T is a cause of D – as where, for example, T represents the incidence of tattooing in a population and D the rate of 'delinquent' behaviour in that same population. For the trouble with mathematics is that a good deal (though not all) of it is based upon assumptions that relationships are *symmetric*: things tend to *equal* one another or to correspond with one another rather than to *force* one another to do things. As Blalock says:[19]

> In mathematics we conventionally mean by a 'dependent variable' whatever variable happens to appear on the left-hand side of the equation. Thus if we write $Y = a + bX$ we are considering Y to be dependent and X independent. We say that Y is a 'function' of X. But we recognise that we could just as easily have written the equation as $X = -a/b + Y/b$, in which case X is taken as dependent. The two equations are algebraically equivalent and can be used interchangeably. In other words, we are ordinarily permitted to treat X and Y perfectly symmetrically.

So, as the sums, or equations, or graphs become more and more complicated it is likely that you will find it more and more difficult to remember which were the causes and which the effects in your causal story. MacIver made this point persuasively when he said:[20]

> In no sense does the mathematical function symbolize our experience of time, the irreversible order that moves from present to past, *from cause to effect* . . . It is a fine instrument for expressing the calculable elemental attributes of physical mechanics, but it is futile to seek to apply it to the processes, trends, and happenings of the complex time-bound constructs within which we have our being.

So, unless we sociological RABBITS exercise *very great care*, the result of our forays into the mathematical warrens could end in hopeless stretchings of analogies and terrible confusions.[21] Visions of SPIDERS drowning in BATHWATER rise up to haunt those of us bold enough to venture into the mathematical tunnels.

A review of the sorts of causal FAIRY TALES employed by RABBITS in general, and sociologists in particular, would not be complete without a brief look at the sort of theories which emphasize the term 'function' in a sense in some ways different from that implied by the mathematicians.[22]

The so-called '*functional*' theories are attempts to circumvent the knotty problem of causal priority. They claim not that one happening is responsible for *making* another happening, but that a number of relevant happenings are related together in a systematic fashion and that the state of balance of this total conglomeration of happenings – this '*system*' – is 'a function of' the behaviour of the constituent parts.

Some methodologists and theorists have insisted that this sort of theorizing is different from, and even superior to, ordinary causal thinking.[23] But this is a curious view. For, unless some assumption of *automatic* self-regulation, balance, or 'equilibrium' is made, functional theories do no more than rudely sidestep the major questions about what-makes-what-else-happen. As many commentators on the behavioural sciences have pointed out, functional theories in sociology are no more than first steps on the way to the drawing of more explicit causal sketches, which are themselves steps on the way to the production of logically convincing, that is deductive nomological explanations.[24]

For example, if I say that *'the social institution we call the family functions to control affection and sexual behaviour as well as to socialize individuals into the norms of the society in which they live'*, I have certainly *not explained* anything about either the being or the becomings of families in society. I have *not* said that *only* families can perform those functions – so I have given no good reason why families might not be replaced by, say, production communes – and even if I *had* made that rash claim[25] I would still have failed to give an adequate explanation either of why families exist or of why they have taken various forms in history. For – unless I imply that society has a mind and will of its own, or that God has taken a particularly detailed fatherly interest in the affairs of man – I have merely restated the questions about what makes families happen in the ways they do. Now it may be that no adequate answers *can* be given to those causal questions, but this is no reason to treat functional sketches as though they are complete explanations, rather it is a reason to admit our inability to invent sufficiently ingenious FAIRY TALES which are adequate to explain even the more obvious appearances.

When theorists stop short of determining the causes of the phenomena in which they are interested they naturally run the risk that others, reading their explanatory sketches, will turn them into more complete explanations by adding causal notions of their own. And even Bunge admits the fundamental tendency to subsume less-than-causal generalizations under more general causal judgments.[26]

This brings me to my third and final argument for the importance of causal notions. The first two arguments may be said to have their roots in some ideas about the history of thinking. Both common sense and, as we have just seen, scientific thinkers have tended in the past to yield to the temptation to invent stories about the *makings* of happenings. The third, and intrinsically related, argument for thinking causally lies, as Nettler has put it, not in our pasts but 'in our futures'.[27] For 'causation is part of the vocabulary of intervention':[28] it is only when we believe that A is *a cause* of B that we can happily alter A with reasonable confidence that B will alter in response. Knowing merely that A and B are in some sense 'related' to one another is clearly not a sufficient basis for effecting any deliberate changes in reality. Nettler quotes Nagel who says, 'It is because some things can be manipulated so as to yield other things, but not conversely, that causal language is a legitimate and convenient way of describing the relationships of many events.'[29]

This then is the final reason why scientists, who do not express their FAIRY STORIES as causal explanations, must expect others, both laymen and other scientists, to do that job for them. Thus if, for example, a sociologist publishes his finding that measurable intelligence (IQ) is related to social class or to race, he must expect that there will be at least some who will read this to mean that certain social classes or races remain socially and educationally deprived *because of* their lower intelligence, and he should be sharp enough to fear that some educational policies may even be based upon this belief. If he wishes to avoid this outcome then he must *either* make explicit his alternative FAIRY TALE (for example that social and educational disadvantages *produce* a relative inability to obtain high scores in intelligence tests); *or* he must simply shut up!

In terms of the perspective offered by the paradigm being displayed here then, the attribution of causes to happenings turns out – *in the last analysis* – to be much more of a metatheoretical business than a logical one. For stories about causes can be constructed on various levels of generality. When we invent causal stories we simply arrange those ¿variables? in which we are interested in a pattern of varying complexity or simplicity. This pattern is, of course, produced by selection and abstraction: we choose those features of those happenings in which we are most ¿interested? and allocate the roles of causes and effects according to our moral, theoretic, and aesthetic preferences. The resulting sequences then refer only to a particular story told from a particular angle. Thus any causal story represents no more than one *moment*[30] in a wider and more marvellous tale created by myriad storytellers whose combined voices yield a saga of 'universal action and reaction in which causes and effects are eternally changing places, so that what is effect here and now will be cause there and then and vice versa'.[31]

Clearly then, one causal story can always be subsumed under another one. Thus, for example, judgments about causes and effects which operate between sociological ¿variables? can in principle usually be deduced from higher-level generalizations about the nature of man. So there is some reason for the claim that sociological judgments are 'reduceable' to the terms of psychology.[32] George Homans goes so far as to say that satisfactory explanations cannot really be achieved until a theory has been constructed which can be validly derived from such propositions.[33] And, in so far as people may indeed go on asking in terms of human motives, then he is right. (For instance, an explanation of the falling birth-rate in Britain at the turn of the century would remain inadequate unless it included some story about *why individual people were motivated* to reduce their families.[34])

But it would be a mistake to think that this means that the whole of the existing stock of theory kept as knowledge by sociologists could be subsumed within the established theories of psychologists. For socio-logical paradigms are in many ways 'roomier' than psychological ones. After all, inspiration for the weaving of FAIRY TALES often seems to come from below as well as from above, from experiences of the real world of appearances as well as from preconceptions derived from the FAIRY-TALE world of theory. When one looks at a real world through the eyes of a normal rabbity sociologist one sees things that would not be apparent to a normal rabbity psychologist.[35]

Nor does this mean that there is little point in constructing ¿socio-logical? FAIRY TALES at low levels of generality without explicitly relating these to higher-order propositions. For very low-level generalizations may result in the broadening and enriching of more general theories and paradigms.[36] Consider, for example, the following case in which socio-logists produce a set of low-level generalizations to explain a puzzling phenomenon, namely, that *those who have least to lose by revolution are not the most inclined to produce it.* The story might be simplified as in Figure 8.

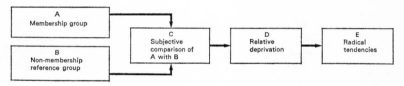

FIGURE 8

This story might well yield testable hypotheses, and evidence from these tests might result in this little FAIRY TALE finding its way into the honoured company of *KEPT KNOWLEDGE* where future sociologists could draw upon it, happy to find a few nice ready-made links which may help them construct their own causal chains.[37]

So causal stories can usefully be invented at low levels of generality. But they can also be posited on planes of thought which are very general. Indeed it is right up in the cloudy realms of metatheory that theorists may eventually halt their feverish regresses of 'Why?'s by invoking final or *ultimate causes.*[38]

Ultimate causes are notions about the first and last reasons or purposes which men have believed to govern all things. Created and sustained by everything and nothing, these omnipotent fictions are taken to explain all conceivable states of affairs, and to these terminal forces alone men attribute the awesome power of creation-of-something-out-of-nothing.[39]

For some sociologists the ultimate goal is ¿society?; they believe all things social to be handmaidens of this ubiquitous fiction. Yet for others the ultimate cause is a creation which, though no easier to pin down, is definitely more lovable. Here it is ¿man? who is the final cause, the sole creator of his worlds and of himself. Across eight centuries these sociologists would echo the call of the sibyl of the Rhine:[40]

Oh man look at man!
For man has in himself heavens and earth
. . . and in him all things are latent.

And, in resounding this metatheoretical commitment, they join with a company of writers who have attributed magical properties to ¿man? and who, in modern ¿time?, express themselves in sentiments like these:

It is not a question of putting something into nothing, but the creation of something *out* of nothing. *Ex Nihilo*. Man, most fundamentally, is not engaged in the discovery of what is there, . . . he is enabling being to emerge from nonbeing . . . man, as creator, must invent, conjure up meanings and values, sustenance and succour out of nothing. He is a magician.[41]

A man sets himself the task of portraying the world. Through the years he peoples a space with images of provinces, kingdoms, mountains, bays, ships, islands, fishes, rooms, instruments, stars, horses and people. Shortly before his death, he discovers that patient labyrinth of lines traces the image of his face.[42]

Let me summarize the argument. Human beings, whether disguised as rabbits or not, like to pretend that the things that they can observe in the real world are explicable. Basically they consider that happenings – whether beings or becomings – have been explained when they have been incorporated in a plausible FAIRY TALE about what caused them. These FAIRY TALES need not be simple monocausal and unidirectional theories. More often, particularly among the bob-tailed folk, they involve complex webs of causal influences and interrelations operating in several directions and with complicated feedback loops, dialectical syntheses and what-not.

Now we have seen that any theory is *open-at-the-top* unless it happens to have been arbitrarily closed up by the force of some mighty ultimate cause. But some theories are more open than others. For, where a theory has been explicitly formulated as a set of logically related causal judgments there is less danger that someone will read into it causal implications which the theorist did not intend. On the other hand, where a theory has been stated in a vague and incomplete fashion there is an alarming possibility that more general theoretical assumptions, and particularly metatheoretical judgments, will be slipped into the theory –

if for no reason more sinister than to cement the gaps and prevent the mind from falling through into an infinite regress of Why?-questions. Such *hidden causal judgments* are not unnaturally regarded as fearsome bogeys by GOLD-STAR RABBITS who believe that fair play requires openness and honesty.[43] And this is one of the dominant reasons for their preference for *EXPLANATORY* rather than *IMPLICIT* theorizing, that is for their firm belief that 'only *EXPLANATORY THEORIES actually explain*'. Thus, according to the GOLD-STAR rule-book,

EXPLANATORY THEORIES INVOKE CATEGORICAL CAUSALITY WHILE IMPLICIT THEORIES EVOKE CASUAL CAUSALITY.

But what of *ANALYTICAL THEORIES* or models? These are after all a very common kind of FAIRY TALE, particularly among sociologists, and, as you will probably have noticed, a favoured way of *presenting* causal stories is in terms of diagrams, that is two-dimensional models. Is the causal status of these pictures-of-boxes-and-arrows *categorical*? – or is it merely *casual*?

Of course it may be either. An *ANALYTICAL* theory may be derived from an *EXPLANATORY* theory, or it may be drawn directly from an *IMPLICIT* theory. In the first case the model will represent a valid causal explanation which has been expressed in the form of a picture simply for reasons of speed, pedagogy, or elegance in communication. Such a model can naturally be treated as though it were an *EXPLANATORY* theory, since the possibility of translating it into a chain of propositions forming a deductive system is always present. On the other hand, the *ANALYTICAL* theory which is based on an *IMPLICIT* theory (whose validity, of course, cannot be directly checked by the logic of science) may or may not be a true$_3$ causal FAIRY TALE.

ANALYTICAL THEORIES MAY BE EITHER CASUALLY OR CATEGORICALLY CAUSAL.

Obviously then the very *testability* of an *ANALYTICAL* theory depends upon its causal status. A model may *look* most impressive – it may involve sophisticated feedback loops, or, say, breathtaking algebra – but it may still be only casually causal: it may be nothing more than an *IMPLICIT* theory in fancy dress. In that case hypotheses derived from it might yield ¿interesting? observations which could serve as puzzles for the initiation of further theorizing, but those observations could not be taken as tests of the model. Such a model cannot be tested, for it can never be put properly at risk. Hypotheses drawn from it, cannot be assumed to be logically related to the whole, and therefore the entire structure of the model is never intrinsically connected with the points at which it is claimed to be contingent.

So it must be clear that, while *not very much* can be said with absolute certainty about the truth$_4$ of proper *EXPLANATORY THEORIES*,[44] *even less* can be said of the evidence which is produced by research guides which are merely casually causal, that is by *IMPLICIT THEORIES*, and those *ANALYTICAL THEORIES* which are no more than pictorial impressions of *IMPLICIT THEORIES*.

So it seems that, for GOLD-STAR RABBITS, the theory construction process must not end until the level of *EXPLANATORY THEORY* has been reached. Only when an *EXPLANATORY THEORY* has been produced can the rituals of testing be performed properly. According to the GOLD-STAR rule-book, the process of theory construction should begin with a puzzle and end with a true$_3$ deductive nomological explanation. If *ANALYTICAL THEORIES* are employed in scientific work then, these should be regarded either as temporary devices which may be of help in the intellectual process of constructing more complete causal explanations, or as methods of *presenting* causal theories in a 'graphic' form, for heuristic reasons. Another way of making that point is to say that *ANALYTICAL THEORIES, or models, are devices which should be regarded as aids to thinking rather than as completed thoughts.*

What did I mean by 'aids to thinking'? Well, I hope that you will now feel able to draw out some further implications of the distinction between *thinking* and *thought* which was introduced in chapter 4. For it is through the magical process of *thinking* that individuals manage to relate particular thoughts to more general ones, and thus to effect (causal) understanding of the former.

Now, we have already seen that there is no *logical* way to move from any particular set of thoughts-already-thought to a more general level of analysis. We have seen that,

GENERALIZING IS NOT A REASONABLE PROCESS.

The scientific *RADII OF REASONING* are no more able to provide recipes for theorizing than are the ordinary common-sense *RULES OF REASONABLENESS*. There is only one way in which an individual ever grasps a connection between a particular notion and a more general idea. That way is the way of *transcendence*. It is through an imaginative leap, an encounter with the FAIRIES. For, as we have seen, *imagination is a necessary prerequisite for thinking*.

Now it is as heuristic – or, more precisely, as '*mnemonic*' – devices that models or *ANALYTICAL THEORIES* come into their own. We may use such images to record something of our imaginative experi-

ences, simply so that we do not forget them. But we will be in deep
BATHWATER if we become so enamoured of the elegance of these models
that we try to pretend that they are either *full* or *reasonable* causal
accounts of the imaginative experiences which they were designed to
evoke. *Models should never be used as means of persuasion in science*, for,
to consider that *ANALYTICAL THEORIES* represent true$_3$ links
between Truths$_1$ and truths$_4$ – or between truths$_4$ and Truths$_1$ – is to
disregard the true$_2$ spirit of GOLD-STAR science.

In order to assess its truth$_4$ (its utility for describing and predicting
reality) a theory must first be rendered true$_3$. That is to say that before a
theory can be tested it *must* be formed as a deductive nomological explanation, as an *EXPLANATORY THEORY*, in which the *explanandum*
(the particular which was to have been explained) is validly deducible
from the *explanans* (some general propositions combined with limiting
conditions).

Logic is not, then, a means of deriving a theory but a method of
checking the validity, or truth$_3$, of a completed, that is *EXPLANA-
TORY*, theory. It is only by *thinking* that an *EXPLANATORY
THEORY* can be produced and, of course, thinking cannot occur in
advance of *imagination*. A successful GOLD-STAR theorist is one who has
transcended a particular set of thoughts by an act of imagination. Then,
not wishing to forget the implications of his imaginative experience for
the thoughts which he had formerly been taking for granted, he has
attempted to sketch his vision by means of some artistic, literary, or
mathematical device: he has employed a metaphor or model to jog his
memory. But, realizing that such a device is not scientific, our GOLD-
STAR theorist does not pretend that his mnemonic images are proper
subjects for science, he does not offer them as thoughts for others to
ponder upon. For he knows that *ANALYTICAL THEORIES* cannot
be subjected to the scientific ritual methods of determining truth$_3$ and
truth$_4$: their logical validity is not open to examination, and thus testing
can provide no real criterion for their acceptance or rejection. Knowing
this, then, the successful GOLD-STAR theorist proceeds to *think*, that is to
transform his *ANALYTICAL THEORY* into an *EXPLANATORY*
one. Once it has been so rendered the theory will be truly$_3$ exposed to
the critical scrutiny of the community of science. A novel FAIRY TALE
will have achieved the status of a scientific thought.

So,

THINKING IS NEITHER DEDUCTIVE NOR INDUCTIVE.

It is a mistake to consider that either deductive or inductive methods of
thought can lead to thinking and thus result in the creation of new

theories. *Deduction*, the logical movement from a general to a more particular level of analysis, is not a recipe for *producing* theories but is, simply, the proper GOLD-STAR method of *checking* the truth₃ of a theory once it has been thought. What then of *induction*, the so-called method of movement from a particular to a more general level of analysis? Induction is quite simply *codswallop*! It is a monstrous potion, a SPIDERY hash, which some of the RABBITS have been trying to cook up as a protection against the everpresent threat of realization that the movement from particulars to generals can never occur *within* a paradigm of thought. Fearing to admit that you cannot move from a 'lower' to a 'higher' level of analysis without transcending *both*, and moving out of the realm of the taken-for-granted altogether, these silly bunnies have pretended to develop dependable routines for creating new theories out of old. But the absurd recipe they have been using could no more produce a new theory than a blancmange!

Now permit *me* to resort to another mnemonic, not, of course, as a means of persuasion, but simply as a convenient method of summarizing what I have been saying about the part played by causal thinking in the magical union of particulars and generals which produces understanding (Figure 9).

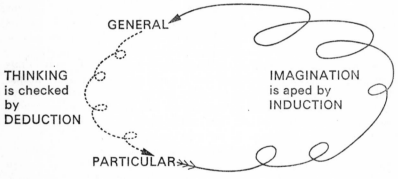

FIGURE 9

The point to be remembered is that the process of theory construction is neither deductive nor inductive. New theories result from a synthesis of the taken-for-granted and a transcendent realm. This synthesis is effected first by a leap of the *imagination*, and then by a careful attempt to reconstruct the newly envisaged relationship between generals and particulars, by means of *thinking*. Once the thinking is complete the result is a set of thoughts which can be expressed within the framework of reason. Valid scientific thinking is always expressible in the form of a deductive nomological explanation, that is as a series of logical steps from the *explanans* to the *explanandum*.

Following Clarence Schrag,[45] I have chosen to refer to this strange synthesis of the rational and the more-than-rational by the thoroughly unimaginative term *'retroduction'*. Of course the word explains nothing, it is only a model chosen to remind you of something that you may have grasped in your imagination. But perhaps that word is *too boring* to trigger off your memory? In that case you may find the illustration on page 138 more ¿interesting?.

Did you recognize the illustration? I am sure you did: it is just another perspective on a familiar *CONUNDRUM*!

Now if you are wearing a GOLD-STAR badge at the moment you will certainly be dissatisfied with my model of theory construction. You will be cross with me for cheating, for slipping in an *ANALYTICAL THEORY* where only a proper *EXPLANATORY THEORY* will do. Indeed you may even consider me rather rude. For, if you are to consider what I have been saying about theory construction and causal thinking as a collection of *scientific thoughts* (rather than as the conglomeration of unscientific images which you find here) then you will have to do the thinking yourself!

If you have decided that that is a mean trick, then I agree with you. And it is no excuse at all for me to say that this is what all the other normal bunnies usually do. Of course, I could point out that the LIBRARY is overflowing with models; that most of the ¿time? most of us have to be content with them because we do not have the wits and energy to do the thinking that should be done; that our models may provide much needed fuel for each other's imagination; or that at least *I* have been honest in admitting that the theory is not a finished product, not a set of scientific thoughts. But those would be excuses. In truth$_2$ I must admit that I am guilty of violating the GOLD-STAR code.

Perhaps you have already transcended my puzzle, seen it on a more general level of analysis as a *CONUNDRUM*, instantly redefined it as a *PARADOX*, sketched your new perspective as a rival model, and are now engaged in the difficult process of thinking it into shape as an *EXPLANATORY THEORY*. If so I wish you luck.

If not, then I offer you a choice: you may borrow my BATHWATER to drown some SPIDERS, or you may face the SPIDERS without it. For, have no doubt about it, the discussions of the process of theory construction which are to be found in the LIBRARY at present are overwhelmingly confused when it comes to the question of inductive versus deductive methods. There are SPIDERS all over the place!

Perhaps the most mean-minded SPIDER in the LIBRARY is the one who lurks in the supposition that rules can be created for the true$_3$ induction of generalizations from the worlds of appearances, and that, once created

The Gyre Descending

according to those rules, theories will necessarily reveal truths$_4$. For we have already seen that the way in which a theory is created is a matter which has no bearing upon its truth$_4$. In order to make a reasonable decision about the truth$_4$ of a theory, that theory *must* be subjected to proper testing rituals. And, of course, before hypotheses can be derived from a theory in such a manner as to put the whole explanatory structure at risk, the theory must be expressed as a deductive nomological explanation. Those RABBITS are horribly mistaken who rely upon so-called procedures of induction (such as, for example, J. S. Mill's modes of the 'comparative method')[46] for the 'discovery' of true$_4$ theories. These methods can lead no one to discover anything. Anyone who considers that he has 'discovered the ¿truth?' by means of induction has fallen into a coney-catch: he has 'discovered' nothing; what he has done is to link some observations together in a haphazard way and then *invented* a FAIRY TALE to 'explain' them. Whether or not the FAIRY TALE so fabricated is ¿interesting?, nothing at all is known about its status with respect to the scientific criteria of truth$_4$.

Of course, the most common type of inductive speculation in the ¿social sciences? is that which takes a *statistical* form. Here the frequency of the occurrence of some happening in the past is used as a basis for a generalization about the likely frequency of its occurrence at all ¿times?. This latter judgment is usually termed a '*statistical law*', and further judgments predicting the '*probability*' of other happenings are inferred from such laws according to certain rules about statistical probability.[47] Such laws are often combined into theories which, on closer inspection, turn out to be models which are not only falsely$_3$ believed to be true$_4$ when they have never been tested, but which are also attributed the power to *explain* things – a quality which they cannot possibly have.[48] Those sociologists who rely upon this form of theorizing naturally consider that the process of inquiry starts with the bare facts and ends with a true$_4$ explanation. They often use most complicated and impressive statistical methods to apprehend their data, believing that inductive statistical analysis is 'like radar turned upon a fog . . . it necessarily reveals to us whatever organization or structure is present.'[49]

That SPIDER must be heartlessly ground underfoot for it frequently tricks RABBITS into dangerous and dishonest ways. The dishonesty lies in the pretence that the facts that generated the theory lie in the real world itself, and that the theory is an accurate description and explanation of what *really is*, rather than a figment of the theorist's imagination. The danger lies in the unhappy likelihood that other run-of-the-mill RABBITS, and even laymen and policy-makers in the worlds outside the scientific MOUNTAIN, will take the theorist seriously – will believe that he has ¿discovered? true$_4$ facts about their real worlds.[50]

There is another SPIDER that should also be squashed while we are in a SPIDER-bashing mood.[51] This one is rather more furry, the better to confuse the RABBITS! Its favourite haunts are in those parts of the LIBRARY where '*empirical theories*'[52] and the more fashionable '*grounded theories*'[53] are to be found.

The arguments of those who advocate such theorizing are not *out-and-out* inductivist ones. Indeed, their claims that elements of theory generation and testing should coexist sound at first entirely reasonable:

perhaps these are no more than statements of the idea of retroductive theorizing? But no. In their feverish attempts to steer clear of an imaginary SPIDER these RABBITS run straight into a genuine one. Their fear is of 'logically deduced theories based on ungrounded assumptions'[54] but of course this is mere paranoia since no such theories exist, all are produced in attempts to save at least some appearances.[55] In place of such theorizing these thinkers advocate what amounts to a methodology of induction, where 'grounded theory is *derived from data* and then *illustrated* by characteristic examples of data'[56] (*sic!*). Though they do occasionally talk of 'testing' – by which they mean a search for verification rather than falsification – most of their methodological rules are specifically directed to the question of how theories are created in the first place. For, unlike Weber and other GOLD-STAR RABBITS, they believe that 'the adequacy of a theory for sociology today cannot be divorced from the process by which it is generated.'[57]

Let's go and fetch one of Alice's favourite cricket UMPIRES and grant him the pleasure of stomping on *this* SPIDER. Over to you Professor Popper:[58]

> what about the method by which we *obtain* our theories or hypotheses? What about *inductive generalisation,* and the way in which we proceed from observation to theory? . . . I shall give two answers. (a) I do not believe that we ever make inductive generalisations in the sense that we start with observations and try to derive our theories from them. I believe that the prejudice that we proceed in this way is a kind of optical illusion, and that at no stage of scientific development do we begin without something in the nature of a theory . . . which in some way *guides* our observations, and helps us to select from the innumerable objects of observation those which may be of interest . . . (b) that it is irrelevant from the point of view of science whether we have obtained our theories by jumping to unwarranted conclusions or merely by stumbling over them (that is, by 'intuition') or else by some inductive procedure. The question, 'How did you first *find* your theory?' relates, as it were, to an entirely private matter, as opposed to the question, 'How did you *test* your theory?' which alone is scientifically relevant.

Theories, then, are thoughts which, like all the other thoughts which have ever been thought, have resulted from the synthesis of non-rational leaps from particulars towards generals, and rational steps back to the taken-for-granted particulars. The outward leaping of imagination is, of course, a matter for which all rules and advice are irrelevant. Science may achieve miracles but it cannot circumscribe and define the Human Imagination. The *process* of thinking cannot be formalized either, but the *results* of thinking should be chains of reasonable judgments arranged in such a way that the particulars can be deduced from the generals without logical error. That is to say that thinking should result in the production of explanatory theories. Strictly speaking, no theory can be tested adequately until it has been expressed in a deductive, and therefore causal, form. But testing rituals are normally going on all the ¿time? in science, and premature testing may have the incidental outcome that it reveals some of the mistakes which might otherwise have remained unnoticed.[59]

> *ME:* I can't see any SPIDERS about now. Do you think it is safe to proceed?
>
> *YOU:* Proceed with what?
>
> *ME:* With our quest to discover the nature of *¿variables?*.
>
> *YOU:* Oh *that*: I don't really see that as a difficulty any more somehow. In fact I'm beginning to think that I knew the answer before you asked the question.

Of course you did! Unlike the foolish inductivists – or as one RABBIT once called them, the idiotic idiographers[60] – you never considered for a moment that ¿variables? were inhabitants of real worlds. You were happy to accept that theirs is a FAIRY-TALE existence. And now somehow it seems that you had realized all along that they are nothing more or less than aspects of happenings which theorists abstract from a totality of appearances in their attempts to construct plausible causal stories. *¿Variables?* are created through a retroductive synthesis of 'invention' and 'discovery'. They are simply those characteristics of those happenings that some RABBIT happens to be ¿interested? in when he views a world of appearances from the standpoint of a paradigm. Quite simply,

A VARIABLE IS A FEATURE OF A HAPPENING SELECTED TO PLAY A PART IN A CAUSAL STORY.

As we shall see later, RABBITS assign different names to variables according to the different parts which they wish them to play in their causal stories. If something is considered to be a *cause* for the purposes of a particular story then it is referred to as an *independent variable*; an *effect*, on the other hand, is called a *dependent variable*. And in most FAIRY TALES a whole structure of *intervening variables* is placed between the independent and dependent variables. In addition to these major sorts of variables, thoughtful scientists also include certain spurious factors to play the parts of the naughty elves and mischievous FAIRIES without which any FAIRY TALE would be less than convincing. These are generally termed *extraneous variables*, and some of them are sometimes called *antecedent variables*.

Well, does it seem a little odd to talk of 'catching' variables, or even – forsaking analogies – to talk of *measuring* them? It certainly does! If variables are FAIRY-TALE entities generated in the process of theory construction, how *in the world* can they be manipulated in rituals for the purpose of theory testing?

This is certainly a difficult problem, and in attempting to come to terms with it we shall have to face a few more horrors. For, just as our discussion of the role of variables in the process of *theory construction* revealed a wide SPIDER-infested gap between *inductive* and *deductive* arguments so, when we come to look at the way variables are 'caught' for *theory testing* another crevice yawns before us: this time there are *positivistic* arguments on one side and *idealistic* ones on the other – and crawling out of the breach are horrible hairy SPIDERS.

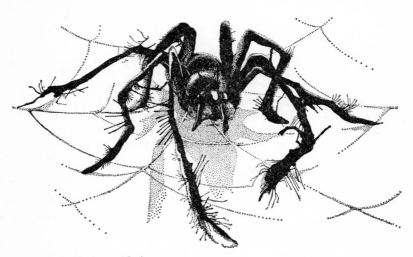

A 'horrible hairy spider'

Chapter 8

Battles for the Bridges

Our desire to find out something about the nature of variables in ¿*sociology?* has led us into the FAIRY-TALE land of theory. In this weird land we have gained a glimpse of the ways in which ¿*sociological?* RABBITS weave variables into causal theories. But, in order to *test* those theories, the RABBITS must obviously find some way back from this fantasy realm into a real world of everyday life. And, if *we* are to find out how they manage this, then we too must attempt to return to some taken-for-granted reality. Yet the way back looks most forbidding.

Ahead is a bottomless, contentless ditch, inconceivably wide and constantly altering its banks. The air is filled with horrible shrieks and an unbelievable stench. All over and around the dyke the SPIDERS are writhing, a ghastly, hairy mass of red and white.

And *what is happening now?* Out of the red and white ghastliness there limps – a RABBIT! His waistcoat is stained with SPIDER-blood, one ear seems more than usually floppy, and if he ever had a GOLD-STAR BADGE he must have mislaid it in the frenzy. For some reason it is reassuring to see that he is approaching us.

RABBIT: (*Huffing and puffing*) Oh dear, oh dear, oh *dear*! That's quite enough for now. I'll never get through that lot before tea-time. I'm lucky they didn't push me in, they're really foul-minded today.

YOU: Whatever is going on?

RABBIT: (*Still very out-of-breath*) Just the usual philosophical punch-up, I wonder they don't wear themselves out. Come on, let's go and get some tea.

We have not walked very far when the RABBIT stops in front of a gay marquee. A sign says, '*Methodological Rest-Post – First Aid and Refreshments*'. We go in and sit down at a round table with an odd design on the top – rather like a chessboard but with only four squares. Tea and buns are brought promptly, and the RABBIT regains his breath and poise remarkably quickly. Realizing that we are eager to know about the strange goings-on surrounding the ditch, and their implications for our journey home, he gulps his tea and begins to explain. (See the illustration on page 145.)

Apparently the RABBITS have erected a rope BRIDGE across the deep trench and it is by means of this shaky structure that they attempt to establish communication between their FAIRY-TALE world of science and the world of appearances which surrounds their terrain. Specialists in people-language, known as 'operationalizers', translate recipes involving RABBIT variables into lists of ingredients which need to be obtained from the real world. The RABBITS then attempt to get across the wobbly BRIDGE with their lists in order to purchase the goods they will need for their testing rituals.

But, though their way is precarious enough as it is, the situation is made much more difficult by the SPIDERS. These nuisances have decided that the RABBITS should pay them a toll for the privilege of crossing their own BRIDGE, and while the RABBITS would be prepared to do this without complaint, the trouble is that it is difficult to know who to pay. For the SPIDERS form two enemy armies and are engaged in a ceaseless battle about the rights to collect the toll.

So, in order to cross the BRIDGE, the unfortunate RABBITS have to negotiate their way through the carnage. Many fall off into the bottomless ditch, and others, like our RABBIT, deciding that 'discretion is the better part of valour', retreat back into their FAIRY-TALE world, either forsaking the quest entirely or at least procrastinating.[1]

Our RABBIT invites us to climb a tall observation tower which is conveniently placed near the marquee. If you put sixpence in the slot you can use the binoculars – and certainly the view they offer is worth the price. On the bank nearer to us, and along the first part of the BRIDGE, the WHITE SPIDERS are massed under a decorative banner which declares 'Idealism for Ever', while on the further part of the BRIDGE and on the nether bank the RED SPIDERS are re-forming under their banner which states in clear black and white 'Positivism Here and Now'.

Whatever we may think about the ethics of exacting tolls from hard-working RABBITS, the Positivists and Idealists certainly do seem to have something to fight over. This is one point on which both sides are agreed: the BRIDGE is vital, for as one furry observer remarked,[2]

> Our scientific activity . . . is . . . performed . . . in order to acquire knowledge for mastering the world, the real world, not the one created by the grace of the scientist. We want to find out what happens in the real world and not in the fantasies of a few sophisticated eccentrics.

The same point has been made by a number of other commentators on the battle, whichever side they are rooting for. One, whom we have

'Tea and buns were brought promptly'

met before (and who incidentally supports the opposite side from the one just quoted), not only agrees about the importance of the thoroughfare between scientific FAIRY TALE and everyday reality but also accepts the analogy of the BRIDGE. For him, 'bridge principles . . . indicate how the processes envisaged by the theory are related to empirical phenomena'. He continues, 'the various ways in which (or test implications by which) sentences containing the terms of a scientific theory can be tested will be determined by the bridge principles.'[3]

We have seen in chapter 6 that to test a theory is to employ testing rituals to check that the happenings forbidden by that theory do not happen in the real world. The question in dispute now relates to how we can *know* whether they *do* happen. How would we *recognize* the occurrence of a happening that has been forbidden by a theory? How can the variables involved in scientific hypotheses be represented by observable equivalents in the world of appearances? For, as we have just seen, variables are not of the world of appearances; in and of themselves they have only a flimsy FAIRY-TALE existence. The precarious rope BRIDGE between the world of the RABBITS and our own familiar world represents the uncertainty with which scientific hypotheses can be translated into statements about what-ought-to-be-observed-in-what-circumstances in reality. The process of relating the two is the the process of *operationalization*.

There are, then, two extreme views about operationalization. On the one hand there are the RED SPIDERS, *the positivists*. These maintain that knowledge is inherently neutral or *objective*, that is to say that universally applicable rules can be developed for the observation of reality, and that, provided that these rules are followed, non-controversial facts can be discerned, facts which would be evident to any unprejudiced observer. Facts are not, for the positivists, products of the sum of the differences of myriad seeings and believings, nor do they result from the relativity of recognitions from multiple perspectives; facts, on the contrary, exist in and of themselves and it is their existence which defines reality. In short,

POSITIVISTS BELIEVE IN THE NEUTRALITY OF THE SCIENTIST AND THE OBJECTIVITY OF HIS DATA.

Naturally enough those sociological RABBITS who count themselves as supporters of the RED SPIDERS add to these two beliefs a third: they assume that any true$_3$ ¿*social science?* must be modelled according to the dominant paradigm of the physical sciences.[4]

Facing the positivists on the opposite bank of the Great Divide, and swarming towards them along the BRIDGE, are *the idealists*, the WHITE SPIDERS. They are opposed to everything about the positivists' creed. Thus they take a contrary view:

IDEALISTS BELIEVE IN THE PARTIALITY OF THE SCIENTIST AND THE SUBJECTIVITY OF HIS DATA.

They are not fooled by the scientists' impressive shows of technical competence. They believe that what an observer sees is guided by what he believes. Hence, for idealists, far from having objective existence in reality, facts are merely products of the imagination. Thoroughgoing idealists are, however, rather few and far between. It is a well-worn joke amongst their RED SPIDER enemies that these courageous and radical thinkers tend to suffer serious and constant depletions in their ranks because they are more than usually accident prone. The trouble is that they tend to keep smashing their heads against imaginary walls and getting stabbed in the back by illusory positivists.

However, the brave WHITE SPIDERS' loss in numbers is amply compensated by the continuing recruitment of younger subalterns who, while less radical than the old guard, are no less vociferous. These prefer to call themselves *neo-idealists* and, though they are dubious about the wisdom of applying idealistic assumptions to physical data, they firmly believe that social and cultural phenomena are subjective in nature and that the student of man and his history has no special immunity from prejudice.

It is hardly surprising that those sociological RABBITS who would not be seen dead in the company of RED SPIDERS have a tendency to support the neo-idealist section of the WHITE arachnids. Lacking the courage to reject entirely the tenets of positivism, they accept the positivists' views with regard to physical data but consider that ¿social? facts are of a different order.[5] Thus they consider that the strategies of operationalization employed by ¿social theorists? must necessarily depart from the example offered by the paradigm of physical science.

The war has been raging long. (See the illustration on page 148.) And in some small corner of a German field it has recently become rather serious. The Germans, never ones for calling spades spades (except when they are spades), have always referred to the fighting by the euphemism '*Der Methodenstreit*'. And currently their attention has turned to that part of the line that stretches by Frankfurt. Here the dyke divides the Frankfurters from their red spidery foes to the North. And here, along the battlefront currently known as '*Der Positivismusstreit*', the din is particularly loud. The local hero is a bright young general known as Habermas. According to his men he has done well today, but let us hear the report of an eye-witness.[6]

To the battlefield then. Allons marcher aux canons. After all this distant gunfire the reader is entitled to an account of the actual slaughter. But of course no one was killed or even seriously injured. When the smoke had lifted, all the contending parties were seen to be securely in possession of their ground. The great contest had ended in a draw: or perhaps one should say the rival armies never really came to grips. In the end they did not perhaps have enough in common to make a genuine engagement possible.

Might it be that the dispute is fruitless? It certainly seems to evoke memories of another famous battle!

'I know what you're thinking about,' said Tweedledum, 'but it isn't so, no-how.'

'Contrariwise,' continued Tweedledee, 'if it was so, it might be; and if it were so, it would be; but as it isn't, it ain't. That's logic.'

'I was thinking,' Alice said very politely, 'which is the best way out. . . .'

The Long War

Well it is too much to expect that the monstrous crow will come down and shut everybody up! So the only thing to do is to try to find out how the differences between the two sides affect their views about the actual practice of operationalization in science. We can only hope that this investigation will reveal a way out of the débâcle.

Who will speak for the positivists? Ah! Let us hear from someone from that smart regiment over there,[7] the one under the leadership of the Colonel with the appropriate name of Bridgman.

Bridgman's argument is quite simply that to be meaningful a variable must be defined in terms of the measurement operations that would be involved in detecting it in reality.[8] This view is usually termed *operationism* (though it is sometimes referred to as operation*al*ism) and it amounts to the methodological assertion that any variable which cannot be directly represented by a measurement operation has no place in science. Thus a hypothesis like '*Those rabbits will be afraid*' is regarded as meaningless. However, the statement '*Those rabbits will be seen to be emitting more faecal boluses per hour than is normal for rabbits*' is perfectly meaningful as far as Bridgman and his men are concerned. Fear, then, is meaningless to the operationist but an observably increasing defaecation rate does have meaning. (Notice incidentally that Cockneys seem to think that Bridgman has a point: the Cockney rarely says 'Huck is afraid', instead he says 'Huck is shitting himself'.)

It follows from the view that meaning inheres in measurement operations that, to avoid ambiguity, every meaningful term must be defined by *one* operation. Therefore operationists believe that even if two different procedures are found to yield the same results (for example, optical and tactile ways of measuring length, or, say, two different sorts of fitness-for-military-service tests) they cannot be measures of the same thing. To followers of Bridgman they must be, in fact, measures of different things which just happen to be associated together in reality.

Certain ¿sociologists?, bowled over by the neatness of the operationist regiment, decided to take over their tactics for ¿sociology?. Most prominent amongst these were Lundberg[9] and Chapin[10] though others have done the same thing in a less obtrusive manner. These theorists claimed that there is no point in conceiving of some unmeasurable thing (like '*intelligence*' for example) and assuming that this has measurable implications (for example, the skills measured by IQ tests). No, for these ¿social scientists?, IQ is *not* an indicator of intelligence, as the needle of a speedometer is an indicator of speed, rather IQ score is *all* we can reasonably *mean* by 'intelligence'. 'After all', they would say, 'how can you know that anything you cannot see, feel, hear, etc., or at least detect with special instruments, how can you know that it is really *there*?' From this point of view the concept 'intelligence' should be abandoned or simply redefined as whatever-it-is-that-intelligence-tests-measure.

Well, this does seem a reasonable view at first. If something is really there then we must be able to recognize it, and given that, why not define it by the procedures used to identify it? Yet if you ponder on this for a moment or two you will see that it is an approach that cannot be reconciled with the arguments of the preceding chapters.

In the first place it is not a very useful view. For if we limit the variables involved in our ¿sociological? theories to those which can be directly measured, then 'sociology becomes a niggling business, doing the easy thing because it is accurate and avoiding the difficult thing because it is imprecise.'[11] Are ¿sociologists? going to throw away concepts like 'alienation', 'social class', 'deviance amplification', and so on, because they cannot be defined by a single measurement operation? Will they instead merely talk about 'span of control', 'net income', and so on?[12]

Certainly you can't prove that something you can't ¿measure? directly is 'there', but then you can't prove it isn't there either! And, if our travels into the FAIRYLAND of science have taught us anything at all, they should have taught us that nothing can be proved. The point of theorizing is to invent things that might be there, to pretend that they are there, because by imagining the existence of such things we can make better sense of whatever we feel we can observe in the real world.[13] You simply can't write a theory in ¿sociology?, or in any other discipline, without including ¿unmeasurable?, make-believe, or hypothetical notions.[14] Some happenings, as we saw in chapter 7, only happen in FAIRY TALES. We do not even pretend that they have observable equivalents in reality. But these utter fictions are not thereby meaningless as Bridgman and his followers would have us believe. On the contrary they are essential to our sense of understanding of what is going on.

A second problem with the operationist approach can perhaps be more readily grasped from the point of view of the enemy. Many ¿sociologists?, following the lead of the neo-idealist Dilthey and his rabbity supporters, have stressed their belief that ¿social? happenings are inherently different from physical happenings and that the former, unlike the latter, can only make sense when they are considered as a part of the total context in which they occur. To abstract happenings from the context in which they are embedded, especially by attempting to ¿measure? isolated traits or variables is, according to this school, to distort them.

Of course, this is a good point. Social phenomena must be meaningful if people claim to understand them; and, in the context of everyday life, notions like 'intelligence', 'ambition', 'friendship', and so on, make perfect sense. The idealists are quite right to accuse the positivists of spidery thinking on this issue – but according to our tale they are octopods themselves.

Let us take as an example the group which formed itself in the tradition laid down in the nineteenth century by Dilthey.[15] They are usually identified by their friends and enemies as the *Verstehende* school because central to their ideas is a particular notion of *understanding* for which English-speaking SPIDERS and RABBITS prefer to retain the German term.

Like the operationists, the Verstehende lot appear at first to make very good sense. Yet the ideas of the two schools of thought are so far apart that healthy opposition to one inevitably leads to a realization of the absurdity of the excesses of the other. For the Verstehende thinkers are so obsessed with the importance of understanding meanings as they occur in *real* taken-for-granted worlds, that they have no interest in *science*.[16]

To understand a happening, for them, is to grasp it from the point of view of an actor who is *au fait* with the taken-for-granted meanings which define the *¿social?* context in which it occurred. They believe that they can explain *¿social?* happenings not by the imposition of abstract analytical frameworks or deductive nomological explanations, but simply by taking part in the taken-for-granted reality of life in the *¿social world?* in which those happenings occur.

Thus Dilthey posits the existence of an 'objective mind' which is 'the manifold form in which what individuals hold in common has objectified itself in the world of senses'.[17] And, though his terminology may be off-putting to the modern reader, his sense is clear: a shared reality is a prerequisite for understanding. No supporter of the Verstehende school would delude himself into thinking that he could pretend to be a visitor from outer space, an impartial alien observer of a *¿social?* scene; he would be well aware that unless he had learnt the meanings of a particular *¿social world?* he would be at a loss to understand anything that happened within it. And such an investigator would never make the mistake of thinking that he could simply 'objectify' the situation with a tape-measure or its equivalent. All Dilthey's brave men are familiar with the following cautionary tale.[18]

A rabbit was once landed by parachute in the world of the Bongy Wongy. Deciding that this might be a good opportunity to gather some information on these exotic people, he soon became friendly with them. They didn't seem at all surprised at his floppy ears or funny way of getting about, and he for his part soon became used to their irritating way of drying their babies' bottoms on his fluffy white bobtail. While the unmarried women got on with the all-important task of standing on their heads, the men spent their time transporting bundles of noodles about. The rabbit soon discerned that the noodles were being stacked in heaps of arbitrarily varying height, and sold at prices fixed according to the ground area covered by the piles. When the intrepid parachutist (now familiar with a little Bongy Wongese) asked why this was done, the men replied, 'if you buy more noodles you must pay more.'

The implications of this approach for the bridging process of operationalization must be obvious. Not only can you not reduce the number of meaningful concepts to those which can be defined by a single operation, but, for this school, most meaningful concepts are considered not to be operationally definable at all. Thus, many of the ¿sociologists? who work in this tradition do not even attempt to ¿measure? ¿social? phenomena, they merely observe ¿social? patterns and interpret them *ex post facto* in a framework which feels ¿true? to them.

Obviously the problems raised by the Verstehende approach are in one sense the antithesis of those thrown up by operationism. For, if the observer must be familiar with the culture in order to understand, and if his data are essentially subjective, the question of universally acceptable testing rituals looms large. What happens when two observers familiar with the same culture interpret a particular happening in different ways? How can they decide between their two opposing theories?

Clearly they cannot do so at all – unless they develop testing rituals which are entirely independent of the methods used to construct the explanation in the first place. Even when a ¿sociologist? is pretty certain that his theory is ¿true? because he feels that he has meaningfully interpreted the signs and come to a realistic appraisal of what is going on in a real ¿social world?, he still has a need to test that explanation, and the pure Verstehende approach gives no guide as to how to do so.[19]

But maybe you are beginning to think that this particular band of WHITE SPIDERS is making more than one sort of spidery error? The battle seems to have become complicated by some additional confusions. Surely there is more at stake here than simply positivism versus idealism?

Indeed the Verstehende school seem to be fighting on two fronts at once. Not only are they battling to protect the tenets of *idealism*, at least in so far as ¿social? phenomena are concerned, but also they seem eager to defend the principles of *inductivism* at the same time. They obviously believe that theories are induced from observations of reality, rather than derived from pre-existing theoretical structures, and they go so far as to consider that the proper inductive procedures (to wit, their special methods of 'understanding') are a sufficient guarantee of the truth$_4$ of the resultant explanations!

Perhaps we would do better to escape from the nitty gritty of the actual fighting. For, unlike the Verstehende folk, I get the feeling that we would have a clearer picture of the whole scene if we were *less* immersed in it! Let's climb up the MOUNTAIN a bit and see if we can get a better view from there.

Aha! From up here we can see that the dreadful dyke does not run in a straight line at all; it is a great, empty, circular moat which surrounds the mountain of science, cutting it off from all the lands of reality. Connecting the mountain with the outside worlds is not one BRIDGE but two, and on each a SPIDER BATTLE is raging. The bridges connect up with two RABBIT holes in the side of the MOUNTAIN. Above these gateways are signs: one is marked '*Theory Construction*', and the other '*Theory Testing*'.

On the former BRIDGE a bloody battle is taking place between the *deductivists* and the *inductivists*. But it seems to be a fight between two flanks of Fred Karno's army who set off in opposite directions to look for the enemy. Blindfold, because they had their balaclavas on back to front, each flank marched a full circle, coming face to face with the other on the return journey. Still not knowing their philosophical ear'oles from their spidery arse'oles they proceeded to lay into one another and hack bits off one another. Some of them are still at it!

On the other BRIDGE, marked '*Theory Testing*', an equally nasty fracas is in progress, this time between the *positivists* and the *idealists*. Within the positivist army the real extremists are the operationists. These take their positivism so far that they claim to be unable to understand most of what anyone says to them. In fact, when commanded to 'Make mincemeat of the bastards!', they rush about examining birth certificates and demanding mincing machines from the exasperated generals. But, of course, the idealist army has its share of eccentrics too. Among them are the Verstehende boys. They seem to be intoxicated with some mind-blowing substance that the Witchfinder General has dropped in their tea. They just sit on the bridge blowing bubbles and tickling the soles of each other's multiple feet with their swords, believing so firmly that the battle is won that they see no point in defending the bridge.

But, fruitless though both these battles may be, they evidently do not occur in isolation from one another. By some strange coincidence I have in my pocket an old map of the campaigns for the bridges. This shows that the warring armies in both battles have formed alliances with their nearest neighbours for purposes of defence against a common foe. (See the illustration on page 154.)

It is clear from the map that the battle area can be divided into four territories as the division between the ground held by the deductivists and that held by the inductivists cuts across the front dividing the positivists from the idealists. Within these territories the SPIDERS have set up four encampments. Unfortunately they have chosen some confusing names for their camps, but that is the way of SPIDERS!

Nearest to us is the camp they call Camp Colza, but let's not bother about the name, we will call it '*C*'. In this camp are those of the *idealists* who have retreated as far back into FAIRYLAND as they can get. They have met up with those of the *deductivists* who have also drawn back towards the MOUNTAIN as they too have a preference for FAIRY TALES rather than reality. These two groups are happy to share a camp, and proud of their joint battlecry: 'Our intellect does not draw its knowledge from nature but imposes its knowledge on nature.'

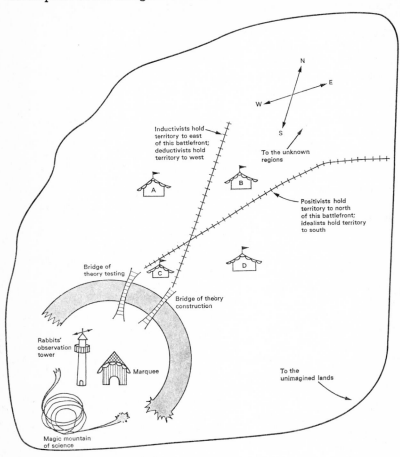

An Old Map

Others of the *deductivists* have been bolder. They believe so strongly in their right to define reality that they have extended their ranks right out into the area which the *positivists* are defending against the idealists. Here they have made a convenient and necessary alliance with some of the positivists and together they have set up a camp which glories in the name of Camp Colander. Let's call this lot '*A*'.

Across the other side of the battlefront these deductive positivists can spy a camp called Camp Collation (we will call it '*B*'). Here other *positivists* have joined forces with some of the *inductivists* to build a solidly practical base with its foundations resting directly on the yellow sand which they believe to be reality.

A fourth camp, Camp Collyrium, which we shall call '*D*', stands in the remaining quarter, and here a thriving community of *inductivists* and *idealists* have settled in. It is rumoured in the *¿sociological?* warrens of the RABBIT MOUNTAIN that more and more furry *¿sociologists?* are paying their tolls to this group every day. This seems to have been especially so since the Collyrium soldiers have been decorated with phenomeno-bars and their helmets newly plumed with ethno-feathers. (But, after all is said and done, SPIDERS in soldiers' uniforms look somewhat ridiculous whatever else they are wearing.)

The *Map of the Campaigns for the Bridges* can of course be simplified for our purposes. In bald form it looks like the design on the tables in the RABBITS' refreshment marquee. It is what in the rabbity world is usually called a *typology*,[20] a device for expressing a number of distinct but simultaneous classificatory distinctions. We have already encountered one typology[21] and we have seen the same principle in operation in the construction of tables for purposes of statistical comparison.[22] But perhaps our SPIDERS have failed to confuse us for once, and have instead unwittingly helped to clarify the way in which typologies are constructed.

There are, then, four obvious types of solution to the two basic methodological dilemmas which haunt the GOLD-STAR RABBITS and taunt the normal ones. These represent four different sets of metatheoretical assumptions about the relationship between paradigms and appearances. Each school of thought has its *¿sociological?* supporters, but none is without problems. In the first place there are those *¿sociologists?* who, like George Homans[23] and Hubert Blalock,[24] follow the strictly respectable lead of philosophers of science such as Hempel, Popper, and Braithwaite.[25] These opt for the *Type A solution*. Of these some are very run-of-the-mill RABBITS who have produced actual *¿sociological?* research which is based on deductive and positivistic assumptions.[26] Such writers suffer from many adverse consequences which come from trying to test deductive nomological explanations by *¿measuring?* happenings like 'occupational choice', 'friendship preference', and 'social class' with ruler-like instruments. (But one of their worst faults is that their work is unrelievedly boring.) On the other hand, others in this group consider that their GOLD-STAR BADGES provide them with exemption from the drudgery of testing and these continue to produce theories which they believe to be testable-in-principle, in the hope that others will oblige with *their* ¿sociological? measuring rods.[27]

Typology of methodological dilemmas

	Deductivism	Inductivism
Positivism	**Type A solution** Deductive Positivism	**Type B solution** Inductive Positivism
Idealism	**Type C solution** Deductive Idealism	**Type D solution** Inductive Idealism

Even more misguided, at least as it seems from my perspective, are those ¿sociologists? who adopt the *Type B solution*. Some of these, like Lundberg and Chapin,[28] carry their positivism to the point of operationism in honour of one of their mentors, Bridgman (who was also a confirmed inductivist). But this sort of extremism is rare these days, as is the outspoken empiricism of writers like Pearson and Cattell who advocated the use of statistics for the induction of explanations from collections of arbitrarily ¿measured? happenings.[29] Indeed few well-worn textbooks on ¿sociological? methodology actually advocate this approach, though many texts slip about between this and the *Type A solution* without ever coming to grips with the difference between the two.[30]

What ¿sociological? RABBITS say they do and what they actually do are, however, quite different things.[31] And it is unfortunately the case that much ¿sociological? research still adheres to the following inductive and positivistic formula:

1. Decide what you want to ¿measure?.
2. Obtain research facilities for so doing.
3. Think of a few more things that might be ¿interesting? to ¿measure? at the same time.
4. ¿Measure? all these.

5. Scan your data for relationships between the various ¿measurements?.
6. Construct an *ex post facto* explanation of your 'findings'.
7. Present this as a 'verified' theory.

Diametrically opposed to these naughty bunnies are those who adopt the *Type C solution*. These consider ¿measurement? to be a thoroughly contemptible occupation. Their interest is in Truth$_1$ rather than truth$_4$. For them, reality only has relevance for theory in so far as the former is dependent upon the latter, different Truths$_1$ produce different worlds and it is solely a matter of metatheoretical decision which truths$_4$ prevail. Such theorists boldly repudiate the positivists' claims that science can be objective or value-free, and assert, contrariwise, that it is a matter of ideological and political dialogue: once one has decided upon one's ideology, deduction of the facts is a relatively simple step, there is no question of *investigating* reality, reality is *produced* by the thinker, the ideopraxist.

This is indeed a courageous stance to take. But it is not without its problems. For under one methodological banner the most contradictory views find shelter, and no rules can exist to guide one in choosing between them.

How, for example, is any RABBIT who takes this position to select his theory? He may accept the conservative bias of functionalist grand theorizing on the one hand, or he may endorse the radicalism of certain current interpreters of Marx on the other.[32] Whichever decision he makes must be affected by his own biases and prejudices which will themselves be partly patterned by his own everyday experiences of a real taken-for-granted world.[33] And this is courage indeed! For the RABBIT committed to this methodological viewpoint is willy nilly committed to constant theoretical bloodshed. He cannot accept any rules for the arbitration of dialogue other than the notions of truth$_3$ which his own chosen Truths$_1$ appear to imply. Thus he must continue to draw the blood of his opponents because, vampire-like, he can have no control over his own destructive power: as long as others exist who disagree with him the bleeding must continue.[34]

Finally there is the *Type D solution* to the two methodological dilemmas. This is currently the most fashionable view amongst sociological RABBITS. In the past it has found philosophical expression in the work of writers like Winch, Antoni, and Hughes,[35] and has been implicitly behind the studies of those ¿sociological? researchers who, like Goffman and the younger Becker, are sometimes identified as the 'New Chicagoans'.[36] More recently it has found methodological apologists amongst a generation of unorthodox American ¿sociologists? who are generally labelled 'ethnomethodologists'.[37]

The ethnomethodologists seem to have constructed their particular methodological jelly pie from three ingredients: the 'ethnoscience' of certain anthropologists,[38] an interpretation of some of the flavours of European phenomenology,[39] and some of the assumptions of linguistics.[40] The resulting confection bears a remarkable similarity to the work of many currently fashionable anthropologists who, while differing amongst themselves in many respects, collude in their idealism and their inductivism.[41]

There are many reasons why the *Type D solution*, particularly ethnomethodology, may rightly be regarded as a more appropriate ¿sociological? approach to methodology than those offered by the other three resolutions of the two basic dilemmas. Ethnomethodologists have the great merit of marrying theory with methodology to produce a unity of thought which is rare amongst the other schools: they allow their theoretical conceptions of the nature of ¿social? reality to guide them in developing procedures for operationalization. Thus, conceiving of ¿social? reality as a precarious and ever-changing web of ideas, they never make the mistake of supposing that ¿social? beings and becomings can be readily subjected to objective ¿measurement? procedures. Moreover their emphasis on a dynamic conception of ¿social? reality leads them to stress the on-going *processes* of reality construction and this has resulted in the production of a number of fascinating studies of emerging ¿social? realities which could certainly not have been produced by ¿sociologists? committed to *either* positivism *or* deductivism.[42]

But I wonder if you have ever seen a jelly pie? The ¿interesting? thing about a jelly pie is that, to the extent that it is a good jelly it cannot be a good pie, and in so far as it *is* a good pie it is bound to be a lousy jelly. For the best jelly is notoriously wobbly, yet perfect pastry must stay still or it will crumble apart. The *Type D solution* – like the other three types – cannot possibly be maintained either as an aim or as an actual method for apprehending ¿social? reality. The form of idealism assumed by the ethnomethodologists cannot get along with inductivism any more than their prescriptions for inductive field-work procedures can get along with their idealism. This is the ethnomethodological Catch 22!

Let me explain. In so far as they believe that ¿social? reality is a human construction, a complex of judgments about ordinary and extraordinary happenings which 'does not exist apart from the objectives and motives of human beings',[43] then the ethnomethodologists make a methodological assumption of idealism.[44] Now it follows from this assumption that ¿social? happenings cannot be apprehended, as it were, 'in the raw'; they can only be constructed by human beings who are familiar with the taken-for-granted background of reality which illuminates them and who are also practised in the methods-of-judging-happenings[45] normally

employed by participants in that reality. This is, of course, the Verstehende view, and it amounts to saying that if the ethnomethodological researcher is to understand what is going on in a ¿social world? he
must be a 'member' of that world, at least in the sense defined above.

Yet, at the same time, the ethnomethodologists are aware that they
must, as scientists, *transcend* the real world-taken-for-granted which
circumscribes the objects of their study at any particular ¿time?. They
must adopt a scientific point of view.[46] For they wish to do more than
to describe aspects of a ¿social world? from the point of view of an
ordinary participant in that world, they also wish to *explain* how those
happenings come to appear like that to such an ordinary participant,
how he takes part in the making of his world. Now in order to put forward a satisfactory explanation they need, of course, to produce a
theory, and Garfinkel is explicit about the way in which the ethnomethodologist strives to take a number of separate observations as
pointers or ¿indicators? in order to build up his own theoretical picture
of the '*underlying pattern*' whose discovery will make sense of the
¿social world? under scrutiny. *But whose pattern is it?* Does the pattern
inhere in the reality itself, or is it a product of the ethnomethodologist's
emerging theory? Of course, from our point of view, it must be the
latter. Yet Garfinkel and many of the ethnomethodologists seem to
think that it is the former, they seem to be implying that the underlying
forms or 'deep structures'[47] can be *discovered* by the scientist applying
inductive procedures to his data, that is to someone else's reality.

In this respect the ethnomethodologists' practical methods-of-doing-
research contradict their theoretical idealism. They intend to do one
thing but they – almost literally – *find themselves* doing another. Their
logic-in-use turns out to be inductive after all, a logic of discovery rather
than invention and one in which research is used to *illustrate* theoretical
generalizations, rather than to *test* deductively valid inferences.

Let us take an example. Aaron Cicourel, in his excellent text on
Method and Measurement in Sociology, carefully distinguishes theory
induction from testing procedures: he talks of testing hypotheses and
discusses operationalization as though he conceives of this as a deductive
translation procedure. He also stresses the way in which pre-existing
theoretical assumptions affect the research process, and he does so in a
manner which certainly renders this book a significant advance on previous texts directed to the same end. In a subsequent work, *The Social
Organization of Juvenile Justice*, Cicourel develops some of his methodological ideas more fully, while attempting to apply them to the study of
a specific kind of meaning-construction in a real world of his acquaintance.

In this book he emphasizes the way in which the processes of classification and interpretation employed by the ¿sociologist?-trying-to-make-

sense-of-official-statistics *parallel* those of the members-of-the-real-world-under-scrutiny-when-compiling-the-statistics-in-the-first-place. In both cases decisions have to be made about how happenings can be meaningfully subsumed under general categories, and, in both cases the final judgment is arbitrarily imposed upon the available information. Cicourel illustrates this point by referring to the following conversation he had with one of his research assistants.[48]

> After the data were coded, punched, and tabulated, I asked the head assistant about the difficulties involved. He began to catalogue a long series of problems that occurred at every step of the data-processing procedures. He described how he and his wife and another graduate student would have continual argumentative sessions wherein categories, raw data [*sic!*], and coding procedures were disputed. Many impasses occurred, and these were finally resolved by the head research assistant more or less by fiat in order to settle the matter and so that they could all get on with the work. The assistant remarked: 'I decided that I was responsible for getting the work done and had to take responsibility for having it make sense. So I would simply make an arbitrary decision that seemed to settle matters at that point.' The head assistant made the remark that: 'My approach was that since I didn't know what would be most important to you I was going to bleed everything out of those files that I could possibly get, even if it seemed a waste of time to even code it. I just tried to bleed everything I could out of it and let you do what you wanted with it. . . . '

He then sums up the problems involved in interpreting such data as follows:[49]

> The entire set of procedures *for coding and probation records constituted a continuous improvised set of decisions, whose primary purpose was to achieve practical solutions to problems whose outcomes or resolutions could not be decided according to explicit criteria based upon an explicit theoretical position* vis-à-vis *the intended meaning of the data.*

And, of course, this conclusion is intended to be read with an awareness that all this hassle and uncertainty in categorization is paralleled in reality:[50]

> *Here I assert that the ways in which such factors are identified and 'known' by the researcher are similar to the ways in which they are invoked by the practitioner to justify his actions.*

But let us pause for a moment whilst we attempt to give an account of Cicourel's account of his researchers' accounts of police and probation officers' accounts of juveniles' accounts of their actions. *Whatever is going on?* Yes, indeed! Cicourel is attempting to describe a process of *induction*, or rather, several parallel processes of induction.

He is perfectly aware that the subsumption of particulars under generals is not a random business, he knows full well that it is, rather, a theory-guided and paradigm-determined activity. Yet he believes that the theories applied to observations in order to structure them into meaningful patterns are *in reality* imprecise and ambiguous – they are, in other words, merely *implicit*, their causal status is casual rather than categorical. Of course, no one would argue with him about *that*! Most of us are agreed that common-sense logic-in-use is, from a RABBIT viewpoint, tacit rather than explicit and ambiguous rather than syllogistic. But in his eagerness to stress the parallelism of judging-in-¿sociological?-FAIRY TALE and judging-in-the-reality-of-everyday-life Cicourel forgets that admirable methodology in the former is distinguished from actual methodology in the latter by an insistence on deductive validity and on the explicit theoretical derivation of genuinely risky hypotheses.

Now if *all* that Cicourel is doing here is to describe some of the problems of inducing-a-provisional-and-implicit-¿sociological?-theory-prior-to-rendering-it-in-testable-form, then he need not have bothered! For, as we have already seen, this is essentially a private activity, the properly-brought-up RABBIT should be no more interested in it than he is interested in the state of Professor Cicourel's underpants – neither is the sort of thing that one likes to discuss publicly.

But I don't think that this *is* all that Cicourel is doing. I believe that he considers that he is formalizing procedures for the valid induction of theories which are a true$_4$ representation of reality. The question of independent testing of those theories seems to me to have been forgotten in the general brouhaha. And, though Cicourel himself is perfectly capable of bringing this matter back to mind when discussing how research *should* be done, most of his admirers do seem to show an extraordinarily perverted interest in UNDERWEAR. They avidly pursue inductive fieldwork in the misguided belief that what is hidden beneath the fabric of the members' accounting procedures will eventually be exposed in all its glory. Naughty *naughty*!

Cleanse your mind of this unsavoury idea: concentrate on the judgment that ethnomethodology (however *risqué* it may be) is by no means *risky* enough! After all, if you were to put a jelly pie in a shockproof glass case then it might well survive a while. (It *might* even do a useful job in disabusing onlookers of some of their comfortable taken-for-granted assumptions: 'What? *Jelly pie?*! Pull the other one, it's got bells on.') But an adequate methodology should not resemble a preposterous proposal for the preservation of precarious pastries. It should aim at the *maximization of risks*, not their virtual abolition.

Can such a methodology be devised for ¿sociology?? I believe that it can. The shortcomings of the four solutions to the two methodological dilemmas which have been examined so far need not be taken as pointers to the impossibility of creating any more adequate methodological position. There is always the additional possibility of avoiding both dilemmas by refusing to accept the choices.

'I like the Walrus best,' said Alice: 'because he was a *little* sorry for the poor oysters.'

'He ate more than the Carpenter, though,' said Tweedledee. 'You see he held his handkerchief in front, so that the Carpenter couldn't count how many he took: contrariwise.'

'That was mean!' Alice said indignantly. 'Then I like the Carpenter best – if he didn't eat as many as the Walrus.'

'But he ate as many as he could get,' said Tweedledum.

This was a puzzler. After a pause, Alice began, 'Well! They were *both* very unpleasant characters – .'

Chapter 9

The Magic of Meanings

We have already seen that the arguments over the question of inductive versus deductive theory construction can be resolved, not by choosing one or other spidery contraposition, but by accepting both methods as essential components of one synthesis. In making a metatheoretical commitment to a *retroductive* approach to theory construction we chose to treat the processes of generalizing and particularizing as mutually entwined aspects of the creative art of composing FAIRY TALES, both in the rarefied domain of science and in the taken-for-granted world of everyday life. From our methodological viewpoint such tales are neither wholly invented nor wholly discovered, they are articulated as a result of deduction from more basic beliefs combined with induction from the worlds of appearances. They are neither exclusively *a priori* nor entirely *a posteriori*; they comprise a *bricolage* of seeings and believings, an abstraction of believings and seeings.[1]

If we can transcend one SPIDER BATTLE, can we transcend the other? Is there some way of avoiding the dreary implications of positivism on the one hand without condemning ourselves to the purgatory of idealism's collective solipsism[2] on the other?

This was the major problem which beset those early ¿sociologists? who have subsequently been endowed with the honorific title 'Founding Fathers'. The most influential[3] of these were Marx, Durkheim, Simmel, and Weber, each of whom composed his own synthesis and, in the course of so doing, attempted to define the distinctive subject-matter of his discipline, and hence to provide a definition of ¿sociology? itself. Some lesser RABBITS have occasionally attempted to classify these original thinkers in terms of the polarity of positivism-versus-idealism – for example many assume that Marx was unequivocally a positivist, others that Weber and Simmel were idealists, and others still that Durkheim began his work as a positivist and ended it as an idealist. This is nonsense. For, while self-styled disciples of these gurus may mistakenly grant allegiance to one or the other SPIDER camp, none of the 'Founding Fathers' conceived of the issues in such simple RED and WHITE terms.

EXERCISE
Go back to the LIBRARY and study the works of the 'Founding Fathers'.

How did Marx, Durkheim, Simmel and Weber effect their syntheses of positivism and idealism?

How far did their substantive work conform to their own methodological prescriptions?

Phew! That was tough, wasn't it? Never mind, you will feel better after a nice cup of tea. When you are well rested and have shaken the cobwebs out of your hair we can go on to attempt to summarize the lessons learned in the LIBRARY. For, if you have paid good attention to the writings of the early sociologists, you will have absorbed the essence of a set of metatheoretical assumptions which has guided *¿sociological?* theorizing and research methodology for well over a hundred years. These assumptions have been expressed in varying terminology, and have generated many (often conflicting) theoretical viewpoints. But all those *¿sociologists?* who have managed to avoid both the positivists' frying pan *and* the idealists' fire seem to me to have looked in this direction before leaping.[4]

So the metatheoretical tale I am about to tell is not a new one. I do not propose to endow it with a brand new label and attempt to promote it as the latest methodological fashion in *¿sociology?*. Contrariwise! What you are about to read is just another revised version of an old, old story.

Where shall I begin? Karl Marx, who posed himself the same question, concluded that it was futile for his purposes to take his questioning beyond the point of asking about the nature of *¿man?* (*das menschliche Wesen*). To anyone who would seek an anterior beginning by asking of the *genesis* of humanity and the *¿physical world?*, Marx has this to say,[5]

Your question is itself a product of abstraction. Ask yourself how you arrived at that question. Ask yourself whether your question is not posed from a standpoint to which I cannot reply, because it is wrongly put. Ask yourself whether that progression as such exists for a reasonable mind. When you ask about the creation of nature and man, you are abstracting, in so doing, from man and nature. You postulate them as non-existent, and yet you want me to prove them to you as existing. Now I say to you: Give up your abstraction and you will also give up your question. Or if you want to hold on to your abstraction, then be consistent, and if you think of man and nature as non-existent, then think of yourself as non-existent, for *you too are surely nature and man*. Don't think, don't ask me, for as soon as you think and ask, your abstraction from the existence of nature and man has no meaning . . . [for] *the entire so-called history of the world is nothing but the creation of man* through human labour, *nothing but the emergence of nature for man*, so he has the visible [indication] . . . of his birth through himself, of the process of his creation.

For Marx, then, the appropriate beginning for a metatheoretical saga about the relationship between FAIRY TALE and reality – that is between constructions of the human mind and the sensuous, perceptible world of appearances – is ¿man? himself. And Marx's assumption about the fundamental nature, or 'essence' of humanity can be put very simply:

MAN IS CREATIVE.

According to his view it is in the nature of man to express his creativity in ¿physical? and symbolic representations of the forms of his imagination.[6] Thus *homo faber* creates and externalizes himself in the reality which becomes his taken-for-granted environment. So it would appear that, 'Man ought to honour himself and deem himself worthy of the highest. He cannot think too much of the greatness and power of the spirit.'[7]

But, though we may take it as a True$_1$ judgment that *man* is the author of the beings and becomings which constitute his world, we may also believe that *men* are everywhere oppressed and constrained by happenings which they cannot merely 'wish away'.[8] *I* find it hard to escape the observation that we real people suffer from exploitation, degradation, poverty, and disease. *I* believe that we are at the mercy of inept (and sometimes malicious) governments, bureaucracies, and law-enforcement agencies. *I* fear that we are threatened by the consequences of our own inability to control ourselves; that war, pollution, and overpopulation may finish us all off before we even have time to wake up to the implications of the erosion of our civil liberties which is currently taking place over the whole ¿planet?. Even if you do not share these judgments you may still perceive a discrepancy between the belief that man is creative and the observable circumstances of mankind.

How can this be? The answer offered by Marx is the same as that put forward by Simmel, Durkheim, and Weber. All of these ¿sociologists?

recognized that the act of creation results in the objectification or *exteriorization* of its product. Once made, a human artefact – be it object or idea – is no longer a part of its maker, it 'confronts [him] as something alien, as a power independent of the producer'.[9] Thus it comes about that you and I, each individually, experience ourselves as confined within the limitations of a world which is not of our own making. We experience ourselves as existing in a real world outside of our dreams, a world which is both 'exterior' to us and, in that sense, 'constraining' upon us.

EACH MAN EXPERIENCES HIMSELF AS AN INHABITANT OF A REAL WORLD OF HAPPENINGS.

Such a world thus becomes a 'given' environment within which each person must fashion a mode-of-being. And, in order to live in his world, each must apprehend it, that is he must successfully accomplish its *interiorization*. Of course this doesn't happen all at once, the human is not dropped as a full-grown adult into some strange reality and left to get on with it. From babyhood he grows in understanding and awareness of his surroundings as he grows in bodily stature and ¿social? and motor skills. But in the absence of some coherent paradigmatic assumptions, observations must necessarily be experienced as unco-ordinated and unpredictable – that is as chaotic.[10] For,

EACH HAPPENING IS EXPERIENCED AS OCCURRING UNIQUELY IN ¿SPACE? AND ¿TIME?.

How, then, do men make sense of the idiosyncratic happenings which appear to them? How do they interiorize the reality which, though man-made, is not of their making? How do they each establish a background of appearances which can be taken for granted as the routine and pre-dictable context of life, and against which the extraordinary and un-predictable will be thrown into relief? According to the views expressed by the 'Founding Fathers', men accomplish this by *ongoing* acts of creation. Out of the potential chaos of appearances men create meanings and via these abstractions they fashion patterned regularities from the unique happenings that seem to crowd upon them. It is through signify-ing generalizations, types, categories, forms, or *meanings* that men make sense out of the senseless, order out of disorder, and routine out of singularity.[11]

Our intellect forms perceptions into objects, systems and unifor-mities. . . . In order to know a man, we see him not in terms of his pure individuality, but carried, lifted up or lowered, by the general

type under which we classify him. . . . [The meanings] form immediate
data into new objects . . . [and] make the given world into a knowable
world.

Happenings, then, though they are *experienced* as unique cannot be
apprehended as such,[12]

UNIQUE HAPPENINGS CAN ONLY BE APPREHENDED THROUGH MEANINGS.

Sometimes the meanings assigned to appearances are merely vague as
when, for example, one notices 'a man in the middle of the road doing
something with a round yellow thing'. Yet, even in these cases, happenings are not apprehended 'in the raw' but structured in terms of meanings, albeit ambiguous and provisional ones. More often, however, we
human beings are quite unaware of the process of subsuming appearances under meanings: we experience-interpret-and-apprehend in one
unreflective operation which may, perhaps, best be termed *'recognition'*.
The reality of normality is an immediacy of recognition in which seeings
and believings are not separated but combined in one set of sensations.[13]

I say I 'hear a thrush singing outside my window'. But do I? He is
invisible, and it might perhaps be a blackbird; I have begun the business of thinking and believing already! The same thing happens to a
lifelong birdwatcher. He does no thinking at all. He *recognizes*. He
hears a thrush singing.

When the unusual disrupts routine then recognition is no longer
automatic and the assignment of meaning becomes a reflexive process.
Now the appearance in question has become a puzzle for common
sense which can only be solved by conscious reasoning. So the observer
will attempt to develop or apply some theory which enables him satisfactorily to assign meaning to the puzzling happening.

THUS, IN THE REALITY OF EVERYDAY LIFE, MEANINGS ARE ASSIGNED TO HAPPENINGS.

¿Sociologists? believe that real people in real worlds create, recognize,
and act upon meanings. Some of these are shared, some are private;
some are freely expressed, others remain hidden. It is through meanings
that human beings experience, understand, and manipulate themselves,
each other, and their worlds. Sometimes these meanings are frozen or
reified, they are taken-for-granted and conservative, they serve to maintain existing states of affairs and limit life-possibilities within well-worn
patterns. Sometimes, however, through the energy of imagination, men

fashion innovatory meanings from the substance of appearances, causing changes in patterns of human life and radical revisions of worlds-taken-for-granted. Thus meanings are socially constructed, maintained and revised, and

MEANINGS ARE SOCIAL.

So, from the ¿sociological viewpoint?, it is meanings which define the realities of everyday lives, whether these be the *ordinary taken-for-granted* meanings which form the recognizable backgrounds of normality, or the *extraordinary thought-about* meanings which generate puzzles for common sense and change-possibilities for real worlds. These meanings must therefore be the subject-matter of the ¿sociologist?. And, since to define the subject-matter is to define the discipline, the 'Founding Fathers' ' conception of ¿sociology? can now be simply summarized.[14]

SOCIOLOGY IS THE STUDY OF MEANINGS.

That is to say that the happenings sociologists take as data are the meanings that real people in real worlds assign to those happenings that interest them. Sociology operates at another level of abstraction. The sociologist must assign meanings to meanings, create 'typifications of typifications' and theorize about theories.

So the sociologist is not interested in real-world happenings 'in themselves'. For these cannot be known except through the network of meanings which is operative in any particular real world. The specifically sociological focus is on the meanings which provide the keys to a world, and which therefore, in a very important sense, *constitute* a world. These meanings become happenings at another level of analysis: let us call them *second-order happenings*. The sociologist then has to apprehend these second-order happenings by attributing to them *second-order meanings*, that is meanings which make sense not in terms of common-sense causal stories but in terms of sociological FAIRY TALES which transcend the reality of everyday life.[15]

As we have seen, some sociologists make the mistake of supposing that they are on a quest of discovery rather than creation. They think that sociology consists in the *search* for *first-order meanings* (or if you like, second-order happenings) which can be gathered together and *subsequently* structured by means of the second-order meanings of sociology. But, of course, sociologists are actually *constructing* meanings out of ideas and observations in a manner which parallels the construction process occurring at the first-order level. Whether from the second-order point of view of sociology or the first-order perspective of common-sense realities,

WE THINK WE ARE LOOKING FOR MEANINGS WHEN WE ARE CREATING THEM.

The construction of meanings, the selection and apprehension of happenings through typifications, is not a random business either for the real person in a real world or for the sociologist attempting to transcend, and thereby theorize about, that world. Rather the attribution of meaning is paradigm-determined. Within a paradigm a sediment of meanings-which-have-worked-all-right-before are collected together as *KK* and these, together with the *RR*, the *BB* and the *FF* of the paradigm also serve to circumscribe what new meanings may be devised. Thus in the science of meanings, as in common sense, meanings are neither invented nor discovered; they are products of a fusion of *expectations* regarding *what is likely*, and *observations* of *what appears to be*.

And, just as in common sense our theories inform us what to expect and our observations serve as running tests of those theories, so in sociology. But how does the sociologist go about the business of linking expectations with observations? How does he select from the appearances of reality which present themselves to him (that is, from his observations of one or more worlds of first-order meanings) those features which are relevant to the variables implicated in his hypotheses (that is, to his FAIRY-TALE arrangements of second-order meanings)? For, as we have seen, variables exist in FAIRY TALE not in reality. Thus sociological variables are features of second-order meanings, which are themselves constructions put by sociologists upon first-order meanings.

Alfred Schutz, whose constant interest is in the processes involved in relating meanings from one order to the other, suggests some metatheoretical assumptions which may guide us. He puts forward a second-order story about the way in which first-order appearances are subsumed under sensible first-order meanings, and this tale may help us to follow the way in which the 'Founding Fathers' and many subsequent sociologists have gone about subsuming second-order appearances under second-order meanings.

Schutz points out that, as real people in real worlds, we *could* be faced with dreadful problems. We *could* find communication of meaning, and hence action and interaction with other human beings, impossible. We *might* be unable to decipher the signs and sounds made by other humans (or perhaps even unable to see or hear them), and we *might* have no way of knowing how our own meaning constructions related to those of other humans. Thus, on ¿seeing-another-human-approaching-me?, I *might* have no way of knowing what was likely to happen next. The

range of meanings from which I had to choose would in fact be guided
only by that range of meanings which I had ever in the past attributed
to ¿other-people-walking-towards-me?. And that could be a pretty wide
selection! I could be in for a cordial greeting, a slap around the face
with a wet haddock, a manacling and pressganging into service for the
Government Social Survey, or a taste of a soul brother's home-grown
mushrooms. (What steps should I take to deal with the situation? Large
and speedy ones in the opposite direction? But which would be worse,
to face the risk of the Social Survey – or chance missing out on the
mushroom?)

Luckily for us, life is *not* like that. At least it is not *normally* like that!
For anyone who is not excessively ¿paranoid? – nor unduly awestruck
by Harold Garfinkel and his gang – can avoid the malign anarchy described above by simply taking it for granted that *all-normal-situations-
are-normal*. So Schutz's tale has it that Mr and Mrs Norman Normal
normally do their bit for the normality of normal life by making two
normal assumptions about the normality of the normal. These two basic
assumptions serve to crystallize the range of first-order meanings which
are routinely assigned to first-order happenings or appearances.[16]

1. The idealization of the interchangeability of the standpoints: I
take it for granted – and I assume my fellow-man does the same –
that if I change places with him so that his 'here' becomes mine, I
shall be at the same distance from things and see them with the same
typicality as he actually does; moreover, the same things will be in
my reach which are actually in his (the reverse is also true).

2. The idealization of the congruency of the system of relevances:
Until counterevidence I take it for granted – and assume my fellow-
man does the same – that the differences in perspective originating
in our unique biographical situations are irrelevant for the purpose
at hand of either of us and he and I, that 'We', assume that both of
us have selected and interpreted the actually or potentially common
objects and their features in an identical manner or at least an 'empirically identical' manner, i.e., one sufficient for all practical purposes.

Let me combine these two idealizations in another circularity,

**WHEN YOU AND I ARE IN AND FROM THE SAME ¿ SOCIAL
WORLD ?**
I TAKE IT FOR GRANTED THAT
YOU TAKE IT FOR GRANTED THAT
        WHAT I TAKE FOR GRANTED
          YOU TAKE FOR GRANTED AND
            WHAT YOU TAKE FOR GRANTED
              I TAKE FOR GRANTED.

So, when you and I meet as members of a *¿social world?* described by our common sensibilities, your reality and my reality are interchangeable. I believe that 'if I were in your shoes' I would have the same information upon which to act as you actually do have, you who are standing there in your own shoes. And, when you and I meet as sociologists, we assume that those real people who operate with a shared and reciprocal taken-for-grantedness have come together in a common social time and social space. That is to say that we assume that they are in and of the same *¿social world?* (or, if you like, 'background', 'society', 'culture', 'subculture', 'social milieu', 'social system', or whatever).

From the second-order perspective of the sociologist, then, it is taken-for-grantedness which defines membership in a *¿social world?*.[17] In other words,

A SOCIAL WORLD IS A SET OF TAKEN-FOR-GRANTED-MEANINGS.

Within a social world we real people share a background of relevant meanings which not only tell us what to expect of ourselves, each other, and our surroundings, but also give us some criterion for distinguishing the problematic from the unproblematic. When happenings appear for which we are not prepared by our common-sense expectations these become puzzles for us both. If one of us succeeds in constructing a satisfactory FAIRY TALE out of the available first-order meanings in order to account for these puzzles, then we succeed in incorporating these accounts themselves into our shared *KK*, our background of normality, our world-taken-for-granted.[18] But when you and I meet as members of *different* social worlds things are much more difficult for us. Depending on the width of the gap between our cultures, the difference between our normal expectational criteria produces a situation in which it becomes – to a greater or lesser extent – hopeless to try to take things for granted.[19] Indeed, whatever-it-is-that-you-take-for-granted becomes, itself, a problem for me, and vice versa. We both have to guess, test our guesses, and guess again.

So, when the sociologist attempts to apprehend aspects of a given social world, he is in a situation which parallels that of the real-life stranger. Just as *at the first-order level*, the stranger has to make guesses about an alien social world and cope with the fact that its natives are simultaneously guessing about his own background of taken-for-granted assumptions, so with the sociologist. But the sociologist has a double problem: he is not only attempting to grasp *first-order* meanings but, treating these as happenings at another level of abstraction, to order, interpret, and theorize about them in terms of *second-order*, or socio-

logical, meanings. Thus the *first-order* guessing and testing he performs
as a real stranger in a real world is only a preliminary to a more abstract
process of theorizing, which is itself only the first stage in his scientific
activity. Once he considers that he has subsumed the *first-order* meanings in which he is ¿interested? under plausible *second-order* constructions, he must attempt to formalize this implicit *second-order* theory,
deduce hypotheses from it and then refer back to the *first-order* meanings
in order to test his hypotheses.

   This is precisely what Durkheim meant when he claimed that the
sociologist must 'regard social facts as things'. A 'social fact' for
Durkheim was a *'representation'*, that is a first-order meaning. Durkheim's representations were neither 'objective' in the sense of having
an existence independent from the creative action of the human mind,
nor were they 'subjective' in the sense of private to a particular perceiver
or interpreter. They were, rather, shared and reciprocal, that is *'collective'*, taken-for-granted interpretations of commonly agreed appearances. The sociological task which Durkheim outlined consisted in an
attempt to *'duplicate consciously on the analytical level the process of representation as it takes place on the action level'*.[20] That is to say that he
advocated the conscious mimicking of first-order meaning construction
at the second-order level.

   On the first-order level, then, there is a knower (the real person), a
known (the first-order happening), and a connection between them
(the first-order meaning). First-order meanings are combined into
common-sense theories (KK) which in turn provide a background of
taken-for-granted assumptions affecting the very perception of appearances (first-order happenings). On the second-order level corresponding
processes may be posited. There is a knower (the sociologist), a known
(the second-order happening, that is, the first-order meaning), and a
connection between them (the second-order meaning, or sociological
concept). Sociological concepts (second-order meanings) are combined
into sociological theories (KK) which in turn provide a background of
taken-for-granted assumptions affecting the sociologist's very perception of appearances (second-order happenings).[21]

   From the classic sociological metatheoretical perspective then,
sociological FAIRY TALES may be regarded as isomorphs of the real-life
fairy tales which constitute social realities. But we have already seen that
the leap from one realm to the other must be made not once but twice.
It is not only in the process of *constructing* his second-order theories
that the sociologist must be aware of his dependence upon 'correct'
interpretation of first-order meanings. His interpretation of first-order
meanings is also vital when he comes to *testing* his second-order theories.
In both cases he must take care to see that he has subsumed first-order
happenings under first-order meanings in the manner which is generally

taken-for-granted by the real members of the social world about which he is theorizing.

But we have learnt that the process of constructing theories is a private and idiosyncratic one. Scientists do not judge the truth$_4$ of each other's theories according to criteria defining the 'proper' methods of generalizing from appearances – at least they *should* not do so! The truth$_4$ of theories is judged by *tests*. What we are interested in now is not the way sociologists go about subsuming first-order under second-order meanings in order to *develop* sociological theories, but the way in which they choose first-order meanings in real worlds to *represent* the second-order meanings in their FAIRY TALES in order to *test* hypotheses derived from their theories.

Let us suppose that you have a theory from which you have derived the hypothesis that '*academic success amongst sociology students increases with political involvement*'. Here you have two variables, 'academic success' and 'political involvement'; their meaningfulness derives from their location in a sociological FAIRY TALE; they are second-order meanings. How then do you find real-world, or first-order, meanings in terms of which to test your hypothesis? What second-order happenings will count as instances of 'academic success' and of 'political involvement'? How, in other words, can you ¿measure? the variables 'academic success' and 'political involvement'?

Neither positivism nor idealism will help you here. But the metatheoretical synthesis developed by the 'Founding Fathers', and outlined above, may be of assistance. According to this view you must treat second-order FAIRY TALES as isomorphic with first-order realities. Thus, in selecting first-order meanings (second-order happenings) to *represent* or *stand for* second-order meanings, you are performing an arbitrary operation. In fact your task parallels that of the magician or astrologer, for you are using your second-order theory to make predictions about patterns in the real (first-order) world, and choosing aspects of that real world to serve as pointers to the remainder of that reality. If you have chosen well – and your theory was plausible – then your first-order meanings will be observed to 'behave' in a manner which parallels that posited by your second-order FAIRY TALE. An example may be helpful.

At Rome in 1628 a certain magician called Tommaso Campanella had urgent reason to test his hypothesis that a particular rearrangement of celestial events would ward off an imminent eclipse. (His reason was desperate indeed, for according to another part of his theory that eclipse would inevitably result in the death of the Pope, Urban VIII.) In order to test this hypothesis Campanella could not actually arrange a trip to the heavens for purposes of rearranging the spheres into a more benign combination. The best he could do was to simulate celestial happenings in terms of sublunary ones. So he and the Pope sealed off a chamber against the outside atmosphere and draped it with white hangings. Then they took two lamps, one to stand for the sun and one for the moon, and five torches to stand for the planets. They then assembled jewels, plants, and colours connected with the benevolent planets Jupiter and Venus and with the Sun, drank alcohol distilled under the influence of Jupiter and Venus, and played 'Jovial and Venereal' music. Thus they reproduced the hypothesized celestial arrangement in terms of tangible appearances and manipulated the latter in order to test the hypothesis.

Though Urban VIII survived for another sixteen years, this test of the theory would not convince modern scientists who would point out the faulty logic by which Campanella had compounded two separate events (the occurrence of the eclipse and the death of the Pope) and who would no doubt echo Aquinas in emphasizing that some other hypothesis could equally serve to save the same appearances. But the procedure is none the less similar to that of the modern scientist who, wishing to test the hypothesis that '*a metal will expand if heated*', takes a piece of real iron to represent the hypothetical 'metal', the effect of a laboratory Bunsen burner to represent the FAIRY-TALE idea 'heat', and a change in the ruler measurement of the iron to represent the theoretical notion of 'expansion'.

And the procedure which you would have to use in order to test your sociological hypothesis about political involvement and academic success amongst sociology students is also similar. Like the alchemist who takes lead to represent Saturn, urine to represent water, etc., you would have to take something(s) from your real (first-order) worlds to represent each hypothesized second-order variable. In this way you could manipulate *¿measurement?* of first-order realities in order to make inferences about the plausibility of your second-order FAIRY TALES.

The first-order pointers which sociologists choose to stand for or represent their second-order meanings are called *indicators*. And the important thing to remember is that

INDICATORS ARE ALWAYS SELECTED BY FIAT.

That is to say that the selection is always arbitrary, and consequently the tests of hypotheses are always performed, as it were, by proxy. The meaning 'academic success' cannot be present at the testing ritual because it cannot get out of its FAIRY-TALE world. So instead of 'academic success' you would choose some first-order meanings, some *indicators*, to represent that notion, say, 'examination results', 'tutors' reports', 'essay grades', etc., and you would perform your testing rituals with these instead of 'the real McCoy'.

The ways in which you would go about choosing your indicators, like the ways in which you went about devising your theory in the first place, would be essentially idiosyncratic and private. The selection of indicators is like an art or craft: you may benefit from the hints which others give, you may even steal some of their ideas, but ultimately you have to rely upon your own creative ingenuity. Whilst any schoolboy could readily think up a way of *¿measuring?* the 'expansion' of a 'metal', it is much more difficult to imagine how one would select indicators of, say, 'alienation', 'deferred gratification', or 'erotic stratification'. Later I shall be suggesting some hints to guide you in this tricky business of operationalization, but at the moment the important point to grasp is that this is an entirely arbitrary operation. 'Examination results', 'tutors' reports', 'essay grades', etc. *are not* 'academic success' except in the sense that one of Campanella's lamps *was* the sun, or the alchemists' lead *was* Saturn. Lead, lamps, and sociological indicators are merely representational stand-ins for grander concepts which cannot be manipulated in so prosaic a manner. The assumption that is being made is simply that, because the FAIRY TALE is constructed as an isomorph of the reality, indicators from the latter level can be treated *as if* they were variables from the former.

This, then, is but another profound reason for caution, for great scepticism in interpreting the results of sociological research. When a sociologist claims that he can show a relationship between, say, 'social class' and 'deviant behaviour' what he actually means is that he has tables relating various indicators of socio-economic status with various indicators of deviance. 'Social class' and 'deviant behaviour' remain sociological (that is second-order) meanings, *they* do not exist in any real world (that is at a first-order level of meaning), though ideas like 'income', 'the-job-that-Dad-does', 'the-sorts-of-schools-that-Mum-and-Dad-went-to', and 'how-many-times-our-Malcolm's-done-the-fag-machine-on-the-corner' *are* real-world (first-order) meanings. What relationship these first-order conceptions, these indicators, bear to the second-order meanings in question is something you are well entitled to feel dubious about.[22]

If indicators are merely arbitrarily selected first-order meanings which act as stand-ins for second-order variables, then what do we mean when we talk of *¿measuring?* them? Clearly *¿measurement?* cannot be the detection and quantification of properties *intrinsic* to a phenomenon. For phenomena are happenings, or appearances, and their properties are bestowed upon them by human imagination and perception. *¿Measurement?*, on the contrary, is simply the evaluation of features of happenings according to arbitrarily devised quantitative scales. To put it another way,

MEASUREMENT IS THE ASSIGNMENT OF VALUES TO OBSERVATIONS.

For example, suppose that I wished to test the silly hypothesis that erotic ranking is negatively related to manifestations of acne. I would first need to choose some indicator of acne. Taking a most unsubtle approach to the subject, I might decide that overt facial spottiness would provide an adequate indicator. Next I would have to decide how to rank individual people in terms of spottiness. And presumably the simplest way of doing this would be to actually count the number of pimples on their faces.[23] I *could* simply use the raw numbers as my scale, but I would probably find the business of making comparisons rather cumbersome when the actual number of pimples counted on one face could range from zero to (say) two hundred (how many pimples *can* crowd on to one unfortunate face?). So I would probably find myself setting an arbitrary limit to my pimple-scale and grouping the actual pimple-counts into a set number of divisions between this upper limit and the zero. Perhaps like this:

Scale	0	1	2	3	4
Actual number of pimples	0	1–5	6–10	11–15	16–20
Scale	5	6	7	8	9
Actual number of pimples	21–5	26–30	31–5	36–40	41+

But why like *that*? Why not like *this*?

Scale	0	1	2	3	4	5
Actual number of pimples	0	1	2–3	4–5	6–20	21+

Or even like *this*?

Scale	8	4	0	3	7	2	5
Actual number of pimples		0	1–35	58–60	36–50	51–7	300+	61–299

If measurement, like the selection of indicators, is an arbitrary operation then surely one *could* use any old number system one fancied? Indeed one *could*. But we must beware. For in our eagerness to avoid the foolish positivistic implications of thinking of measurement as the-detection-of-properties-which-have-varying-values-in-reality, we may go too far – and shoot right over into the egocentric zone of idealism. Measurement may be *arbitrary*, but it must not be private and personal. The point of measuring is, after all, to render observations (that is data) in comparable form, for the purposes of performing universally recognizable testing rituals. Therefore we sociologists have to devise methods of scaling which, albeit arbitrarily, can be readily communicated and understood on the level of second-order meanings.

But, again, beware! For as soon as one constructs a measurement scale to act as an arbitrary yardstick for quantifying the ¿interesting? properties of happenings one is, willy nilly, concretizing and limiting the categories into which observations will be fitted, and hence one is at risk of reifying the phenomena themselves. Care must be taken not to distort hopelessly the first-order meanings which form the second-order happenings of our sociological interest. For, while these are certainly products of *human* imagination, they are not exclusively products of the *sociologist*'s imagination, they exist independently of the presence of sociologists and their measuring instruments, they are, in a most important sense, *really real*. They are real just in the sense that they are real to the participants in the first-order worlds of meaning which they define. They may be 'representations', but they are '*collective* representations', their existence is not dependent upon the presence of any particular knower.

The first-order meanings which provide our sociological data are, then, just as real as stones and grass, and ships and rats, and orange icecream. They exist independently of the sociologist's imagination – he cannot wish them away. They are products of the creative activity of real people in real worlds, people who, incidentally, may or may not welcome his prying.

If he is to test his theories, then, the sociologist must find some way of measuring which is both '*objectifiable*' and '*subjectifiable*'. When I say that it must be 'objectifiable' I mean that it must be communicable to other sociologists without misunderstanding: it must be clear to others precisely what the marks on the sociological 'rulers' mean at a second-order level of meaning. On the other hand, when I say that it must be 'subjectifiable' I mean that it must also make sense to real people at a first-order level of meaning: if I characterize Huck's pimple-score as '4' and his sister's as '2', then I must be sure that real people in the world to which Huck and his sister belong would recognize that he is more spotty than she is.

So, though it is clearly arbitrary, a sociological 'ruler' or measurement scale can certainly not be constructed any-old-how! On the contrary, the construction of such scales is an incredibly tricky business. Perhaps it is true$_4$ to say that it is measurement and scaling, and the associated numerical comparisons, that provide the biggest stumbling block for the development of universalistic testing rituals for sociology? It must be clear that,

SOCIOLOGICAL MEASUREMENT SHOULD BE AN ADEQUATE REFLECTION OF BOTH FIRST- AND SECOND-ORDER MEANINGS.

It is as though the measuring devices must be created as isomorphs *both* of the second-order FAIRY-TALE meanings *and* of the first-order real meanings. That is to say that they must preserve not only the constituent parts of those meanings but also the relationships between them. A tall order indeed! For what is required of sociological measurement is that it be a medium for the translation of meanings from first- to second-order and vice versa. (See Figure 10.)

Yet even this notion of triple isomorphism is a terrible oversimplification. Sociological measurement is not like Esperanto – a universal medium, arbitrarily devised to represent all languages so that through it, say, French can be translated into German and German into Italian, etc. Unlike an ordinary language, the language of measurement has to be able to cope with a translation which is taking place between *levels* of conceptualization, where one level (the second-order) *transcends* the other (the first-order) in the sense that it is not merely a reflection but also an explanation thereof.[24]

After all, measurement takes place in reality as well as in sociological FAIRY TALES. At both levels of meaning men set limits upon what they can conceive of in one ¿direction? and then in the ¿direction? which is – in some sense – 'opposite'. These limits provide the poles between which variation may be gauged. The precision with which that gauging is applied (the *scaling*) may vary from a crude dichotomy to a definite multiple calibration, depending upon the purposes of the measurement and upon who is doing the measuring.

But, whether the scales are vague or precise, they are not ¿interesting? in themselves. Nor are the poles. In fact the poles are meaningless when conceived in isolation from each other: how can you understand the notion 'hot' except by comparison with 'cold', how can you grasp the meaning of 'riches' except with a knowledge of 'poverty'? What is interesting is not the boundaries but the meaning bounded within them, not the gradients but the sense of the ¿direction? they announce. And sometimes these ¿directions? are conceived in a manner which cannot be represented in terms of 'positives' and 'negatives' and they are therefore not amenable to the sort of quantification which ordinary arithmetic can handle.[25]

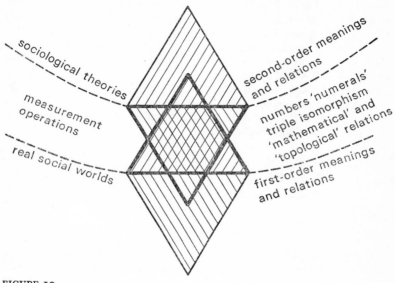

FIGURE 10

Let us have a brief look at the sorts of scales which may be used both by everyday (first-order) and sociological (second-order) theorists in their attempts to measure the features of those happenings which interest them.

Think first of all of the sort of scale that you can find on a tape-measure or a weighing machine. It looks something like Figure 11. Such a scale has three characteristics which are of interest to us here. First, it involves an *unequivocal ordering* of values: a lady with a thirty-six-inch bust measurement unquestionably has a bigger bosom than one with a measurement of thirty-four inches, while Juicy Lucy's forty-two inches would outshine them both. Second, the scale involves an assumption of *equal intervals* between units: an eight-pound mangel-wurzel is heavier than a four-pound one by the same amount as a ten-pounder is heavier than a six-pounder. Third, such a scale has what is sometimes called a 'true zero', that is to say that there is an *unambiguous* point on the scale which is universally regarded as having *zero* value.

Sometimes this form of measurement is called *'pure measurement'*,[26] but this term may be misleading as it seems to imply that the measurement is more than arbitrary. Perhaps the term *'mathematical measurement'* would be more appropriate, since it must be obvious that any scale having those three characteristics (unequivocal ordering, equal intervals, and unambiguous zero) must allow of the use of ordinary arithmetic in the making of comparisons. Because of the assumptions about ordering and equality of intervals you can *add* and *subtract* with such scales: Juicy Lucy's mammary glands are six inches bigger than those of her nearest rival. And, because of the unambiguous zero, you can also *multiply* and *divide* in terms of a scale like this: it makes sense to say that the eight-pound mangel-wurzel is twice as heavy as the four-pounder. For these reasons this, most useful, type of scale is referred to by RABBITS as a *RATIO SCALE*. Ratio scales, then, are scales which operate with ordinary NUMBERS.

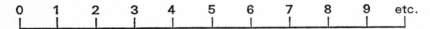

FIGURE II

But neither sociological nor everyday theories of social phenomena offer much in the way of variables which can be usefully subjected to this sort of measurement. Of course, the real person in his real-life activities does use ratio scales for *some* purposes: weights and measures and monetary scales take a lot of the particularism out of domestic economics,[27] and one way of solving the dispute as to whether young Sue is taller than her cousin is to get out a tape-measure. The sociologist may also find occasions for the use of ratio scales. For example, if he enjoys crude 'content analysis' of newspapers he might measure column inches with a ruler – indeed, by the same token, I see no reason why he could not simply cut out selected items from the papers and *weigh* them![28] Yet the occasions on which ratio scales *can* be used form only a small proportion of the actual measurements and comparisons that take place either at the first- or the second-order levels of theorizing and testing. Most quantification is much 'cruder' than this. For instance, you may well claim that HRH Prince Philip is in some sense 'more' conservative than a certain well-known Hell's Angel – but you can't say *how much* 'more'. There is no agreed scale of conservativeness, politeness, respectability, etc. I can't say that you are 4″ polite, 3lbs ambitious, 94° sexy, and ¾ of a pole dense.

Let us call all measurement which falls short of the three criteria for 'mathematical measurement', *'topological measurement'*.[29]

'Topological measurement' may be thought of as employing NUMERALS rather than NUMBERS and, because it always deviates in some respect or other from the features of 'mathematical measurement', it sets limits upon the extent to which ordinary arithmetic can be used to make comparisons.

The simplest kind of numeral scale, or 'topological measurement', is the *NOMINAL SCALE*. In a nominal scale there is naming but not ordering. Properties are broken down into equivalence classes, but these classes are not ranked with respect to one another. Indeed the only rule for the formation of such scales is that the classes be mutually exclusive. In the very simplest case of all there may be only two classes, a dichotomy, as is the case with the classification of socially recognized sex identities into the two categories 'male' and 'female'. On the other hand there may be a greater number of points on a nominal scale as with, say, classifications of government departments, vegetables, or types of drugs. Obviously you cannot perform any ordinary sums using nominal scale values.

But nominal scales have a curious feature. Once a notion has been explicitly conceptualized as such a scale the tendency is for ranking to creep into the scaling. Think for a moment about ethnic groupings: how often and in how many different social worlds have explicit ethnic categories in common use remained free of evaluation? Think also of secondary schools in post-1945 Britain. Three sorts of schools were created, supposedly to cater for three sorts of children, yet, as government propaganda had it, this was a nominal scale for the schools were to enjoy 'parity of esteem'. Of course they did not: the common conception is of a scale which ranks the grammar schools highest, the secondary modern school lowest, and the technical school (by elimination) somewhere in the middle.

I am arguing that there is a tendency for our minds to transform nominal scales into scales which do involve evaluation or ranking. Indeed, it is very difficult to find examples of nominal scales either at the second-order or at the first-order level, for, once categories are *consciously considered as scales*, evaluative comparisons start to be made. I am sure that if you were to ponder for some time on how to present your nominal scales of the features of government departments, vegetables, or types of drugs you would find that even these had somehow been transformed by you into something more than nominal scales. For, of course, you would not be measuring these properties for fun, but because they appeared to be relevant to some test of some hypothesis which you had devised, and that hypothesis and the theory from which it was deduced would guide you in imposing some kind of ranking upon the points of your scales.

What you would probably end up producing would, in fact, be

ORDINAL SCALES, that is scales which simply order the happenings or features of happenings with respect to one another. For example, you might find yourself ranking vegetables according to their price, their tastiness, their fillingness, their supposed protein value, or say, vitamin content.

Let us suppose that I have decided to construct a highly idiosyncratic ordinal scale of the 'tastiness' of vegetables. To make matters easier I have only five vegetables to rank. I do so like this,

1	2	3	4	5
mangel-wurzel	spinach	carrot	potato	french beans

I am saying merely that I like french beans more than potato, carrot better than spinach, and anything better than mangel-wurzel, etc. I am *not* saying that I prefer spinach to mangel-wurzel, by the same 'amount' as I prefer potato to carrot. In creating an ordinal scale, then, I am simply ranking things in some order but I am making no pretence at maintaining equal intervals between the ranks. Clearly such a scale does *not* permit of even simple arithmetic operations like addition and subtraction: the 'tastiness' of mangel-wurzel plus potato is *not* equivalent to that of french beans – not by any stretch of anyone's imagination!

There is, however, a form of 'topological measurement' in which numerals can be assigned to properties in such a way that *some* sums can be performed. *INTERVAL SCALES* may be constructed to rank features in a manner which relies upon the assumption of equality of intervals between classes. Obviously such numerals will permit of simple addition and subtraction, but, because no universally recognized zero is involved, multiplication and division are still ruled out as reasonable operations.

One example of the use of such scales in social science is in IQ scores. Here the assumption is made that the difference between a score of, say, 98 and one of 104 is equivalent to the difference between a score of 108 and one of 114. So in research involving comparisons of IQ scores you will find statements such as 'The children in the experimental group had increased their scores by an average of eight points over the two year period, while those in the control group had only increased their scores by an average of one point.' There is, here, the unambiguous implication that the children in the experimental group have increased their average scores by 'more' than those in the control group. A statement such as 'the experimental group's average increase in IQ scores was eight times that of the control group' would, however, be quite illegitimate.

Let me now sum up the characteristics of these four common types of scales:

RATIO SCALES   assume A unequivocal ordering
                                  B equal intervals
                                  C unambiguous zero

NOMINAL SCALES assume none of these
ORDINAL SCALES   assume A but not B or C
INTERVAL SCALES assume A and B but not C

Much has been written by sociologists about methods of measuring first-order meanings (particularly 'attitudes') in order to justify the imposition of interval and even ratio scales upon the data. But most of this is sheer gibberish. Even notions like age, income, number-of-hours-worked-per-week, family size, etc., notions which seem on the face of it to provide the most hope for the use of mathematical operations at the second-order level, even these raise very difficult problems for the sociologist. It may appear at first that £3,000-p.a.-after-tax is an income which can legitimately be regarded as three times £1,000-p.a.-after-tax – but *is* it? The sociologist is not interested in first-order happenings, like pound notes; he is interested in first-order *meanings*: does a man value three-thousand-a-year three times as much as one-thousand-a-year; does the sociologist's ratio scaling make sense on the first-order level? Again, is the man of forty-five older than his forty-year-old neighbour by the same 'amount' as his ten-year-old son is older than their five-year-old. And, of course, when it comes to 'attitudes' these drawbacks come in spades! Who but a sociologist would be foolish enough to believe that '*Yes, I agree strongly*' is to '*Yes, I agree*' as '*No, I disagree*' is to '*No, I disagree strongly*', or that '*Yes*' is to '*Maybe*' as '*Maybe*' is to '*No*'.

Clearly then, *most* sociological measurement must be limited to nominal and ordinal scaling, for only with these minimal assumptions can the second-order yardstick be imposed upon first-order meanings without doing too much violence to the integrity of the latter. Yet, as I have said, nominal scaling too easily becomes implicit ordinal scaling, so where it is clear that there is a risk that this may occur there are strong arguments for the formulation of explicit ordinal scales.

Ordinal scales are, then, the scales which are most commonly employed in sociological measurement. But how can the sociologist *check* the ordinality of his data? How can he be sure that the rank order he has chosen for items at the second-order level of meaning is, at least minimally, isomorphic with first-order conceptions. A number of techniques are available and I shall return to some of these later. At this stage, however, one trick is worth mentioning – if only because it serves

as a good illustration of the tenacity of the sociologist in his unquench-
able thirst for quantifiable data.

This trick was developed by Louis Guttman and so it has, not unnaturally, come to be known as *Guttman scaling*. Quite simply the technique is to check upon the ordinality of items on a scale by ascertaining
whether or not the lower-ranked items always appear before the higher-
ranked ones. Take my habits about responsible dress for example. I
consider that (weather aside) when an occasion is *'informal'* no clothing
is required, when it is *'slightly formal'* I should be 'decently covered',
when it is *'formal'* I should have clean fingernails, and when it is *'very
formal'* I should wear shoes. That these properties form an ordinal
scale can be ascertained from the fact that no one has ever seen me
naked but shod, nor indeed will you ever catch me wearing shoes unless
my fingernails are clean.

The following example of a more complicated piece of Guttman
scaling which comes from a classic sociological study is, however, much
more entertaining than my idiosyncratic notions about respectable dress.
Stouffer and his colleagues selected the following nine items as points
on a scale indicating the level of stress experienced by soldiers under
fire.[30]

1 Urination in pants.
2 Losing control of the bowels.
3 Vomiting.
4 Feeling of weakness or faintness.
5 Feeling of stiffness.
6 Feeling sick at the stomach.
7 Shaking or trembling all over.
8 Sinking feeling of the stomach.
9 Violent pounding of the heart.

Scoring '+' for the presence of the item and '−' for its absence, the
distribution of these items amongst a sample of soldiers was as shown
in the table on page 185. In other words, there was no group of soldiers
who actually pissed themselves without first experiencing all the
other eight 'reactions' posited as lower points on the scale. Pissing
oneself is a more 'extreme' reaction than shitting oneself – it indicates
'greater' stress.

Perhaps you are wondering if there are *no* limits to the absurdities of
sociological measurement? Well, there are none that the professional
associations are able to impose. Yet limits can be drawn, and their
source is – common sense. Let us remind ourselves of Whitehead's
dictum: 'you may polish up common sense, you may contradict it in
detail, you may surprise it. But ultimately your whole task is to satisfy
it.'

Remembering this, it is up to us to draw the line between sensible measurement and absurdity. We have to find a way of deriving testable hypotheses from our theories, and of obtaining reasonable measurements of the indicators selected to represent the variables in those hypotheses. Of course, we would like guarantees that those measurements *are* both sensible and relevant to the tests we wish to perform. But no such guarantees can be given. The best we can do is to strain towards the

Groupings of respondents	Item number								
	1	2	3	4	5	6	7	8	9
1	+	+	+	+	+	+	+	+	+
2	−	+	+	+	+	+	+	+	+
3	−	−	+	+	+	+	+	+	+
4	−	−	−	+	+	+	+	+	+
5	−	−	−	−	+	+	+	+	+
6	−	−	−	−	−	+	+	+	+
7	−	−	−	−	−	−	+	+	+
8	−	−	−	−	−	−	−	+	+
9	−	−	−	−	−	−	−	−	+
10	−	−	−	−	−	−	−	−	−

unattainable: to maintain vigorously that *FALSIFICATIONIST ATTITUDE OF MIND* which is essential to the true$_2$ scientist, and simultaneously to remain true$_2$ to the *COMMON SENSE* which provides our inescapable grounding in the real world of appearances.

Chapters 10 to 20 contain some simple directions for research rituals which are consistent with these aims. They form a sort of *grimoire* of sociological spells. For, as I shall argue in chapter 20, the sociologist is in a position similar in many ways to that of the witch. We shall see that this raises for the sociologist, as for the witch, a question about *ethical responsibility*. And this question is troublesome enough to keep any honest sociologist awake well past the witching hour!

Notes

1 I Beg Your Pardon

1 Thomas S. Kuhn, *The Structure of Scientific Revolutions* (University of Chicago Press, 1962).

2 It is well known that Kuhn's usage of the term paradigm in *The Structure of Scientific Revolutions*, op. cit., is somewhat ambiguous. See for example Margaret Masterman's rather pedantic paper, 'The nature of a paradigm', in Imre Lakatos and Alan Musgrave (eds), *Criticism and the Growth of Knowledge* (Cambridge University Press, 1970). However, subsequent clarifications by Kuhn leave me confirmed in this seemingly flippant interpretation. See 'Reflection on my critics', in Lakatos and Musgrave, op. cit.; 'Second thoughts on paradigms', in Frederick Suppe (ed.), *The Structure of Scientific Theories* (Urbana, Ill., 1971); and the 1969 Postscript to the 2nd edn of *The Structure of Scientific Revolutions*. This issue will be discussed further.

3 It is arguable that Bacon's treatment of the concept 'laws of nature', in the *Novum Organum*, marks a crucial turning-point in the history of Western thought. Without the replacement of the natural forms of the ancients by 'laws *of* nature' Western epistemology could not have ¿advanced? to its present position.

4 Alfred Schutz, *Collected Papers*, vol. 2 (The Hague, Martinus Nijhoff, 1964), p. 88. Much of what follows is heavily dependent on Schutz's work.

5 Berger and Luckmann express the same idea in a less objectionable metaphor; they argue that this epistemological issue is as absurd a practical dilemma as trying to push a bus in which you are riding. See Peter Berger and Thomas Luckmann, *The Social Construction of Reality* (London, Allen Lane, 1967).

6 For an introduction to Husserl's method see C. N. Mohanty, *Edmund Husserl's Theory of Meaning* (The Hague, Martinus Nijhoff, 1964). It has been argued that Husserl did not go far enough, and that his method is not as radical as it at first appears. For one angle on this see Jürgen Habermas, 'Knowledge and interest', in Dorothy Emmet and Alasdair MacIntyre (eds), *Sociological Theory and Philosophical Analysis* (London, Macmillan, 1970).

7 This trick is pinched from the field of literary criticism. See I. A. Richards, *Speculative Instruments* (University of Chicago Press, 1955),

pp. 17–56. Here, however, we invert the first interrogative to give a Mediterranean feel.

8 Harold Garfinkel and Harvey Sachs, 'On formal structures of practical actions', in J. C. McKinney and E. A. Tiryakian (eds), *Theoretical Sociology: Perspectives and Developments* (New York, Appleton-Century-Crofts, 1970).

9 Voltaire once said 'If you would converse with me you must first define your terms'; but it is difficult to see what kind of a demand that is.

10 Berger and Luckmann's definition of reality 'as a quality appertaining to phenomena that we recognize as having a being independent of our own volition' avoids the circularity of this one at the expense of begging the question so elegantly analysed by Martin Buber. See Berger and Luckmann, op. cit., p. 13, and Martin Buber, *I and Thou* (trans. R. G. Smith, Edinburgh, T. & T. Clark, 1937). As Kuhn has said, 'Not all circularities are vicious', op. cit., 1969 edn, p. 176.

11 Ibid., p. 13. The following argument draws heavily from this work.

12 A. N. Whitehead, *The Aims of Education* (London, Benn, 1932).

13 See Scott Greer, *The Logic of Social Inquiry* (Chicago, Aldine, 1969), p. 149 and p. 173. Another modern sociologist whom one would not have expected to find playing at Martians is Jack D. Douglas, 'Deviance and respectability: the social construction of moral meanings', in *Deviance and Respectability* (New York, Basic Books, 1970).

14 J. W. Dunne, *Nothing Dies* (London, Faber & Faber, 1940). See also his *An Experiment With Time* (London, A. & C. Black, 1929) and *The Serial Universe* (Cambridge University Press, 1942).

15 This is the view of Maurice Merleau-Ponty. See his two major works, *The Structure of Behavior* (Boston, Beacon Press, 1963) and *Phenomenology of Perception* (London, Routledge & Kegan Paul, 1962).

16 John Dewey, *Logic: The Theory of Inquiry* (New York, Holt, Rinehart & Winston, 1938).

17 Cf. Henri Bergson, *Matter and Memory* (London, Allen & Unwin, 1911).

18 My apologies to others who have used this technique to better effect. I have in mind R. D. Laing, *Knots* (London, Tavistock, 1970); George J. McCall and J. L. Simmons, *Identities and Interactions* (New York, Free Press, 1966); and Aaron V. Cicourel (private communication).

19 The fundamental issue of the relation between Mind and Matter will be treated, albeit rather cursorily, in chapters 4 and 20.

20 Schutz, op. cit., vol. 1, pp. 207–59.

21 N. Polsky, *Hustlers, Beats and Others* (Chicago, Aldine, 1967); R. T. Anderson, 'From Mafia to Cosa Nostra', *American Journal of Sociology*, 81 (1963), pp. 302–10; Hunter S. Thompson, *Hell's Angels* (Harmondsworth, Penguin Books, 1966); Troy Duster, *The Legislation of Morality* (New York, Free Press, 1970); Leon Festinger et al., *When Prophecy Fails* (New York, Harper & Row, 1964).

22 Erich Goode, 'Marijuana and the politics of reality', *Journal of Health and Social Behaviour*, 10 (June 1969), pp. 83–4. Goode argues that reality, scientific and otherwise, is a matter of political bargaining and struggle.

23 There have always been groups of 'heretics' who create their worlds by unorthodox methods. For sociological analyses of some such deviant

world-views see Kai T. Erikson, *Wayward Puritans* (New York, Wiley, 1966); T. Szasz, *The Manufacture of Madness* (London, Routledge & Kegan Paul, 1971); Festinger *et al.*, op. cit.; and Theodore Roszack, *The Making of a Counter Culture* (London, Faber & Faber, 1970).

24 Cf. Stephen Toulmin, *The Philosophy of Science* (London, Hutchinson, 1953); and see also J. Bronowski, *Common Sense of Science* (London, Heinemann, 1951).

25 Goode, op. cit., p. 85.

2 Just Another Fairy Tale

1 Owen Barfield, *Romanticism Comes of Age* (London, Steiner Press, 1944), p. 75.

2 Owen Barfield, *Saving the Appearances: A Study in Idolatry* (New York, Harcourt Brace & World, 1965), pp. 24ff.

3 Ibid., p. 15.

4 Ibid., p. 16.

5 Bishop Berkeley, *Principles of Human Knowledge* (London, Routledge, 1878), p. 12.

6 Barfield, *Saving the Appearances*, p. 20.

7 Turn back to the illustration on page 9!

8 Philip Morrison in a BBC television programme 1972.

9 *The Cambridge History of Later Greek and Early Medieval Thought* (Cambridge University Press, 1970) might provide some useful leads for the ¿interested? reader.

3 A Trip Through the Library

1 From the *Dictionary of Philosophy and Psychology* (J. Baldwin and W. Stout), cited in J. W. Dunne, *Nothing Dies* (London, Faber & Faber, 1940), p. 42.

2 Descartes thought 'I think therefore I am' but he mistook reason for ¿thinking?. In assuming reason to be sufficient for knowledge he took as indubitable the very assumption which thought relies upon but ¿thinking? may reject, that is his own self-consciousness.

3 Cf. Scott Greer, *The Logic of Social Inquiry* (Chicago, Aldine, 1969).

4 For a thoroughgoing analysis of this situation see D. Price, *Little Science, Big Science* (New York, Columbia University Press, 1963).

5 See, for example, Jacques Barzun, *Science: The Glorious Entertainment* (London, Secker & Warburg, 1964).

6 Ibid., pp. 22 and 63. In rejecting this 'cliché inherited from the nineteenth century' Barzun makes the mistake of identifying the scientific enterprise with the *content* of the paradigm, with knowledge kept as science.

7 Notice that this series is incomplete as it stands. I do not intend to stretch a mathematical ¿model? to the extent of projecting, for example, the relationship between today's science and tomorrow's common sense. To do so it would be necessary to evaluate yesterday's science against today's common sense and it is not clear, at least to me, how we do this or, indeed, if we normally do it at all.

8 This notion, of a world-taken-for-granted which is '*external*' and

'*constraining*' by virtue of the 'objectivity' which inheres in the quality of learnability, is a central ¿sociological? judgment which is by no means a mere trend of the phenomenological fashion. I know of no current school which rejects this judgment. For an interesting appraisal of Durkheim's views on this see Paul Bohannan, '*Conscience collective* and culture', in E. Durkheim *et al.*, *Essays on Sociology and Philosophy* (New York, Harper & Row, 1959).

9 For an elaboration of the relationship between 'internal' and 'external' stimuli of scientific theories, see Imre Lakatos, 'History of science and its rational reconstructions', in R. Cohen and R. Buck (eds), *Boston Studies* (Dordrecht, Reidel Publishing Co., 1971). Cf. also Thomas S. Kuhn, *The Structure of Scientific Revolutions* (University of Chicago Press, 1969 edn), pp. 23–34.

10 I am grateful to my colleague, John F. Crutchley, for this, as for many other entertaining snippets of *KK*, for example, that the gentleman in question was the founder of our ontological institute at Ponders End.

11 Cf. the end of Wittgenstein's *Tractatus*. By the way, if Archimedes ever did write 'give me a place on which to stand and I will move the earth' it was probably in the lost work 'On Levers'. See T. L. Heath, *The Works of Archimedes* (Cambridge University Press, 1897), p. xix.

12 If you want ¿evidence? for my claim that ¿sociology? is trendy you have only to look at the article entitled 'How to get your egghead' in the teenage magazine, *Nineteen*, September 1970.

13 G. Psathas, 'Ethnomethods and phenomenology', *Social Research*, 35 (1968).

14 Alfred Schutz, *Collected Papers*, vol. 1 (The Hague, Martinus Nijhoff, 1964).

15 Of course there is nothing novel in this degree of intellectual megalomania. In so far as they hit upon ¿sociology?, Rousseau, Condorcet, and, of course, Comte, were among the social philosophers seeking to define a discipline to 'crown' the sciences.

16 Kuhn's answer nowadays would probably be as follows. If you want to learn about the paradigm of ¿sociology? (always supposing that one has already ¿emerged?) then look at what the people calling themselves 'sociologists' do, and pay great attention to the important *examples* which they hold up to you. By emulating these great examples you will learn to be a ¿sociologist?. The implication is that you should pay heed, for example, to what Marx *did* and what Weber *did*; you know Merton's famous model, Erikson got a MacIver award for his *Wayward Puritans* so that must be good too, then there's this man Cicourel who is also very fashionable nowadays. Somehow, according to Kuhn's view, attention to all those famous examples would make a ¿sociologist? of you. See Kuhn, op. cit., 1969. (Did I say '*attention*'? – There's something ¿fishy? around here!)

17 Kuhn, op. cit. (1969), p. 16 and n. 6.

18 Karl Popper, *Conjectures and Refutations* (London, Routledge & Kegan Paul, 1963).

19 This unintentionally damning description comes from the back cover of John and Elizabeth Newson's *Patterns of Infant Care* (Harmondsworth, Penguin Books, 1960). Not for nothing have this hardy pair earned the title 'The Pearl Carr and Teddy Johnson of English Sociology'.

20 With apologies to Denis Wrong, 'The oversocialized conception of man in modern sociology', *American Sociological Review*, 25–6 (1958).

21 Cf. Wallace's apt summary of Hegel's notion of a 'presentation', 'one of two things: either a particular thing taken under general aspects, or a universal narrowed down into a particular thing', W. Wallace, *The Logic of Hegel* (Oxford, Macmillan, 1873), p. lxxxix.

22 For an interesting discussion of the notion of *commensurability* see Kuhn, 'Reflection on my critics', in Imre Lakatos and Alan Musgrave, *Criticism and the Growth of Knowledge* (Cambridge University Press, 1970), pp. 266ff.

23 By 'the advocate of the scientific approach' I mean those methodologists such as Hempel, Braithwaite, etc. who have taken a strictly deductive view of the process of science. See for example Carl G. Hempel's excellent introductory text, *Philosophy of Natural Science* (Englewood Cliffs, New Jersey, Prentice-Hall, 1966), and R. B. Braithwaite, *Scientific Explanation* (New York, Cambridge University Press, 1953). Leading ¿sociological? exponents of this view are G. C. Homans (see particularly *The Nature of Social Science* (New York, Harcourt Brace & World, 1967)) and H. M. Blalock (see, for example, *Causal Inferences in Nonexperimental Research* (University of North Carolina Press, 1961)).

24 From Mervyn Peake, *Rhymes Without Reason* (London, Eyre & Spottiswoode, 1941).

25 Hempel, op. cit., p. 16. Here I am interpreting 'critical scrutiny' purely as judgments of validity by the criteria of logic which characterize science. Hempel actually means something more than this: he wishes to include judgments about ¿truth? as well as those about validity, thus he sets great importance upon the notion of 'contingency', which, along with that of ¿truth? will be examined below.

26 Hempel, 'The logic of functional analysis', in Llewellyn Gross (ed.), *Symposium on Sociological Theory* (New York, Harper & Row, 1959), pp. 271–307.

27 I have never known a student who has been unable to work this out for himself. If one were really in difficulty then it would be a good idea for him to read the first three chapters of Hempel, *Philosophy of Natural Science*, and then consult the article cited in the preceding footnote.

28 Cf. Hempel, *Philosophy of Natural Science*, Braithwaite, op. cit., Homans, op. cit., Blalock, op. cit. All these writers would include rules about '*contingency*' and ¿*truth*? in these catechisms. We have not yet examined these ideas, and will be postponing this difficult issue until chapter 5.

29 I refer particularly to Blalock's deductive nomological exercise in *Towards a Theory of Minority Group Relations* (New York, Wiley, 1967). It is, of course, a mere matter of taste but many people find this extreme approach unutterably boring. The same is also said of attempts to simplify ¿sociological? statements by expressing them in mathematical symbols. Many of the latter efforts are not, however, *explanations* in our sense at all, they are simply ¿models? which take a mathematical form. The concept of ¿model? will be discussed in a moment.

30 If you are into my extended metaphor, you may like to think of a 'distinction' as something a creature in the catacombs can brandish

at the SPIDER. It is like a crucifix to a vampire, or an ethnomethodologist's wet haddock to an assemblage of ¿sociologists?.

31 Cf. Harold Fallding, *The Sociological Task* (Englewood Cliffs, New Jersey, Prentice-Hall, 1968).

32 Here, of course, 'false' means *invalid* as opposed to ¿untrue?. We have not yet explored the meanings which are given to the idea of ¿truth?.

33 See Carl G. Hempel, 'Explanatory incompleteness', in May Brodbeck (ed.), *Readings in the Philosophy of the Social Sciences* (New York, Macmillan, 1968), pp. 398–414. A similar distinction is made by Aaron Cicourel; see *Method and Measurement in Sociology* (New York, Free Press, 1964), particularly pp. 8–10.

34 Cf. T. Szasz, *The Manufacture of Madness* (London, Routledge & Kegan Paul, 1971).

35 On the way in which similes in everyday speech may be transformed into metaphors and then 'die' as metaphors, leaving a common-sense model with the status of an assumedly literal explanation, see Severyn T. Bruyn, *The Human Perspective in Sociology* (Englewood Cliffs, New Jersey, Prentice-Hall, 1966), particularly *circa* p. 137; and Colin Turbeyne, *The Myth of Metaphor* (Yale University Press, 1962).

36 Cf. May Brodbeck, 'Models, meaning, and theories', in Brodbeck (ed.), op. cit., pp. 579–600.

37 The notion of relationships of scale is here being used as a simple and familiar *model* in order to facilitate communication of the notion of isomorphism. Like anyone else who ever offers a model, I am saying 'Look at it like this . . . for until you can grasp this sequence of ideas in its own terms another seemingly similar sequence may provide a thought-pattern.'

38 If you are familiar with the real British Museum (or are lucky enough to have a super model thereof) you will see what I mean. The point is that the ordering of a certain volume by a reader, sitting in a certain seat, must be accomplished by the movement of the reader's body through a set pattern, this is a property of the fixed position of the catalogues, seating, and 'in'-window.

39 See particularly Hans Zetterberg, *On Theory and Verification in Sociology* (Totowa, New Jersey, Bedminster Press, 1964), and Homans, op. cit.

40 For an interesting attempt to make sense of these early model-builders see W. Buckley, *Sociology and Modern Systems Theory* (Englewood Cliffs, New Jersey, Prentice-Hall, 1967).

41 For a particularly attractive example see George J. McCall and J. L. Simmons, *Identities and Interactions* (New York, Free Press, 1966).

42 We cannot find our way around the LIBRARY properly yet because we do not have a key.

It has often been noted that *taxonomizing* is to be distinguished from *typologizing*. Wandering vaguely around the LIBRARY trying to classify all the sorts of models we could find would be taxonomical activity, akin to classifying butterflies. Taxonomizing is an activity of natural history rather than of science. Typologizing, on the other hand, is a properly scientific activity. For it is deductive rather than inductive, one's paradigm determines one's specific theory and one's theory dictates the dimensions upon which it will be *relevant* to classify the phenomena with which one is concerned. The construction of a logically exhaustive typology of ¿sociological? grand models would be

a simple matter, given a paradigm from which to start. For examples
of this type of typologizing, see H. R. Wagner, 'Types of sociological
theories', *American Sociological Review* (October 1964); W. L.
Wallace, *Sociological Theory* (London, Heinemann, 1969); C. P.
Loomis and R. K. Loomis, *Modern Social Theories* (Chicago, Free
Press, 1959).

43 One famous proponent of this view is R. K. Merton; see his *Social
Theory and Social Structure* (Chicago, Free Press, 1949). But Merton
confuses models with theories and generally misunderstands the issue
of levels of generality. For one critique of Merton's views of so-called
'theories of the middle range', see Fallding, op. cit.

4 Advice from a Caterpillar

1 When Alice encountered the caterpillar she was, like it, 'exactly three
inches high'.

2 That is, the kind of 'normal' growth discussed in the previous chapter,
the progress or advance of knowledge which must appear to the perspective limited by reason.

3 Even that most thoughtful of rationalists, John Stuart Mill, admitted
in his *Autobiography* that, while reading Bentham's view that phrases
like 'law of nature', 'moral sense', etc. were 'dogmatism in disguise,
imposing its sentiments upon others under cover of sounding
expressions which convey no reason for the sentiment, but set up the
sentiment as its own reason. . . . *The feeling rushed upon me*, that all
previous moralists were superseded, and that here indeed was the
commencement of a new era in thought'! [Italics added.] Passage cited
in Barfield, *Saving the Appearances: A Study in Idolatry* (New York,
Harcourt, Brace & World, 1965), p. 70.

4 These range from the intellectual sophisticates such as Krishnamurti,
through L. Ron Hubbard, to the Guru Maharaj Ji.

5 I shall discuss this metaphysic again in chapter 20.

6 I hope to show below that it is not only the unequivocal 'empiricists'
but also the so-called ethnomethodologists who are reduced to this
inductivist strategy.

7 The notion of 'Chance' and its part in statistical methods of induction
will be examined in some detail in chapters 14 and 19.

8 That is, at more than mere 'accretion'. See the collection of papers in
the symposium, *Criticism and the Growth of Knowledge*, ed. Imre
Lakatos and Alan Musgrave (Cambridge University Press, 1970).

9 The exception is the Mad Hatter and he will have a chance to air his
views later.

10 I mean no offence to any of the guests by that remark. Rather I wish
to indicate that I shall be doing them injustice by quoting them out of
context. Obviously ¿time? must preclude a faithful reportage of the
whole débâcle, and all the issues raised will be discussed at greater
length in the following chapters. If you wish to examine the arguments
from some other viewpoint(s) I suggest that you pretend to go to the
party on your own. This you can do by retiring to a quiet spot with
some writing materials, a copy of Lakatos and Musgrave, op. cit., and
some suitable refreshments.

11 Watkins in Lakatos and Musgrave, op. cit., p. 34

12 Ibid., p. 32; Karl Popper, *Conjectures and Refutations* (London, Routledge & Kegan Paul, 1963), p. 53; and cf. Thomas S. Kuhn, *The Structure of Scientific Revolutions* (University of Chicago Press, 1969 edn), p. 242.

13 Popper, op. cit., p. 56.

14 Cf. 'The Newtonians', turning 'each new difficulty into a new victory of their programme' as Laplace put it, back in 1796. Lakatos cites this phrase with some relish, loc. cit., p. 133.

15 Ibid., pp. 97–8. What I have characterized as 'dogmatic deductivism' Lakatos calls 'dogmatic falsificationism'. The label is of no consequence whatever, the view in question is that interpretation of the 'rule-book principles' (discussed in the preceding chapter) which has been associated with the names of Braithwaite and, perhaps less justly, those of Carl Hempel and George Homans. As Lakatos points out, there is *sometimes* a hint of this approach in Popper's work.

Anyone familiar with Popper's methodology may feel that I am trying to put a cart before the horse and that the issues being raised here cannot be considered in advance of an explication of the principles of falsificationism. But this is why I have employed the term 'dogmatic deductivism': I wish to delay a discussion of falsificationism versus verificationism until these are covered in detail below.

16 In chapter 5.

17 Lakatos is firm in his disdain for this view, considering that, 'exactly the most admired scientific theories simply fail to forbid any observable state of affairs', Lakatos and Musgrave, op. cit., p. 100. But he has overreached himself for, in rejecting the criterion of concord with the observed facts as the sole arbiter of theories, he proposes an equally 'empirical' criterion for judging a *series of theories*: 'that it should produce *new* facts'. Thus, says Lakatos, compounding the concepts of ordinary and extraordinary science, 'The idea of growth and the concept of empirical character are soldered into one', Lakatos and Musgrave, op. cit., p. 119.

18 He does discuss the definition of the term 'verisimilitude' in a footnote (pp. 188–9) but he never gets around to asking what it is that he takes for granted about the concept of ¿truth?.

19 Ibid., p. 105. The sources to which he refers are P. Duhem, *The Aim and Structure of Physical Theory* (first published in 1905, first English edition 1954, Princeton University Press) and Karl Popper, *The Logic of Scientific Discovery* (first published in 1935, published in English in 1959, London, Hutchinson). I shall be examining Duhem's and Popper's conventionalism in greater detail below.

20 Ibid., p. 106. The phrases in quotation marks are from Popper, *The Logic of Scientific Discovery*, sections 26–8.

21 Lakatos and Musgrave, op. cit., p. 112.

22 The latter views this methodological position as a game which, though one has 'little hope of winning' one still feels 'that it is better to play than to give up'; and in a footnote he adds 'I am sure that some will welcome [it] . . . as an "existentialist" philosophy of science.' Ibid., p. 113.

23 I.e. 'fallaciously subtle', 'specious', 'adulterated', or 'tampered with for the purposes of argument'.

24 One even more evocative of Herman Hesse's glass bead game than that which we find today.

25 Another way of stating this point is to say that Lakatos's new demarca-
tion criterion cannot be applied universalistically. What does and does
not produce a 'progressive problem shift' is as much a matter of taste
as anything else. Currently, mathematical theories are very fashionable: they are thought to provide more ¿space? because they are
contentless. Yet some ¿times? mathematics are not general enough.
And how can *extraordinary* mathematics arise? I shall return to the
question of extraordinary mathematics in chapter 19.

26 Though one would surely need to weigh that ¿responsibility? against
the other calls on one's ¿time?, pivoting the comparison on some set of
moral assumptions. I shall return to the question of the criteria for
moral theorizing.

27 For one of the most lucid examples see D. Price, *Little Science, Big
Science* (New York, Columbia University Press, 1963). I shall return
to the subject of 'productivity' in chapter 20.

28 I should not need to waste *more* paper to dismiss the objection that I
should cover over my own typewriter. For I have no *new* theories
with which to bore you. Though I may well be boring you I am doing
so by an opposite method. Rather than inventing *new* theories with
'progressive problem shifts' in the hope that these will create room-
to-spare for new facts, I am trying to suggest some ways of storing
the old theories a little more economically thus creating recognizable
lacunae which, rather than being viewed as storage space for more
KK, might be regarded as escape holes.

29 Cf. Kuhn, op. cit., p. 250. Incidentally I have said nothing to suggest
that normal and extraordinary features of scientific work are not
copresent. While deploring Lakatos's plea for a less risky methodology I accept his view that 'proliferation' and 'tenacity' (the proposal of new theories and the effort to bash the old facts into line
with the old theories) are scientific activities which are present at all
¿times?.

30 But Lakatos need not worry that the diligent logical and methodological
efforts to uncover mistakes will *necessarily* result in the premature
rejection of *new* theories. The GOLD-STAR methodology which I have
tried to outline in the remainder of this book *ought to ensure that the
new theories are no more and no less at risk than the old facts*!

31 This point parallels Lakatos's view that '*There is no falsification before
the emergence of a better theory*', Lakatos and Musgrave, op. cit.,
p. 119. But it is not quite the same point. For me, lack of 'fit' between
an empirical hypothesis and 'an experiment, experimental report,
observation statement, or low-level hypothesis' (p. 119) is *only one
kind of anomaly* which may be uncovered *within* a paradigm by a
thoroughgoing GOLD-STAR methodology. This sort of discrepancy
between old theory and observed facts may, from a ¿transcendent?
viewpoint, be both recognized and 'solved' with *one stroke* of the *new*
theory. But in the history of science *not all the anomalies which progress
has picked out as conundrums have had empirical referents*. Some have
been purely 'abstract', for example mathematical puzzles. 'Falsification before the emergence of a better theory' has *often* occurred in
the history of science and, to their detriment, normal scientists
usually attribute such instances to their own shortcomings. But often,
too, scientists have worked on known anomalies until madness,
exhaustion, or merciful serendipity have intervened. But falsified

predictions are not the only kinds of puzzles which drive honest scientists to desperation: some conundrums are 'non-empirical'.

32 Just here the role of Mad Hatter is being played by P. Feyerabend, see Lakatos and Musgrave, op. cit., p. 217. But I disagree with him that this may be 'the only' function of rational discussion. For, as we shall see, reason is an essential check on the ¿thinking? without which inspiration could not culminate in scientific revolution, that is, without which imagination could never be reflected in thought.

33 Kuhn, op. cit., pp. 122–3.

34 For an interesting discussion of the use of chemical substances to produce ASCs for the good of science see Andrew Weil, 'Altered states of consciousness', *New Scientist*, 30 March 1972, pp. 696–8. This is a very risky (though spectacular) method of stimulating the imagination by abolishing the relevance of the taken-for-granted. Most ASCs, those usually produced by cannabis or alcohol, drastically reduce the significance of *KK* and *RR*, leaving *FF* virtually untouched (except in that it may more often be recognized as mistaken: e.g. 'I thought I saw a pink elephant but looked again and found it was . . . '). Other ASCs (those which may be produced by mescalin and, say, rather large doses of opium) may even render most normal *FF* irrelevant. It is for this reason that such ASCs should be utilized with the greatest caution. For where normal figuration is too drastically or too frequently thrown into doubt the consciousness is left with no earthly platform and the adventurer may find that he, like Icarus, is out of his element. If indulged too frequently or intensively any method of attaining ASCs can simply lead to a different kind of imprisonment, as Coleridge knew. On the other hand, used with care, a great 'receptivity' may certainly be effected as Huxley and others have shown.

35 Karl Popper, *Conjectures and Refutations*.

36 Weber also put this point clearly. For an excellent commentary see Talcott Parsons, *The Structure of Social Action* (Chicago, Free Press, 1949).

37 Lukács's definition of alienation was characterized in terms of 'man's self-created environment' becoming 'his dungeon'. See Georg Lukács, *History and Class Consciousness* (London, Merlin, 1971).

38 Owen Barfield, *Romanticism Comes of Age* (London, Steiner Press, 1944), p. 34.

39 In other FAIRY TALES the littoral beings whom I have playfully termed FAIRIES have been summoned by more ponderous nuncupations. More enticingly they have been nicknamed 'Angels', 'Monads', 'Forms', etc. by their mortal friends. If I had wanted to avoid the ridicule which I hope to have invited, I would probably have been content with the innocuous-sounding term '*third-order meanings*'; or, indeed, obliterating all trace of anthropomorphization, with the label 'deep structure' or some equally unattractive, but no less metaphysical, suggestion.

40 For full documentation of the available evidence for the proposition that 'those who eat from the fairies' table may never return to the land of time' see Edwin S. Hartland, *The Science of Fairy Tales* (London, Walter Scott, 1891), particularly pp. 39ff.

41 A parallel to ¿thinking? may be found in the process of '*accounting*' which characterizes everyday life. Through '*accounting*' the extraordinary

is reconciled with the taken-for-granted. Successful 'accounts' soon assume the status of ordinary thoughts, that is to say that they are institutionalized within the taken-for-granted. The behaviours for which they 'account' thus become ordinary and expected rather than extraordinary and problematic or surprising. For a useful introduction to the ¿sociological? concept of 'accounting' see M. B. Scott and S. Lyman, 'Accounts', *American Sociological Review*, 33 (1) (1968), p. 46; and J. Ford and S. Box, 'Some thoughts on the orienting proposition that "there are no 'thems', only us"' (forthcoming).

The part played by ¿thinking? in the dialectics of transcendence may also be compared with P. McHugh's characterization of 'emergence' in *Defining the Situation*, pp. 24–8, and of 'relativity', pp. 28–32 (New York, Bobbs-Merrill, 1968).

42 Thus completely reversing Descartes's viewpoint. In both FAIRY TALES *self-consciousness* is the door to *thinking* but while the founders of 'Enlightenment' thought viewed it as an opening I see it as a very real obstacle, a door which is shut tight by normal thought: 'they thought therefore they were'!

43 Cf. Lakatos and Musgrave, op. cit., p. 152.

44 To transcend a viewpoint is, quite simply, to make generalizations from a different point of view which subsumes all the judgments of the original viewpoint in a more general theory. Generalizing is always a process of transcending a point of view. Thus one may move from one ¿level of analysis? to a 'higher' or more general one. Theories may therefore be conceived as rankable within paradigms according to levels of generality. Thus, for example, propositions about family patterns of interaction may be subsumed under a more general theory of human interaction, and so on. This implies a notion of hierarchies of theories *within* paradigms, and, ultimately, one of an infinite series of paradigms. Though, as I have said, ordinary and extraordinary scientific thought and thinking are present in science at all ¿times?, nothing can happen to science all-of-a-sudden. Gestalt switches are sudden but only for *individuals*, not for paradigms of thought. A Gestalt switch occurs *in an instant*, but a Gestalt switch does not in itself constitute a change in a *shared* paradigm of thought. Before any paradigm change, or indeed any new theorizing, will take place (if it takes place at all), *the individual's imaginative flash must be translated through thinking into shareable thoughts*. The collective result of individual thinking is thus a proliferation of rival theories. The cumulative comparison of rival theories by ¿testing? will, if carried out in a GOLD-STAR spirit, ensure a gradual process of paradigm change. But if the GOLD-STAR spirit is lacking, if loosely inductive and verificationist methods prevail, then the result will be what Lakatos has termed a 'degenerating problem shift'. Here more and more ¿uninteresting? KK will be crammed untidily into the creaking framework which will begin to 'crumble under the weight of "continual repairs, and many tangled up stays" when "the worm eaten columns" cannot support "the tottering building" any longer'. Cf. Lakatos and Musgrave, op. cit. and Duhem, op. cit., chapter 6, section 10. I shall return to the question of individual thinking and the collective results of GOLD-STAR methods of ¿testing? below, and I shall also define the term ¿level of analysis?.

45 J. M. Baldwin, *Thought and Things*. Cited in Barfield, op. cit., p. 74.

46 Ibid., p. 64. Notice that this passage was written in the 1930s. Since then the problems of over-production in Britain were masked for a while by various factors. Perhaps the new economic facts created by the application of the same (degenerating) paradigm of thought to the appearance of a European Economic Community, and the continuing war efforts of various international powers, will succeed in masking them again, thus, for a ¿time?, saving the ¿truth? of the Economists' FAIRY TALES.

47 See Francis Bacon, *The Advancement of Learning* (Oxford University Press, 1906); and Stephen Toulmin, *The Philosophy of Science* (London, Hutchinson, 1953).

48 Alvin Gouldner, *The Coming Crisis of Western Sociology* (London, Heinemann, 1971), p. 3.

49 I shall be content here with just the following example, as I shall return to this subject in chapter 20. The Association of the Prevention of Addiction has, in several different publicity and policy statements, called for the setting up of 'fire brigade groups' to deal with *'drug subcultures'*. And these ¿sociological? creations figure as Frankensteinian monsters in many of the media messages on the subject of drugs.

50 As was Peter Berger's view in his delightful introduction to the subject as he conceived it, *Invitation to Sociology* (New York, Anchor, 1963).

51 See Richard Cavendish, *The Black Arts* (London, Routledge & Kegan Paul, 1967), p. 2.

52 To suppose that it is anything else is to commit what philosophers call 'the naturalistic fallacy': to assume that ethical imperatives can be induced from appearances.

53 Barfield, op. cit., p. 59.

5   Cross My Heart and Hope to Die

1 For example, it is quite well known in certain circles that blackbirds have bright golden beaks in the springtime because they then visit a well of molten gold where they dip their beaks. For other examples see E. S. Hartland, *The Science of Fairy Tales* (London, Scott Publishing Co., 1891) and S. R. Littlewood, *The Fairies Here and Now* (London, Methuen, 1913).

2 Of course, if the child actually discussed his plans for ¿testing? the Father Christmas theory, his parents would probably attempt to dissuade him from carrying out his research on the grounds that Father Christmas might be so annoyed that he would leave the stocking as he found it. *Anticipatory* conventionalist stratagems like that are also common in the domain of academic fairy-tale telling.

3 Further thought on this may lead you to the view that the issue is further complicated if we accept the judgment that 'contingency' is a *practical* dilemma (that is to say that it is a problem of ¿operationalization?) rather than a characteristic of some ontologically discrete reality. The problems revolving around practical questions about the feasibility of ¿adequate operationalization? will be further elaborated in the following chapters.

4 A good indication of this overwhelming tendency to treat science as having a firm foundation in contingent or ¿testable? propositions is the

approach taken by the available textbooks which offer an introduction to scientific method in general or to the methodology of the social sciences in particular. Consider, for example, the following introductions to social science (chosen at random): Alan Ryan, *The Philosophy of the Social Sciences* (London, Macmillan, 1970); David Willer, *Scientific Sociology* (Englewood Cliffs, New Jersey, Prentice-Hall, 1967); Richard Rudner, *Philosophy of Social Science* (Englewood Cliffs, New Jersey, Prentice-Hall, 1967).

5 An interesting example of this overriding 'empiricist' tendency is Bennet's totally unsuccessful attempt to interpret Kant's transcendental idealism as necessarily *implying* answerability to the evidence of the senses. For Bennet 'it is bad logic to say that something might be the case although there was nothing anyone *could* do which would yield sensory evidence for it.' Because of his assumption that Kant, like himself, connects ¿truth? with ¿testability? Bennet has to admit that he actually cannot ¿understand? Kant. 'We understood him just as long as we could guess at what sorts of evidence he believed could be found to support his position; now that he admits that his thesis is not answerable to evidence at all, we do not even know what his thesis is.' See Jonathan Bennet, *Kant's Analytic* (Cambridge University Press, 1966), especially pp. 22–3.

6 The issue of whether the label ¿true? is awarded to an hypothesis or theory as a result of attempts to *prove* ('verify') it or to disprove ('falsify') it will be raised below. The notion of ¿testing? must remain, for the moment, bracketed.

7 Carl G. Hempel, *Philosophy of Natural Science* (Englewood Cliffs, New Jersey, Prentice-Hall, 1966), pp. 30–1. Note Hempel's admission that it is often difficult to distinguish those hypotheses which are testable-in-principle from those which are not (pp. 31–2). It is also interesting that Hempel does not see the terms 'true' and 'truth' as worthy of inclusion in the subject index of this book, and that he seems to be trying unsuccessfully to avoid the use of these terms.

8 Cf. Hegel's distinction between 'correctness' which is ordinarily taken as synonymous with empirical 'truth', and 'Truth in the deeper sense'. See W. Wallace (ed.), *The Logic of Hegel* (Oxford, Clarendon Press, 1874), pp. 262–3 and 306.

9 For an interesting discussion of the practice of 'normal science' see Thomas S. Kuhn, *The Structure of Scientific Revolutions* (University of Chicago Press, 1962), chapter 3.

10 I am, as I have said, referring only to *judgments about* relationships between phenomena, processes and events, not directly to works of art, straight lines, love affairs, or whatever.

11 For example, direct challenges to the sincerity of the sociologists involved on the infamous Project Camelot are rare. The bulk of attacks on this enterprise have been made on other grounds. For an interesting discussion of Project Camelot see I. L. Horowitz (ed.), *The Rise and Fall of Project Camelot* (Cambridge, Mass., M.I.T. Press, 1967). I shall return to the conception of truth-as-sincerity in a minute, and again in chapter 20.

12 See chapter 3. Hacking's discussion of 'necessary' or 'logical truths' as byproducts of notation is interesting in this connection. But his claim that such 'truths' are 'the *only* contingent-upon-nothing truths' is clearly ¿false?. See Ian Hacking, *What is Logic?* (mimeo. from

lectures at the London School of Economics, February and March, 1971).

13 From the television series, *Star Trek*, created by Gene Roddenberry. This is the saga of the USS *Enterprise* and the ethno-Kosmic adventures of its international crew in the twenty-first century AD.

14 See for examples, Charles Squire, *Celtic Myth and Legend in Poetry and Romance* (London, Gresham Publishing Co.) and D. A. Mackenzie, *Egyptian Myth and Legend, Indian Myth and Legend*, and *Teutonic Myth and Legend* (Gresham).

15 For example George C. Homans derives his sociological theories from the 'Truth' that actions which are rewarded are likely to be repeated. See for example *Social Behaviour: Its Elementary Forms* (London, Routledge & Kegan Paul, 1961). Notice that this statement, while having a superficial appearance of being contingent-upon-something-or-other, is not. The only competent judge of whether the first action was rewarding or not is the actor himself. Thus no ¿test? could be devised which would indicate the empirical correctness of the proposition, though several ¿testable? hypotheses have been *deduced from* this judgment and satisfactorily ¿tested?. Homans is fond of remarking that his 'general proposition' is 'True' and, while he may well be right, he clearly cannot persuade us that this is a logical or empirical 'truth'.

16 From tape transcript. Notice, incidentally, that the stockbroker has made an additional ¿mistake?: are the two versions of the story incompatible?

17 Alfred Schutz, *Collected Works*, vol. 1 (The Hague, Martinus Nijhoff, 1967), p. 208.

18 R. D. Laing, *Knots* (London, Tavistock, 1970), p. 30.

19 William Blake, *The Marriage of Heaven and Hell*.

20 See for examples, Karl Marx, *The Economic and Philosophical Manuscripts of 1844*, edited and introduced by Dirk J. Struik (London, International Publishers, 1967), particularly pp. 106–19; L'homme naît inachevé', in Georges Lapassade's *L'Entrée dans la vie* (Paris, Éditions du Minuit, 1963), p. 17; Karl Marx, *The German Ideology* (London, Lawrence & Wishart, 1965); Jean-Paul Sartre, *Critique de la raison dialectique* (Paris, Éditions du Seuil); Peter L. Berger and Hansfried Kellner, 'Arnold Gehlen and the theory of institutions', *Social Research*, 32 (1) (1965), pp. 110ff.; Peter L. Berger, *The Sacred Canopy* (New York, Doubleday, 1967), p. 4; Peter L. Berger and Thomas Luckmann, *The Social Construction of Reality* (London, Allen Lane, 1967); George J. McCall and J. L. Simmons, *Identities and Interactions* (New York, Free Press, 1966), particularly chapter 3; R. D. Laing, *The Politics of Experience* (Harmondsworth, Penguin Books, 1967), pp. 34, 36–7.

21 This view is, in a sense, the opposite of that expressed by modern Christian Existentialists such as Paul Tillich. See particularly *The Protestant Era* (Chicago University Press, 1948), p. 163. The sociologist, Peter Berger, expresses that view clearly by the use of the term 'inductive faith'. He considers that 'Truth' of this sort is not so much *recognized*, as I have argued, as *discovered* by a 'process of thought that begins with the facts of human experience'. See *A Rumour of Angels* (London, Allen Lane, 1969), pp. 75–6, and see also p. 105.

22 See, for example, A. J. Weigert, 'The immoral rhetoric of scientific sociology', *American Sociologist*, 5 (2) (1970), pp. 125–7.

23 The idea of 'probability' and its relationship to truth₄ will be discussed in some detail in chapter 14.

24 For some interesting pointers in ¿these directions? see Lynn Thorndike, *A History of Magic and Experimental Science* (London, Macmillan, 1923); Peter Winch, *The Idea of a Social Science* (London, Routledge & Kegan Paul, 1958); and Robin Horton and Ruth Finnegan (eds), *Modes of Thought* (London, Faber & Faber, 1973).

6 Testing Rituals

1 For a useful exposition of Ptolemy's system see E. J. Dijksterhuis, *The Mechanization of the World Picture* (Oxford University Press, 1961), part I, chapter 3, C, paras 68–85.

2 Al-Bitrogi, *Planetarum theorica, physicis rationibus probata, nuperrime latinis litteris mandata a Calo Calonymos Hebreo Neopolitano, ubi nititur salvare apparentias absque eccentricis et epicyclis* (Colophon: Venetiis, in aedibus Luce antonii Junte Florentini, January 1801), cited in Pierre Duhem, *To Save the Phenomena* (trans. Edmund Doland and Chaninah Maschler) (University of Chicago Press, 1969).

3 Bernard of Verdun, '*Tractatus optimus super totam astrologiam*' (Paris, Bibliothèque nationale), cited in Duhem, op. cit.

4 Ibid., p. 37. Italics added.

5 Thomas Aquinas, *Expositio super librum de Caelo et Mundo* (trans. from Duhem, op. cit., p. 41).

6 Aquinas's views on this matter were that physics differed from astronomy in that the former *was* concerned with 'demonstrating' or 'proving' truths₄. In this he drew close to Averroës's position. This is why I have taken the liberty of interrupting him in mid-argument.

7 Galileo Galilei, *Dialogue Concerning the Two Chief World Systems Ptolemaic and Copernican* (trans. Stillman Drake) (University of California Press, Berkeley and Los Angeles, 1953). See also Thomas S. Kuhn, *The Copernican Revolution. Planetary Astronomy in the Development of Western Thought* (Cambridge, Mass., Harvard University Press, 1957).
In the first century AD the Greek philosopher, Plutarch, had posed a teaser: what would happen if someone fell through a hole in the middle of the earth? Martin Gardner gives Galileo's 'correct' answer together with the estimation that such a trip would take about forty-two minutes. See *The Annotated Alice* (Harmondsworth, Penguin Books, 1965), pp. 27–8, n. 4.

9 Duhem, op. cit., pp. 37–8. Imre Lakatos suggests that this 'unquestioning confidence' is even more pernicious in the social sciences where the function of such 'scientific' devices of 'demonstration' as statistical techniques seems to be 'Primarily to provide a machinery for producing phoney corroborations and thereby a semblance of "scientific progress" where, in fact, there is nothing but an increase in pseudo-intellectual garbage'. See 'Falsification and the methodology of scientific research programmes', in Imre Lakatos and Alan Musgrave (eds), *Criticism and the Growth of Knowledge* (Cambridge University Press, 1970), p. 176, n. 1.

10 Karl Popper, 'Normal science and its dangers', in Lakatos and Musgrave, op. cit., p. 53.

11 See ibid., also *Conjectures and Refutations* (London, Routledge & Kegan Paul, 1963), and *The Logic of Scientific Discovery* (New York, Basic Books, 1959).

12 A broad discussion of the methodology of analysis of historical data can be found in A. C. Danto, *Analytical Philosophy of History* (Cambridge University Press, 1968).

13 Thomas S. Kuhn, *The Structure of Scientific Revolutions* (University of Chicago Press, 1962); 'Postscript–1969' to the 1970 edition; and 'Reflection on my critics', in Lakatos and Musgrave, op. cit.

14 Of course Popper is not unaware of this. See Lakatos and Musgrave, op. cit., pp. 51–2.

15 Watkins, 'Against normal science', in Lakatos and Musgrave, op. cit., p. 32.

16 Kuhn, 'Reflection on my critics', in Lakatos and Musgrave, op. cit., p. 242.

17 Cf. the distinction made by Sjoberg and Nett between the 'ideal' and 'actual' norms of science. Gideon Sjoberg and Roger Nett, *A Methodology for Social Research* (New York, Harper & Row, 1968), chapter 4.

18 For detailed accounts of some of these 'matches' see Lakatos's discussion of Prout's and Bohr's work, in Lakatos and Musgrave, op. cit., pp. 138–54; and Feyerabend's account of classical celestial mechanics and the special theory of relativity, ibid., pp. 220–9.

19 Feyerabend, ibid., p. 211.

20 Lakatos, ibid., p. 130 and n. 2.

21 The term 'roomier' is actually Popper's, not Lakatos's. Lakatos talks instead about 'progressive problem shifts'. See above, chapter 3.

22 Cf. Kuhn: 'The scientific enterprise as a whole does from time to time prove useful, open up new territory, display order, and test long-accepted belief. Nevertheless, *the individual* engaged on a normal research problem *is almost never doing any one of these things*', *The Structure of Scientific Revolutions* (1970 edn), p. 38.

23 It is worth noting that this very general, though entirely testable hypothesis can be deduced equally well from a number of totally different and partially incommensurable FAIRY TALES – 'scientific' and otherwise.

24 Some, of course, deny that sociology can be 'scientific' at all – though it is never entirely clear what they mean by this.

25 Cf. Kuhn, *The Structure of Scientific Revolutions* (1962), chapter 3. Popper has implied the testable hypothesis that the prevalence of a falsificationist atmosphere is greater in the physical than in the social sciences. While posing very difficult problems of operationalization, this would be a fascinating subject for research.

26 For a vague impression of the importance of this activity to sociologists, select sample issues of the *American Sociological Review*, or consult C. M. Bonjean, R. J. Hill and S. D. McLemore, *Sociological Measurement* (New Castle, New Hampshire, Chandler, 1967).

27 The use of models rather than theories and the idea of inductive or 'fact-finding' research in sociology will be discussed in greater detail below.

28 Kuhn refers to this feather-dusting as 'mopping-up'. A classical sociological example is R. K. Merton's *Social Theory and Social*

Structure, revised edn (Chicago, Free Press, 1957). For a more recent 'spring clean', in the field of the sociology of deviant behaviour, see David Matza, *Becoming Deviant* (Englewood Cliffs, New Jersey, Prentice-Hall, 1969).

29 Cf. Zetterberg's complaint that sociologists have failed to establish any 'laws', *On Theory and Verification in Sociology* (Totowa, New Jersey, Bedminster Press, 1964).

30 S. F. Nadel, 'A field experiment in social psychology', *British Journal of Psychology*, 28, (1937), pp. 195–211.

31 That is 'unrelated' from the point of view of an observer like you, me, or Nadel, who has been differently socialized.

32 Irving Piliavin and Scott Briar, 'Police encounters with juveniles', *American Journal of Sociology*, 69 (1964), pp. 206–14.

33 The problems of interpreting tables like this will be discussed in more detail in chapter 19.

34 See Norman K. Denzin, *The Research Act in Sociology* (London, Butterworth, 1970), pp. 315–16; and J. C. Record, 'The Research Institute and the pressure group', in Gideon Sjoberg (ed.), *Ethics, Politics, and Social Research* (Cambridge, Mass., Schenkman, 1967), pp. 25–49.

35 Not that any sociologist who deserved a 'gold star' would ever be satisfied with his research methods, procedures and techniques.

36 See Julienne Ford and Steven Box, 'Sociological theory and occupational choice', *Sociological Review*, 15 (3) (1967), pp. 287–99.

37 Some critics might retort that it is not necessary to have a theory in order to discover tendencies like 'A increases as B increases'. They would probably argue, further, that, once you have 'discovered' that 'A increases as B increases' you have a basis for action regardless of whether or not you have a theory. Dubin, for example, considers that explanation and control are not necessarily *mutually* advanced in theory building. See Robert Dubin, *Theory Building* (New York, Free Press, 1969), chapter 1. This is, however, a dangerous view. A *causal* FAIRY TALE is an essential prerequisite for action in the real world, for without inventing and testing some story about what-causes-what (e.g. 'A causes B') you can neither predict the *sequence* of correlated events, nor control them. What action would Dubin take if, for example, he wished for some reason to decrease the volume of criminal behaviour and he knew only that tattooing and law-violating behaviour were correlated? For a plea for causal theory as a basis for action in sociology see J. F. Short, 'Action research', *Pacific Sociological Review*, 1967. The question of causation will be taken up again below.

38 I will return to this theme, raising the possibility that 'scientific sociology' may be dangerous. See chapter 20.

39 There are horrifying examples from at least one British university of 'homosexual volunteers' being used for a form of 'aversion therapy' experimentation which involves 'punishments' in the form of electric shocks to the genitals. See also J. Vernon's amazing study, *Inside the Black Room: Studies of Sensory Deprivation* (Harmondsworth, Penguin Books, 1963).

40 See Alex Carey, 'The Hawthorne Studies: a radical criticism', *American Sociological Review*, 32 (1967); and Robert Rosenthal, *Experimental Effects in Behavioral Research* (New York, Appleton-Century-Crofts, 1966).

41 Max Weber, *The Protestant Ethic and the Spirit of Capitalism* (London, Allen & Unwin, 1930); *The Religion of China: Confucianism and Taoism* (Chicago, Free Press, 1951); *The Religion of India: The Sociology of Hinduism and Buddhism* (Chicago, Free Press, 1958). See also Talcott Parsons, *The Structure of Social Action* (Chicago, Free Press, 1949).

42 One example of this approach is the structural functional method of comparing cases (that is, whole 'systems') which are considered to be similar except for the partial structures in question. Thus, Whyte compared the social and structural conditions in twelve Chicago restaurants, to 'test' a hypothesis about the degree of contact between waitresses and kitchen staff and its relationship to emotional tension and 'waitress strain'. For an overview of other examples see G. Sjoberg, 'The comparative method in the social sciences', *Philosophy of Science*, 22 (1955), pp. 106–17. It is confusing to reserve the label 'comparative method' for the method of mental experimentation, however, as it should be clear that all methods of scientific hypothesis testing are 'comparative'. See Marion J. Levy, 'Scientific Analysis is a subset of comparative analysis', in J. McKinney and E. Tiryakian (eds), *Theoretical Sociology: Perspectives and Developments* (New York, Appleton-Century-Crofts, 1970), pp. 99–110.

43 Of course several other rival FAIRY TALES have been invented to make Weber blush. See particularly, R. H. Tawney, *Religion and the Rise of Capitalism* (London, Murray, 1926) and H. Trevor Roper, *The Rise of Christian Europe* (London, Thames & Hudson, 1966 edn).

44 A related point is that it is difficult to examine the independent variation of ¿variables? which are clustered together within the chosen 'ideal types'. See Parsons, op. cit.

45 Cf. particularly John Stuart Mill's various modes of the 'comparative method' which are certainly inductive modes of reasoning: *A System of Logic* (New York, Longmans, 1930).

46 The statistical method of testing hypotheses should not be confused with the use of statistics as a basis for *induction*. The use of statistical techniques for testing deductive nomological explanations is not the same as the construction of statistical nomological explanations. Cf. Hempel, op. cit., chapter 5, The question of statistical induction is raised again in chapter 14.

7 The Worlds of Why-Because

1 Unless, of course, these concepts become so disseminated that they eventually creep into everyday accounts of events. The psychological term 'paranoia', for example, was soon adopted as an argot term in a certain deviant world as the members of this subculture found that the experience evoked by this term represented a significant description of their relationship with a hostile out-world.

2 Of course this does not mean that all questions are Why-questions but merely that other sorts of questions (How-, Which-, Where-questions, etc.) rely upon the assumption that Why-questions can be posed and answered by any paradigm.

3 W. Dray, 'The historical explanation of actions reconsidered', in S. Hook (ed.), *Philosophy and History* (New York University Press, 1963), p. 119.

4 Needless to say the use of the word 'inevitably' does *not* imply any ontological assumptions about fate versus free will, etc. The inevitability referred to is of the same order as that which governs the outcome of a simple arithmetic calculation. If the number 7 is multiplied by 3 and the two terms of the product are added together, then – provided the normal rules are followed – there is one *inevitable* outcome: 3.

5 See E. J. Dijksterhuis, *The Mechanization of the World Picture* (Oxford University Press, 1961).

6 For an interesting discussion of the fortunes of man-as-cause in the fairy-tale world of the sociology of deviant behaviour see David Matza, *Becoming Deviant* (Englewood Cliffs, New Jersey, Prentice-Hall, 1969), particularly p. 7.

7 Mario Bunge, *Causality* (New York, World Publishing Co., 1963), pp. 224–5.

8 Cf. 'to deny the psychological phenomenon of understanding is merely foolish. But it is equally foolish, in psychology and elsewhere, to hypostatize it into a category coordinate to scientific explanation.' Gustav Bergmann, 'Purpose, function, scientific explanation', reprinted in May Brodbeck (ed.), *Readings in the Philosophy of the Social Sciences* (New York, Macmillan, 1968), p. 220.

9 P. W. Bridgman, *The Logic of Modern Physics* (London, Macmillan, 1927), p. 37.

10 This contrasts with Bunge's view, op. cit., especially p. 6. C. S. Lewis makes the point that GOLD-STAR scholars are generally aware of the epistemological status of their assumptions, while normal scholars can happily get on with their work under the vague impression that these assumptions are revelations of the essential nature of things. See *The Discarded Image* (Cambridge University Press, 1964).

11 Cf. P. Park, *Sociology Tomorrow* (New York, Pegasus, 1969), chapter 12. See also the discussion about *intervening variables* in chapter 11.

12 Those sociologists who have taken this view have conceived of their task as one of establishing statistical regularities on the basis of which predictions about the future could be made. Their argument is generally that prediction can be satisfactorily accomplished *without* theorizing. Yet prediction based on inductive statistical reasoning is *not* free of theoretical assumptions: such prediction involves always *at least* the FAIRY-TALE notion that 'things-are-likely-to-behave-in-future-as-they-have-been-observed-to-behave-in-the-past. And, if bereft of any explanatory significance, that is a very curious idea! We shall have occasion to return to this issue in chapter 14.

13 Many sociologists treat questions about *being* as illegitimate subjects for sociological thought, fearing that concentration on the reasons for the actual existence of phenomena will lead them inevitably into teleology. There is certainly some justification for this fear and anyway much of the mundane but ¿worthwhile? business of sociology can be done without ever posing such fundamental questions. However, at times of paradigm crisis and paradigm change in sociology, questions of *being* arise in urgent forms and sociologists are not afraid to suggest answers. An example can be found in the upsurge of interest in problems of '*institutionalization*', that is in answers to questions about why certain institutions came into being. See for example P. Berger and T. Luckmann, *The Social Construction of Reality* (London, Allen Lane, 1967).

14 They raise awkward problems about the relationship of C to the initial *being* of E. For example, in a *TYPE 2* story one might wish to ask whether C actually produced E in the first place, or in a *TYPE 4* story about what caused C to change its direction, that is if it did not do so 'of its own accord'.

15 For one of many succinct pleas for a multicausal approach in sociology see Travis Hirschi and Hanan Selvin, *Delinquency Research: An Appraisal of Analytic Methods* (London, Macmillan, 1967).

16 This raises another problem, that of precision versus richness in fairy tales. For one interesting discussion of this see J. G. Kemeny, 'Analyticity versus fuzziness', *Synthese*, 15 (1963), pp. 57–80.

17 Walter Buckley, *Sociology and Modern Systems Theory* (Englewood Cliffs, New Jersey, Prentice-Hall, 1967), pp. 169, 171. This is not Buckley's own fairy tale but a neat presentation of the theory of mental illness which is current amongst sociologists and which has been developed particularly by Thomas J. Scheff, see his *Being Mentally Ill* (Chicago, Aldine, 1966).

18 For a concise introduction to the use of graph theory in the behavioural sciences see Claude Flament, *Applications of Graph Theory to Group Structure* (Englewood Cliffs, New Jersey, Prentice-Hall, 1963).

19 Hubert M. Blalock, *Causal Inferences in Nonexperimental Research* (University of North Carolina Press, 1961), p. 36, and see his 'Further observations on asymmetric causal models', *American Sociological Review*, 1962, particularly p. 543. Blalock is really talking about algebraic models and of course some applications of graph theory do enable expressions of asymmetric relations particularly by the introduction of ¿time? as a variable. The sociological methodologist who has probably pursued this problem further than anyone else is Johan Galtung; see for example his *Theory and Methods of Social Research* (London, Allen & Unwin, 1967). Galtung attempts to draw diachronic conclusions from statistical regularities in order to avoid posing fundamental questions about causation. However, since his method is inductive and his conception of ¿time? a taken-for-granted one, his recipes will not bake the kind of cake which our Alice would be happy to taste.

20 R. M. MacIver, *Social Causation* (New York, Harper & Row, 1964), p. 52.

21 The problems raised by symmetry in mathematics and asymmetry in causal judgments do not exhaust those raised by the use of mathematical analogies. No less of a stumbling block are the issues of *consistency* and *completeness*. For a preliminary glimpse of the nature of these problems see A. V. Cicourel, *Method and Measurement in Sociology* (New York, Free Press, 1964), pp. 31–3.

22 Of course, the term 'function' can be said to have many different meanings; Albert Pierce, for example, lists no less than 13: Albert Pierce, 'Durkheim and functionalism', in Émile Durkheim *et al.*, *Essays on Sociology and Philosophy* (New York, Harper & Row, 1960), pp. 154–69.
But in the context of explanation the mathematical and teleological meanings are the ones of importance and, though these differ, they exhibit more similarities than has usually been recognized.

23 See, for a discussion specifically related to sociological functionalism,

Wsevelod Isajiw, *Causation and Functionalism in Sociology* (London, Routledge & Kegan Paul, 1968).

24 See particularly E. Nagel, *The Structure of Science* (New York, Harcourt Brace & World, 1961), R. P. Dore, 'Function and cause', *American Sociological Review*, 1961, and Carl Hempel, 'The logic of functional analysis', in L. Gross (ed.), *Symposium on Sociological Theory* (New York, Harper & Row, 1959). All these argue that functional statements are inadequate or incomplete causal statements, thus the former can always be translated into the latter by the inclusion of some additional assumptions. Cf. also F. Alder, 'Functionalism made verifiable', *Sociological Quarterly*, 4 (1), (1963), pp. 59–70, for a specific example of the way in which a substantive functional theory can be translated into a testable causal explanation.

It is, however, necessary to distinguish between *micro-* and *macro-functional* theorizing about ¿social phenomena?. It seems to me that a statement to the effect that an individual person performed a specific action *because of the effect* of that action (a micro-functional statement) is a legitimate form of teleological reasoning. After all one is implicitly introducing an obvious link in the causal chain, namely that the individual *believed* that the action would produce the effect in question. On the other hand discussions of the features of social collectivities which posit ends-as-causes (macro-functional statements) are more pernicious because, unless any rival assumptions are introduced in order to create a feasible causal sequence, the danger is that an assumption about 'societal needs' will slip in to fill the gap. *But societies do not have needs, people have wants:* statements like 'society needs X' are usually merely disguised statements of the type 'I want a society in which X'.

A number of writers have recently drawn attention to the fact that loose – and therefore dangerously misleading – functional formulations can be translated into clear-cut, though not necessarily simple, causal sequences by spelling out feedback loops and 'dialectical relationships'. See for examples Buckley, op. cit., p. 79; P. M. Blau, *Exchange and Power* (New York, Wiley, 1967), chapter 12; R. Cole, 'Structural functional theory, the dialectic and social change', *Sociological Quarterly*, 7 (1) (1966); P. L. van den Berghe, 'Dialectic and functionalism', *American Sociological Review*, 28 (1963).

25 As, for example, Malinowski did when he claimed that magic fulfils an *indispensable* function within a culture.

26 See M. Bunge, op. cit. (1963), pp. 258–9 where he discusses some 'non-causal' ideas of planetary motion, and, particularly, pp. 328–9 where he admits the resurgence of causal notions in quantum mechanics.

27 Gwynn Nettler, *Explanations* (New York, McGraw-Hill, 1970), p. 143.

28 Ibid., p. 145.

29 Nagel, op. cit., p. 75.

30 Cf. Hegel, op. cit., vol. 2, pp. 203ff.

31 Engels, *Anti-Duhring* (1878), p. 36 (cited in Bunge, op. cit.). See also Blalock, op. cit., chapter 1 and the discussion of 'extraneous' and 'antecedent' ¿variables?.

32 For just two of the many interesting articles on the questions of sociological and psychological 'reductionism' see George Devereux, 'Two types of modal personality theories', in B. Kaplan (ed.), *Studying*

Personality Crossculturally (New York, Harper & Row, 1961), and E. C. Tolman, 'A theoretical analysis of the relations between sociology and psychology', *Journal of Abnormal and Social Psychology*, 47 (1) (1952), pp. 291ff.

33 See G. C. Homans, *The Nature of Social Science* (New York, Harcourt, 1967). This raises a sticky problem about the *sui generis* nature of social phenomena. Yet it is not necessary to enter into the well-worn debate about methodological holism versus individualism. For, in concrete terms, this boils down to a question about the present state of adequacy of our existing sociological theories of *institutionalization*: the theories which link individual behaviour to social phenomena over ¿time? and via the mysterious processes of reification and socialization. Some of the most interesting recent contributions to this field are those of P. M. Blau, *Exchange and Power in Social Life* (New York, Wiley, 1967), P. Berger and T. Luckmann, *The Social Construction of Reality* (London, Allen Lane, 1967) and Thomas J. Scheff, 'Towards a sociological theory of consensus', *American Sociological Review*, 32 (1) (1967), pp. 32–45.

34 Cf. the so-called theory of 'demographic transition' which offers no such explanation but merely relates fluctuations in the birth-rate to overall fluctuations in population, occasionally threatening to slip in macro-functional judgments about the self-regulation of systems of population.

35 The reverse may also be the case. One paradigm transcends the other with respect to a particular problem.

36 Cf. Fallding's excellent discussion of Merton's famous but confused plea for the development of 'middle range theory'. Harold Fallding, *The Sociological Task* (Englewood Cliffs, New Jersey, Prentice-Hall, 1968). See also David Willer, *Scientific Sociology* (Englewood Cliffs, New Jersey, Prentice-Hall, 1967), pp. xiv–xvi, where a similar argument is put forward.

37 I have somewhat rewritten the story of the development of the concept of relative deprivation and its routine incorporation into subsequent sociological theorizing. The classic statement of the notion is to be found in S. A. Stouffer *et al.*, *The American Soldier*, vol. 1 (Princeton University Press, 1949); a subsequent empirical test was that of A. J. Spector, 'Expectations, fulfilment and morale', *Journal of Abnormal and Social Psychology*, 52 (1956), pp. 51–6; and the specific application of their notion to radical political attitudes was probably most ¿interestingly?, if not first, made by W. G. Runciman in his *Relative Deprivation and Social Justice* (London, Routledge & Kegan Paul, 1966).

38 The notion of final cause is, of course, usually associated with Aristotle. However I do not wish to imply that these venerable fictions are *necessarily* of a tellic nature. For a discussion of this notion which is more germane to the line of thought expressed here see one of the available commentaries on the work of Saint Thomas Aquinas. For example, Lynn Thorndike, *A History of Magic and Experimental Science* (London, Macmillan, 1923), vol. 2, pp. 593–615, but particularly p. 609 and notes 1 and 2.

39 A review of the role of such dignified concepts as God and Nature in the causation of everyday worlds taken-for-granted would be fascinating – but quite outside the scope of this book. Here attention will be

restricted to the concepts implicated by those metatheoretical judgments which have most commonly enlightened ¿sociological? theorizing.

40 Saint Hildegard of Bingen, *Causae et Curae* (1903 edn), p. 2; Cf. also Giordano Bruno, '*De la Causa, Principio e Uno*', in *Opere Italiane* (1584), vol. 1, p. 180; and in our own century Gordon Childe, *Man Makes Himself* (London, Watts, 1965, 4th edn).

41 R. D. Laing, *The Politics of Experience* (Harmondsworth, Penguin Books, 1967), pp. 36–7.

42 From the *Epilogue* to Jorge L. Borges's *Dreamtigers* (University of Texas Press, 1964), p. 93.

43 Thus, since G. Myrdal's *An American Dilemma* (New York, Harper & Row, 1944), honest-minded sociologists have variously attempted to make their most fundamental and 'value-laden' causal judgments as explicit as possible. Alvin Gouldner, who has written many conscience-prodding articles on this subject, has recently stated the principle in a memorable way: he says 'The important thing . . . is to have *the insight to see what one believes* and the *courage* to say what one sees' (italics added), and he continues with the warning that 'since insight and courage are scarce moral resources, the important thing in reading someone else's account . . . is to be continually aware that at some point you are going to be deceived'. See his *The Coming Crisis of Western Sociology* (London, Heinemann, 1971), p. 35, but also consult pp. 29–60 for an excellent account of the role of what Gouldner calls 'domain assumptions' in ¿sociological? theorizing.

44 Refer back to chapter 5.

45 See C. Schrag, 'Elements of theoretical analysis in sociology' in Llewellyn Gross (ed.), *Sociological Theory: Inquiries and Paradigms* (New York, Harper & Row, 1967), pp. 220–53.

46 Practically all elementary textbooks on ¿sociological? research methods include a run-down of Mill's four modes of the comparative method. On the other hand I am not aware of any such discussion which attacks the issue of the relationship between the use of comparisons for inductive *versus* deductive purposes or which adequately pinpoints the verificationist implications of Mill's famous methods. For two of the better discussions see Bernard S. Phillips, *Social Research Strategy and Tactics* (London, Macmillan, 1966), pp. 87–90; and William J. Goode and Paul K. Hatt, *Methods in Social Research* (New York, McGraw-Hill, 1952), pp. 74–91.

47 The inductive-statistical approach to explanation should not be confused with the use of statistical methods in the *testing* of *deductive* theories. See, for an explanation of this distinction, Carl G. Hempel, *Aspects of Scientific Explanation* (London, Macmillan, 1965) or the two pieces entitled 'The logic of functional analysis' and 'Explanatory incompleteness' which appear in May Brodbeck, *Readings in the Philosophy of the Social Sciences* (New York, Macmillan, 1968), pp. 179–210 and 398–415.

48 To my way of thinking inductive-statistical explanation consists in an attempt to explain happenings according to the formula: 'Yes, those things *usually do* behave like that.' According to this formula something which is not unusual requires no explanation for, being *familiar*, it is already 'understood'.

49 Raymond B. Cattell, *Factor Analysis* (New York, Harper & Row, 1952).

50 The serious responsibility which the ¿sociologist? must bear for the uses to which his work is put will be the subject of chapter 20.

51 Incidentally, the SPIDERS to which I refer are giant FAIRY-TALE monsters. Real spiders in the real world of my belief are the friendliest of creatures – I am very fond of them. I wonder, however, what is Professor Popper's attitude to real *tiny babies*. See his *Of Clouds and Clocks* (Arthur Holly Compton Memorial Lecture, Washington University, 1966), p. 17.

52 See, for one example, M. Prezelecki, *The Logic of Empirical Theories* (London, Routledge & Kegan Paul, 1969).

53 I am thinking particularly of the widely read *The Discovery of Grounded Theory* by Barney Glaser and Anselm Strauss (Chicago, Aldine, 1967). See also Anselm Strauss, 'Comment on a review of . . .', *American Journal of Sociology*, 74 (4) (1969), p. 419.

54 Ibid., p. 4.

55 Anyway the examples Glaser and Strauss produce are not of deductive nomological explanations but of analytic theories woven around 'grand' taxonomic systems such as Parsons's *Social System*. They seem to fear that theories may be produced as a result of 'happenstance, fantasy, dream life, common sense or conjecture' (ibid., p. 6), but fail to realize that no amount of codification of inductive procedures can possibly produce theories which are 'grounded' on anything firmer than these shaky footholds in the shifting realm between FAIRY TALE and reality. For, contrary to Glaser's and Strauss's implicit belief, data do not exist *in* reality but are constructed by human minds in their attempts to grasp reality.

56 Ibid., p. 5. Italics added.

57 Ibid.

58 Karl Popper, *The Poverty of Historicism* (London, Routledge & Kegan Paul, 1960, 2nd edn).

59 It is arguable that premature testing, like so-called inductive methods, may *accidentally* trigger off theoretical advance. Serendipity *can* intervene at any stage of the scientific game and thus it is not at all unlikely that the blissful ignorance of GOLD-STAR methodology may occasionally lead the run-of-the-mill RABBITS to the portals of imagination. However it seems to me that the possible advantage is, on the whole, vastly outweighed by the dangers of premature testing. These dangers inhere in the probability that others will mistake the results of premature tests for relevant evidence against the hypothesis that the theory in question is false$_4$; thus erroneously taking to be true$_4$ a theory which is not even true$_3$.

60 Percy Cohen, *Modern Social Theory* (London, Heinemann, 1966).

8   Battles for the Bridges

1 Cf. Hans Zetterberg, *On Theory and Verification in Sociology* (Totowa, New Jersey, Bedminster Press, 1964).

2 Alfred Schutz, *Collected Papers*, vol. 2 (The Hague, Martinus Nijhoff, 1964).

3 Carl G. Hempel, *Philosophy of Natural Science* (Englewood Cliffs, New Jersey, Prentice-Hall, 1966), pp. 72 and 100. I have oversimplified the view he explicates in this text: he uses the term 'bridge

principles' to refer to a relationship between theory and reality in a double sense. Actually this makes an even better parallel with what is to follow.

4 Two other commentaries on positivism in the ¿social? sciences make essentially the same point. See Trent Schroyer, 'Toward a critical theory for advanced industrial society', in Hans P. Dreitzel (ed.), *Recent Sociology* (London, Macmillan, 1970), p. 210; and Gideon Sjoberg and Roger Nett, *A Methodology for Social Research* (New York, Harper & Row, 1968), p. 7.

5 In his discussion of the development of Weber's methodology Don Martindale offers a useful introduction to the neo-idealist position. Unlike some of the later texts which are confused on this point, Martindale's does not conflate the neo-idealism of Dilthey and his followers with the Neo-Kantianism of thinkers like Rickert who took a more thoroughly idealist view. See Don Martindale, *The Nature and Types of Sociological Theory* (London, Routledge & Kegan Paul, 1961).

6 'Dialectical methodology: Marx or Weber? The new Methodenstreit in postwar German philosophy', Ponders End, Monograph, 1970.

7 Of course our spokesman for the positivists will have to shout very loudly indeed, for we are still on the opposite side of the dyke! The relative positions of the armies will be clarified by means of a map – just as soon as we are in a position to view the ¿whole? scene.

8 'the concept is synonymous with the corresponding set of operations', P. W. Bridgman, *The Logic of Modern Physics* (London, Macmillan, 1927), p. 5.

9 George A. Lundberg, *Foundations of Sociology* (London, Macmillan, 1939).

10 F. S. Chapin, *Experimental Designs in Sociological Research* (New York, Harper & Row, 1955, revised edn).

11 J. P. Nettl, *Political Mobilisation: A Sociological Analysis of Methods and Concepts* (London, Faber & Faber, 1967).

12 'Span of control', for example, *could* be defined operationally as the answer to the single question 'How many workers are under your orders?'

13 Conventional scientific believers would be most alarmed at this suggestion that their normal activity is akin to that of, say, Charles Fort, or of Velikovsky. See, for accounts of the works of these original thinkers, Damon Knight, *Charles Fort, Prophet of the Unexplained* (London, Gollancz, 1971), and L. C. Stecchini and R. E. Juergens, *The Velikovsky Affair: The Warfare of Science and Scientism* (New York, University Books, 1966).

14 Physicists got bored with operationism and gave it up long before the ¿sociological? RABBITS got hold of it.

15 See Wilhelm Dilthey, *Gesammelte Schriften*, especially vol. 7.

16 Weber, though usually regarded as a founder of this 'school' is, of course, not guilty on this charge. He not only distinguished causal adequacy (that is scientific validity) from adequacy on the level of meaning (in an intra-cultural sense) but he also stressed that the Verstehende method gave no automatic guarantee of truth[4] – independent *tests* had still to be devised. To anticipate the arguments presented later in this chapter, C. S. Hughes was correct when he stated that Weber was able to 'bridge the chasm between positivism

and idealism', but he was wrong in supposing that Weber was 'alone among his contemporaries' in so doing. See *Consciousness and Society* (New York, Random House, 1961).

17　Ibid.

18　I admit to having stolen this tale! But, unlike Wittgenstein, I find the idea of vast quantities of *timber* too boring to contemplate, so the reader will have to make do with noodles instead!

19　Cf. Theodore Abel, 'The operation called Verstehen', *American Journal of Sociology* (1948), and Talcott Parsons, *The Structure of Social Action* (Chicago, Free Press, 1949). But remember that Weber *had* clearly distinguished the two issues, though the methods of testing which he developed and applied in his own work are less than adequate.

20　There is some confusion amongst ¿sociologists? about how the term 'typology' is to be used and where it differs from the word 'taxonomy' which also refers to a classification device. In my usage a typology is a set of categories produced as a result of logical *deduction* of a number of possibilities from a number of dimensions of analysis. A taxonomy, on the other hand, is an *ad hoc* classificatory device produced by the *induction* of a number of categories from empirical observations, as, for example, in botany.

21　See chapter 7.

22　See chapter 6. By 'the same principle' I mean the idea of location in that kind of FAIRY-TALE space which is known as Cartesian space to distinguish it from physical ¿space?. See Allen H. Barton, 'The concept of property-space in social research', in Paul F. Lazarsfeld and Morris Rosenberg (eds), *The Language of Social Research* (Chicago, Free Press, 1955), pp. 40–62.

23　G. C. Homans, *The Nature of Social Science* (New York, Harcourt, Brace & World, 1970).

24　See H. M. Blalock, *Causal Inferences in Nonexperimental Research* (University of North Carolina Press, 1961), and, for a substantive example of Blalock's work, see *Towards a Theory of Minority Group Relations* (New York, Wiley, 1967).

25　Of course I don't mean to imply that these cell-mates are in agreement on all matters. Popper, as we have seen above, has developed a methodology of falsificationism which is in many respects the antithesis of the unashamedly verificationist approach of some of the ¿sociologists? in the cell. See, for example, Zetterberg, op. cit.

26　For an example see Julienne Ford, *Social Class and the Comprehensive School* (London, Routledge & Kegan Paul, 1970).

27　Zetterberg, op. cit., who has himself argued for an extension of testing in ¿sociology?, has elsewhere asserted: 'A theorist is supposed to link together ideas and propositions from various fields into a parsimonious bundle that then is handed over to researchers, who guide further investigation. . . .' See 'The secret ranking', *Journal of Marriage and the Family*, 28 (1966), p. 142.

28　Lundberg, op. cit. and Chapin, op. cit.

29　See Karl Pearson, *The Grammar of Science* (London, A. and C. Black, 1911), and Raymond B. Cattell, *Personality: A Systematic and Factual Treatment* (New York, McGraw-Hill, 1950). See also Santo F. Camilleri, 'Theory, probability and induction in social research', *American Sociological Review*, 27 (1962), pp. 170–8.

30 The two examples which come most readily to hand are the old standard, William J. Goode and Paul K. Hatt, *Methods in Social Research* (New York, McGraw-Hill, 1952), and the more recent Morris Rosenberg, *The Logic of Survey Analysis* (New York, Basic Books, 1968).

31 Cf. B. Kaplan's distinction between '*logic-in-use*' and '*reconstructed logic*' in *The Conduct of Inquiry* (San Francisco, Chandler, 1964), pp. 6–11 and Sjoberg and Nett's discussion of '*ideal versus actual norms*' in op. cit., pp. 72–6.

32 Notice that Gouldner whose own metatheoretical commitment is both deductive and idealistic identifies two major paradigmatic trends in current sociology, the 'Marxists' on the one hand and the functionalists on the other; standing for opposing idealisms these two represent antagonistic ideologies. On the idealism of the 'Marxists' see also Alfred Schmidt's preface to *Beiträge zur Marxistischen Erkenntnistheorie* (Frankfurt, Suhrkamp, 1969).

33 Thus comes about that strange synthesis of certain aspects of functionalism and the 'Marxism' which is nowadays popular amongst a group of intelligentsia who share a mode-of-being in the taken-for-granted world of Western Capitalist society. For an academic example see Lucien Goldman, *Marxisme et sciences humaines* (Paris, Gallimard, 1970).

34 This is seen in sharp contrast to the gnostic mode of dialogue where each thinker directs his critical efforts towards the destruction of his own opinion and the vindication of that of his 'opponent'.

35 See Peter Winch, *The Idea of a Social Science* (London, Routledge & Kegan Paul, 1958) and Carlo Antoni, *From History to Sociology* (trans. White) (Detroit, 1959).

36 For two of the best-known examples of the work of this group, see Erving Goffman, *Encounters* (New York, Bobbs-Merrill, 1961) and Howard S. Becker, *Outsiders* (New York, Free Press, 1963).

37 The term 'ethnomethodology' is attributed to Harold Garfinkel: see his *Studies in Ethnomethodology* (Englewood Cliffs, New Jersey, Prentice-Hall, 1967). However, a more lucid account of this methodological view can be found in the work of Aaron Cicourel: see particularly his *Method and Measurement in Sociology* (New York, Free Press, 1964). And, compare these with Severyn T. Bruyn, *The Human Perspective in Sociology: The Methodology of Participant Observation* (Englewood Cliffs, New Jersey, Prentice-Hall, 1966).

38 See W. C. Sturtevant, 'Studies in ethnoscience', *American Anthropologist*, special publication, 66, part II.

39 Particularly as this is interpreted through the work of Alfred Schutz, op. cit.

40 Most especially Noam Chomsky: see, for example, *Syntactic Structures* (The Hague, Mouton, 1957).

41 I am thinking particularly of Lévi-Strauss, but see T. O. Beidelman, 'Some sociological implications of culture', in J. C. McKinney and E. A. Tiryakian (eds), *Theoretical Sociology* (New York, Appleton-Century-Crofts, 1970), for an excellent introduction to some of the methodological trends in current anthropology. 'Jelly pie' is, incidentally, a Lévi-Straussian concept – it is a *liminal categorization*. I am grateful to Robin and Elizabeth Theobald for introducing me to this culinary and conceptual delight.

42 For some examples see Egon Bittner, 'Police discretion in emergency apprehension of mentally ill persons', *Social Problems*, 14 (1967), pp. 278–92, and 'The police on Skid Row', *American Sociological Review*, 32 (1967), pp. 669–715; Craig MacAndrew, 'The role of "knowledge at hand" in the practical management of institutionalized idiots', in H. Garfinkel and H. Sachs (eds), *Contributions to Ethnomethodology* (Bloomington, Indiana University Press, 1971); David Sudnow, *Passing On: The Social Organization of Dying* (Englewood Cliffs, New Jersey, Prentice-Hall, 1967) and 'Normal crimes: sociological features of a penal code in a public defender's office', *Social Problems*, 12 (1965), pp. 255–76.

43 Cicourel, op. cit., quoting from R. M. MacIver's *Social Causation* (Boston University Press, 1942), pp. 20–1.

44 In fact they are *neo*-idealists because they generally distinguish ¿social? from ¿physical? phenomena. For example, Peter McHugh talks about the way in which ¿physical time? and ¿physical space? are 'transformed' into ¿social? time and space. Yet quite what the status of that ¿physical time? and ¿space? is remains unexplained. See 'A common-sense perception of deviance', in Dreitzel (ed.), op. cit., and cf. also J. C. McKinney, 'Sociological theory and the process of typification', in Tiryakian and McKinney (eds), *Sociological Theory, Values and Socio-cultural Change* (New York, Harper Torchbooks, 1970), particularly p. 245.

45 These are what are often termed '*accounting procedures*' in current ¿sociological? parlance.

46 See Cicourel, op. cit., pp. 51–2 and Garfinkel, op. cit., chapter 8.

47 The notion of 'deep structures' is derived from Chomsky, op. cit. This comes into the work of many of the ethnomethodologists, but see Cicourel's denial in *The Social Organization of Juvenile Justice* (New York, Wiley, 1968), pp. 332–3.

48 Ibid., p. 106.

49 Ibid., p. 107, italics in the original.

50 Ibid., p. 100, italics in the original.

9   The Magic of Meanings

1 Cf. Owen Barfield, *Saving the Appearances: A Study in Idolatry* (Harbinger paperback edn, New York, Harcourt, Brace & World, 1971).

2 If you can't take the idea of *collective solipsism* then you have an unnecessarily limited imagination. A crash course of science-fiction reading seems to be indicated.

3 By 'influential' I mean those whose ideas have been incorporated into subsequent work to the greatest degree, not necessarily those who are most widely acclaimed. Simmel is rarely stressed in undergraduate teaching to an extent which would lead one to consider him to be as 'influential' as the others. However there are strong grounds for believing that much of the methodology attributed to Weber was derived from an early reading of Simmel's work.

4 Of course I have no intention of citing textual references in an attempt to '*prove*' this claim. Any references given in what follows are provided merely in an illustrative capacity. However, I invite the reader to

subject my hypothesis to a genuinely *risky test* by searching the works of the 'Founding Fathers' for statements which contradict it.

5 See Karl Marx, *The Economic and Philosophical Manuscripts of 1844*, New World paperback edn, Dirk J. Struik (ed.) (New York, International Publishers, 1964), 'Private property and communism', p. 145. Italics added.

6 This ontology is so central to Marx's thought that, whatever else may have changed between 1844 and the production of *Capital*, this did not. In that later work the following revealing passage appears: 'A spider carries on operations resembling those of a weaver; and many a human architect is put to shame by the skill with which a bee constructs her cell. But what distinguishes the most incompetent of architects from the best of bees, is that the architect has built a cell in his head before he constructs it in wax. The labour process ends in the creation of something which, when the process began, already existed in the worker's imagination, already existed in an ideal form. What happens is not merely that the worker brings about a change of form in natural objects; at the same time, in the nature that exists apart from himself, *he realises his own purposes . . .*' (italics added).

7 Hegel, Inaugural Address, Berlin, 1818, Mueller ed. *Encycl.* p. 61.

8 Cf. Peter Berger and Thomas Luckmann, *The Social Construction of Reality* (London, Allen Lane, 1967).

9 Marx, op. cit., p. 108.

10 I say that it is *experienced* as chaotic, I do not say that it *is in reality* chaotic, at least not in any way that implies that a real chaos exists in a real world independently of human experience. Compare this with McKinney's view, p. 245 of *Sociological Theory, Values and Sociocultural Change* (New York, Harper Torchbooks, 1970).

11 From Georg Simmel, 'How is society possible?', *American Journal of Sociology*, 14 (3) (1910), pp. 372–91.

12 Cf. Alfred Schutz, *Collected Papers*, vol. 1 (The Hague, Martinus Nijhoff, 1964), p. 60.

13 Barfield, op. cit., p. 34.

14 While all four of the 'Founding Fathers' which I have chosen as exemplars necessarily based their definition of their discipline on their conception of the units of analysis proper to their subject-matter, only Durkheim, Weber and Simmel were *explicit* in characterizing sociology as the study of meanings. Weber is most commonly recognized in this connection but many have misinterpreted Durkheim's 'social facts' and Simmel's 'forms', giving them respectively strong positivistic and extreme idealistic interpretations. On Marx, however, the reader should consult 'Die Entfremdete Arbeit', the first of the *Economic and Philosophical Manuscripts*.

15 Cf. Schutz, op. cit.

16 Ibid., pp. 11–12.

17 This view is by no means unique with the modern ethnomethodologists. Similar ideas can be found in the work of Durkheim, Simmel and Weber and in Marx's discussion of the superstructure, as well as – more obviously – in the writings of James, Cooley and Mead.

18 Cf. the recent sociological interest in 'accounting'. See for example M. B. Scott and S. Lyman, 'Accounts', *American Sociological Review*, 33 (1) (1968). They define an account as 'a statement made by a social actor to explain unanticipated or untoward behavior – whether that

behavior is his own or that of others, and whether the proximate cause for the statement arises from the actor himself or from someone else'.

19 For a brief introduction to the sociological concept of *'marginality'* and a summary of some of the literature, see Steven Box and Julienne Ford, 'Commitment to science: a solution to student marginality?', *Sociology*, 1 (3) (1967), pp. 225–38.

20 Paul Bohannan, *'Conscience collective* and culture', in Émile Durkheim *et al.*, *Essays on Sociology and Philosophy* (New York, Harper & Row, 1960), p. 90. Of course I could equally well have performed this translation exercise using the methodological statements of Weber, Simmel *or* Marx. I chose Durkheim because the proto-ethnomethodological aspects of the others' works are more widely accepted by current sociological fashion.

21 Cf. ibid., p. 90.

22 See, for an example of this argument applied to a substantive area of sociology, Steven Box and Julienne Ford, 'The facts don't fit', *Sociological Review*, February 1971.

23 Actually I have oversimplified the matter here. I would not really be entitled to assume that *I* knew what counted as a pimple in the social world which was providing the universe for my observations. Rather than attempting to apprehend first-order happenings directly, then, I ought to do so via the judgments of members. Thus a panel of natives ought to be persuaded to count the pimples.

24 Of course this is not to say that Western common sense does not in some sense transcend sociology! For the man-in-the-pub may well theorize *about* sociology and sociologists, devising explanations of their peculiar ways. Some of these theories may even result in the formulation of genuinely risky hypotheses: for example, 'I bet he'll be wearing a pink shirt and a flowered tie' (yer actual sociologist usually does), or 'He most probably watches the Thomas Hardy things on BBC 2' (they do that too!).

25 Readers interested in *extra*ordinary arithmetic should consult Herman Weyl's work. For example, see 'The ghost of modality', in M. Faber (ed.), *Philosophical Essays in Memory of Edmund Husserl* (Cambridge, Mass., Harvard University Press, 1940), pp. 278–303. And for a concise introduction to non-arithmetic methods of expressing and calculating ¿directions?, see Bernard Burgoyne, *Spaced Out* (London, Thames & Hudson, forthcoming).

26 Cf. Peter Abell, 'Measurement in sociology: I measurement systems', *Sociology*, 2 (1) (1968), especially pp. 2–3.

27 Cf. Gideon Sjoberg, *The Preindustrial City* (New York, Free Press, 1960).

28 A weird, and interesting, collection of 'oddball' quantitative measures like this can be found in Eugene Webb, Donald T. Campbell, Richard D. Schwartz and Lee Sechrest, *Unobtrusive Measures: Nonreactive Research in the Social Sciences* (Chicago, Rand McNally, 1970). Their aim is to devise ways-of-measuring-things which are free of researcher effects, that is to measure 'traces' of human activity in physical manifestations, 'traces' which, unlike human judgments, do not alter as a result of the act of measurement. We shall return to this later, chapters 16 and 17.

29 I am not directly referring to the subdiscipline of topology. The idea

is that 'topological measurement' is *spatial* rather than simply quantitative, it deals with notions conceived about ¿directions? of variation
rather than directly with questions like 'How much?'.

30 S. Stouffer *et al.*, *Measurement and Prediction* (Princeton University
   Press, 1950), pp. 13–14 and 140–2.

Glossary of
Fairy-Tale Words

AMAZING SERENDIPITY BUZZER Transcendental flash.

BATHWATER *see* BATHWATER FALLACY

BATHWATER FALLACY Fallacy of misplaced concreteness.

BRIDGE Operationalization: the magical link between ideas and appearances.

CRICKET PITCH Test ground for scientific theories.

DANCE *see* DERVISH DANCE

DERVISH DANCE Formal choreography of testing rituals.

DIGGING Knowing, feeling, understanding.

DIRTY LINEN *see* UNDERWEAR.

DO-IT-YOURSELF-MULTI-PURPOSE-DATA-MATRIX Classification of modes of data stipulation which may be appropriate for social science purposes.

DWARVES Operationalizers by appointment to the FAIRY courts.

FAIRIES Ideas, potentially thoughts and/or images, manifestations or appearances.

FAIRY TALE Connection of ideas in the form of an explanatory story, or theory.

FAIRYLAND Land of ideas. Any realm of thought. Alternative universe.

GOLD STAR Honorific title awarded for faithfulness to deductive methods in science.

GOLD-STAR BADGE Mark of GOLD-STAR status.

GOLD-STAR RABBIT One recognized as of GOLD-STAR merit.

GRYPHON Chance.

LAUNDRY *see* UNDERWEAR.

LIBRARY Storehouse of written thoughts kept as knowledge.

LIGHTS Guides.

MATRIX *see* DO-IT-YOURSELF-MULTI-PURPOSE-DATA-MATRIX.

MAGICAL MOUNTAIN *see* MOUNTAIN.

MOCK TURTLE SOUP   Positivistic inductivistic universe.

MOUNTAIN   Solid conventions of academic scientific thought.

RABBIT   Scientist.

RED   Positivistic.

RED HERRING   Red herring.

SAMPLING GAME   Process of selecting 'representative' samples.

SOUP *see* MOCK TURTLE SOUP.

SPIDER   Confusion or intimation thereof.

SPIDER BATTLE   Philosophical brawl.

STATISTRICKS   Statistical tricks.

THIRTY-NINE STIPS   Contents of DO-IT-YOURSELF-MULTI-PURPOSE-DATA-MATRIX.

UMPIRE   Philosopher of science.

UNDERWEAR   Theory construction procedures.

WHITE   Idealistic.

WHITE RABBIT   Science teacher.

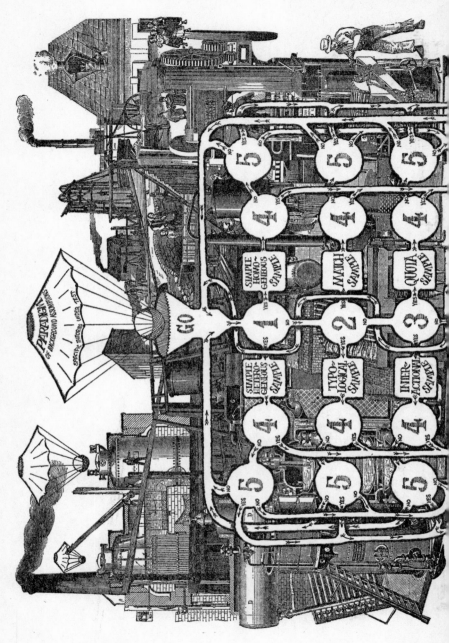